"A wonderful follow-up to Greenfire. *It's refreshing, with a healthy, balanced and insightful view of the arts of sex and love. Sirona approaches relationships in harmony with nature and the cycles of the Moon, drawing on Celtic Druid Tradition to weave a rich tapestry celebrating all aspects of life ...* Moonflower *will enhance all lovers' shared experiences—it's a book that makes you want to take your lover and journey to another realm."*

— Michael Peter Langevin
Publisher, *Magical Blend* magazine

YOUR QUEST FOR ULTIMATE ONENESS BEGINS HERE

The goddess tradition and magic are ancient lovers. In *Moonflower,* their union creates a tool you can use to enjoy a more fulfilling sexual *and* spiritual partnership with your mate. This book blends concepts from the Celtic Gwyddonic Druid Tradition with guided imagery and practical techniques to merge with oneness, your lover, yourself, and with the Divine.

Beginning with the first Full Moon of the lunar year—the Wolf Moon, whose renewing energies are embodied by the warrior deities Medb and Nuada—you will take a stirringly sensual journey with the goddess and her consort through each High Moon cycle. Every journey illuminates another aspect of the goddess and the god, with rituals and suggestions for merging with these aspects—such as dynamic energy, purity, strength, abundance, and perfect love—to activate them in yourself and in your love relationship.

Dream magic is another tool you can use to ultimately connect with the divine aspects within yourself. *Moonflower* will teach you how to guide the energy of your dreams into viable patterns to change your life in positive ways. Learn how magical dreamwork can be practiced to travel through time and space, to gain rapport with a particular aspect of the goddess—even to shape your future.

Moonflower is an invaluable reference source to those who wish to enrich their sexual and spiritual relationships while exploring an innovative approach to the goddess tradition.

About the Author

For more than twenty years, Sirona Knight has been studying psychology, folklore, and religion with a personal interest in goddess tradition. She has traveled to Europe, Mexico, the Pacific Northwest, and Alaska on her quest for knowledge of the goddess. She is a published poet, writer, teacher, hypnotherapist, and lecturer and holds a master's degree in psychology and leisure studies from California State University. Knight is a Third Degree Craftmaster and High Priestess of the Celtic Gywddonic Druid Tradition. She has made radio and television appearances in Northern California, has been an active workshop leader for several years, and has created a series of guided imagery self-help tapes. She lives in the Sierra Foothills with her husband and their son, two dogs, and family of cats. Her writing room is situated next to an ancient Native American site, where she devotes her time to her art and craft and to enjoying life, moment by moment.

To Write to the Author

If you wish to contact the author or would like more information about this book, please write to her in care of Llewellyn Worldwide, and we will forward your request. Both the author and the publisher appreciate hearing from you and learning of your enjoyment of this book and how it has helped you. Llewellyn Worldwide cannot guarantee that every letter written to the authors can be answered, but all will be forwarded. Please write to:

Sirona Knight
℅ Llewellyn Worldwide
P.O. Box 64383-K385, St. Paul, MN 55164-0383, U.S.A.
Please enclose a self-addressed, stamped envelope or $1.00 to cover costs.
If outside the U.S.A., enclose international postal reply coupon.

Free Catalog from Llewellyn

For more than 90 years Llewellyn has brought its readers knowledge in the fields of metaphysics and human potential. Learn about the newest books in spiritual guidance, natural healing, astrology, occult philosophy and more. Enjoy book reviews, new age articles, a calendar of events, plus current advertised products and services. To get your free copy of *Llewellyn's New Worlds of Mind and Spirit*, send your name and address to:

Llewellyn's New Worlds of Mind and Spirit
P.O. Box 64383-K385, St. Paul, MN 55164-0383, U.S.A.

MOONFLOWER

Erotic Dreaming With the Goddess

꧁

Sirona Knight

1996
Llewellyn Publications
St. Paul, MN 55164-0383, U.S.A.

FIRST EDITION
First Printing, 1996

Cover Painting: Moon Deer
Cover Design: Anne Marie Garrison
Illustrations: Lisa Hunt
Book Design, Layout, and Editing: Pamela Henkel

Library of Congress Cataloging-in-Publication Data
Knight, Sirona, 1955—
    Moonflower : erotic dreaming with the goddess / Sirona
Knight. — 1st ed.
        p.   cm.
    Includes bibliographical references (p.   ) and index.
    ISBN 1-56718-385-9
    1. Witchcraft and sex. 2. Moon—Religious aspects.
    3. Dreams. 4. Goddess religion.   I. Title.
    BF1572.S4K55   1996
    299—dc20   95-42623
                                                          CIP

Printed in the United States of America

Llewellyn Publications
A Division of Llewellyn Worldwide, Ltd.
P.O. Box 64383, St. Paul, MN 55164-0383

Dedication

To Michael, my spiritual partner,
and to my bright son, Skylor,
for their ever-growing,
ever-lasting
love, light, and laughter.

Other Books by the Author

Greenfire: Making Love with the Goddess

Acknowledgements

To Oneness—the goddesses and gods of light—especially the masterful Lugh, my special friend and guardian, and to the lovely Lady Rosemerta for her generosity and knowledge. I would like to thank Carl Llewellyn Weschcke for his publishing efforts in spirituality and carrying the light forward. Bright blessings and many thanks to Nancy Mostad for her rapport and confidence in my abilities, and to Nan Skovran for her humor and wonderful stories. A warm thank you to everyone at Llewellyn Publications, especially Andrea Godwin for her efforts and fellowship; Pamela Henkel, my editor who is a dream to work with; Lynne Menturweck for her creative insight; the enthusiastic sales staff—Von Braschler, Luann Wolfe, Lily Winter, and Eric Sneve; and Jim Garrison for furthering the work of the Lady. I would like to also extend my never-ending appreciation to Lisa Hunt and Moon Deer for their magical paintings and artistic vision.

A heartfelt thanks to Jerry Snider for seeing me as a creative resource and helping me to perfect my art and craft, and to everyone at *Magical Blend* magazine—Matt, Yuka, Susan, Kathy, Brian, and Christian—for their unique talents and open minds.

I would also like to thank my Mother, Father, family, and friends for their continued encouragement, and acknowledge my teachers in all dimensions and my students, especially Selene, a most promising pupil. Many blessings and respectful thanks to D.J. Conway for her ever-growing friendship and for sharing her wisdom, and to Silver Ravenwolf for her assistance and goodwill. I would like to express my appreciation to Julian Cope for carrying the Bardic Tradition into the twenty-first century, and to R.J. (Bob) Stewart for awakening the "light within the land." I want to express my gratitude to Margo Anand and Dr. John Gray for their work in uniting spirituality and sexuality. Also, thank you to Cory (Tiger Man) Meacham for his efforts to save the Tiger, and to Merilyn Tunneshende for her time and energy. Finally, I want to extend a very special thank you to Donovan, Heidi Ellen

Robinson, and Rick Rubin for making my 40th birthday a night to remember, filled with enchanting music and magical conversation. All of you have inspired my creativity and helped me on my spiritual quest. For this, I thank you. May you forever walk and dream in perfect love and perfect peace.

Blessed be!

Contents

Introduction

I am the serpent queen
The sun's halo
A moonbeam.

Introduction ॐ

Spirals of white light weave through the woman's soft flowing hair, caressing the top of her head before slowly sliding down to touch her face. The moonlight gently kisses her lips and then moves sensuously down her throat like a warm tongue. Waves of ecstasy course through her body as moonbeams stream over her mountains, cascading down into her flowing river canyons and fertile valleys.

The luminous moonlight dips even deeper, bathing her supple body with moon dust as silken fingers of starlight tenderly touch her velvety petals. In the radiant night, she becomes the moonflower and the moonflower becomes her. Opening fully in the lustrous light, her bell-shaped flower gently envelops the milky fullness of the gleaming moon.

Her lover's hands become the moonlight, caressing her delicate petals. Softly kissing her nose and mouth, his lips travel down her like moon fire, mingling in the warmth of her stamen as he tastes her sweet nectar. The lovers drink each other in and the scent of wildflowers floats over them, filling their senses. Their bodies twine together and spiral out into the luminous night as they merge into the intimate harmony of oneness.

The word *Moonflower* means "to flow with the cycle of the moon." As *Greenfire: Making Love with the Goddess* follows the path of the sun through the eight Great Days of power, *Moonflower: Erotic Dreaming with the Goddess*, flows with the seasons, cycling through the thirteen High

ॐ
1

Moons. Once again renewal and creation in the mating of female and male energies is the focal point with dreaming and healing acting as modes for personal exploration. Celtic Gwyddonic Druid Tradition speaks of the perfect love of the goddess and the perfect peace of the god as divine concepts existing within each one of us. Beginning with the first full moon, the Wolf Moon, you will travel on the moonlit path of the night luminary, achieving complete harmony with your sexuality and experiencing the ultimate bond with oneness.

Like the petals of the delicate moonflower, whose bell-shaped blossoms only unfold with the light of the moon, open and expand your mind. Move beyond your imagination and travel in a crystal ship of starlight across the night sky into the boundless multi-verse of oneness. Using your dreams as a guidebook, nature becomes your road map on the Great Adventure. Knowledge and wisdom abound in the great rivers and shallow streams, teeming in the ever-changing tides of the oceans. Perceive the subtle flows of awareness and patterns of energy in the branches of a tree and in the wings of a dragonfly. Experience the essence of love and peace residing in the clouds sweeping across the skies and in a young child's laughter.

As with nature, the cycle of the moon is one of birth, life, death, and rebirth. This lunar cycle correlates with sexual orgasm, *le petite mort,* where you are continually reborn from your sexual experience. Through each rebirth, your thirst and hunger for expression and knowledge grow and evolve, waking you from your conditioned sleep. Love relationships, where spiritual partners engage in sacred sexual exploration, act as stimulating bridges between the conditioned world and oneness. In the fluid state of spiritual love and orgasm, you see both the physical dream you live in and the divine dream of the goddess and her consort.

The combined powers of female and male, joined together when making love, causes a vast surplus of energy. Making love implies you are making light. True sexual satisfaction comes as you freely give and receive this divine light. The information in the following chapters suggests various ways for you to direct this energy and light towards specific patterns and outcomes. A continually evolving spiritual partnership requires constant effort and a strong positive desire from each participant. Through consideration, build a latticework of love, trust and respect with your mate, remembering that sacred love is everlasting. As the goddess and god, move beyond your self-imposed walls and merge together in a union of perfect love and perfect peace.

Travel to new realms of sensation and perception through erotic dreaming with the goddess. Each High Moon illuminates another aspect of the goddess and the god, unveiling an additional face of oneness and of yourself. As the moonflower unfolds, realize there is no rigid definition between waking and dreaming. Experience all worlds simultaneously as you start to dream with your eyes open.

3

We come from light. We live in light and return to light, becoming one with the divine source of energy. *Moonflower* symbolizes this source through its embodiment of the perfect spiritual union of the goddess and her consort. In the mating of the watery moon and fiery sun, joining goddess and god and female and male energies together, we are all inherently perfect in our connection to oneness. Each one of us wants and needs to connect, remembering who we really are. Through this divine wisdom of oneness, we once again become children of the light.

Moonflower: Erotic Dreaming with the Goddess follows the path of the moon as it moves though the cycle of the sun. The guided journeys and practical knowledge in the following pages blend the ancient with the present, creating a new synthesis for a New Age. Starting on Yule, the Great Day which also marks the beginning of the sun's path, the sensuous adventure of the High Moons moves you from the energetic renewal of the Wolf Moon, to the vibrant stirring of the Storm Moon, flowing into the pure potential of the Chaste Moon. From the sprouting creation of the Seed Moon, to the abundant fertility of the Hare Moon mated to the perfect union of the Dyad Moon, each High Moon brings to light a different face of the Great Goddess. The Mead, Wort, and Barley Moons depict aspects of the harvest while the Wine, Blood and Snow Moons characterize the faces of prophecy, maternity, and ancestry, necessary for the renewal of the cycle. The Oak Moon is the wild card thirteenth moon, occurring approximately every three years. This High Moon represents the mating of the sun and moon in the sense that it shifts the lunar cycle, balancing and harmonizing the moon with the solar cycle. Otherwise the two cycles, through the course of time, would fall out of synchronicity.

The Great Goddess Kerridwen mates with her consort Kernunnos each year on the winter solstice, initiating both the *Greenfire* and *Moonflower* experiences. Just as a goddess and consort symbolize each of the Great Days, the aspects and qualities of a particular goddess and god also embody each of the High Moons. Accordingly, the divine lovers guide you through the great journey of the sun and the moon, propelling you through new realms of awareness and spiritual union. Dreaming and healing become stimulating wells of awareness for patterning your world and actualizing your inner love and light. So cast your line out into the waters of oneness, flowing with the boundless river of dreams as you sing, "Row, row, row your boat, gently down the stream, Merrily, merrily, merrily, merrily, life is but a dream."

The Wolf Moon

Medb & Nuada

The distant voice called my name
a name I had never heard
like a pebble skipping over the water
or the flapping wings of a great bird.

CHAPTER ONE

The Wolf Moon ☙

Medb & Nuada

Full Moon in Cancer, Sun in Capricorn
Cardinal negative water and negative earth elements

The Goddess and Her Consort

Mated to the land, the wolves run together through the winter night. They move over the small meadow, and then pause at the edge of the trees. Settling down on their haunches, the powerful Hounds of the Norns howl in unison to the full Wolf Moon. In the light of the cold night, the mighty hunters call out to the Great Goddess, and to the wolf and raven queens. Their voices echo across the never-ending ever-flowing stream of life.

The goddess sings out in the icy winter wind, answering the wolves' cries. She is the Mother of All Things who issues from that which has no name. As such, she represents the Great Goddess who cares and provides for all nature. She calls to the wolves in an ancient tongue. They respond, yipping and howling excitedly.

Shapeshifting into a great white she-wolf, the goddess runs with the pack. The pack's speed and endurance seem unending as they move swiftly over the snowy expanse, leaving a trail of deep footprints in the frigid crust.

As the All Mother, the Great Goddess represents the nature of all things, and strives for energetic balance and harmony. She desires the All Father, a mate she creates as a reflection of herself. In this way, every aspect or quality of the goddess has a male counterpart known as the god or consort.

Anchoring her mate's and her own nature to the seasons and rotation of the heavens, the Great Goddess expresses herself through the ever-changing ever-growing cycle of life. Her bright nature fully awakens in Spring, and reigns over the season of the greening. As winter approaches, her dark nature roams the land while her bright self enters sleep, reawakening again in the spring.

Rituals and celebrations on the High Moons and the Great Days act as the symbolic bodily expression of the ancient love between the all-knowing goddess and her powerful consort. Repeated through time and generations, ritual energy becomes a powerful change element for self-discovery and development. As a mindful act of creation where energies mate and combine, ritual attunes you to the flow of external nature while increasing your inner awareness. Furthermore, each time you perform ritual you merge with the goddess and god. In this way, you become one with the divine light of all things.

The ancient druids knew the secrets stored in cyclic patterns in nature and in the starlit heavens. Carefully observing the sun, moon, and stars, they devised an extremely functional timekeeping system. Starting with the winter solstice, they watched the changing phases of the moon. They noticed that depending upon the angle at which its luminous face is seen from earth, the moon provided a accurate means for monitoring time, relative to the sun's positioning.

Beginning at the winter solstice, they watched both the cycles of the sun and moon to determine when to plant, to harvest, and when to celebrate the gods. The lunar cycle, which is approximately twenty-nine and one-half days, is about eleven days short of the 365-and-one-quarter-day solar cycle. By watching the north-south course of the sun at the stone circles at Stonehenge and Callanish, the druids were able to observe the path of the sun as it moved through the Great Days. This, in conjunction with the phases of the moon, produced a sophisticated method of measuring time and seasonal cycles. Accordingly, the further north you are on the earth, the more the sun moves from north to south. Only on the equinoxes does the sun rise and set due east and west. If the standing stones in their present configuration had been on the equator, they would have been of little to no use.

Notice the qualities of the moon as it progresses across the earth's sky, rising in the east and setting in the west. Taking into account the earth's rotation, the moon itself actually flows energetically from the water element to the air element. From the streaming primordial waters of oneness, springs the breath of life.

Moon, month, and *menses* all stem from the root word *me* meaning "to measure." The Sanskrit derivative *Mami* means I measure. Interestingly, the Old English word for moon is *mona* which is the ancient name for the Isle of Man, Manannan's home, situated on the Irish Sea. In turn, the Old English word for *man* spelled *monn* is closely akin to *mona.*

Measurer of time, either the full or new moon almost always cycles thirteen times within a given year. Beginning with the first High Moon after Yule, the names of the thirteen moons are as follows: Wolf, Storm, Chaste, Seed, Hare, Dyad, Mead, Wort, Barley, Wine, Blood, Snow and Oak. At the full moon, the sun and moon shine exactly opposite each other. On twelve moon years, each full moon occurs in the same astrological sun and moon sign. When there are thirteen full moons within a year, the cycle changes, flowing backwards after Lughnassad, usually on the eighth full moon. Strongest in the sign of Cancer, each moon radiates unique light, with every moon reflecting its individual combinations of energies, and aligning its qualities with the seasons. The blue moon occurs when two High Moons rise in any one month. Eclipses of the moon occur only on the full moon when the earth travels between the sun and the moon.

The moon becomes reborn out of its own shadow in an ever-lasting cycle of becoming. Follow the eight-fold moon phase cycle, and notice how it corresponds to the eight Great Days. Yule symbolizes the new moon while Bridget's Day embodies the crescent moon. The first quarter of the moon relates to spring and Hertha's day while the gibbous moon parallels Beltane. The full moon relates to Letha's Day or Midsummer, and the disseminating moon represents Lughnassad. Hellith's Day corresponds to the last quarter of the moon and the harvest, just as the balsamic or dark moon personifies Samhain.

Associated with instincts, intuition, imagination, and receptivity, moonlight acts as a regulator of the human body. As solar and lunar beings, women and men experience cycles corresponding to the light of the sun and moon. More obvious in women because of their monthly menstrual flow, the moon affects everyone due to the fact that humans are comprised of approximately seventy percent water. The moon influences the natural flows of all fluids on the earthly plane, within and without the human body. In concurrence, Welsh tradition holds that people are born when the tide comes in, and they die when the tide goes out.

Traditionally the right hand symbolizes the waxing moon, and the left hand represents the waning moon. Follow the shape of your hand from the thumb to the index finger, and see the natural crescent moon reflected in your physical body. Be mindful of your intimate connection with nature's patterns as you incorporate moon energy, utilizing this power and awareness to create stronger and brighter personal and universal patterns. Initiate, build, direct, and dissolve energy as the moon shines new, waxing to full and waning back to new. Follow the birth, growth, maturing, and rebirth of moon energy as it dissipates its collected solar potential.

Observe your personal cycle as you travel with the moon in a ship of gemmy starlight. Sleep in the light of the moon. Fully engage your attention, and notice shifts in your bodily sensations, moods, emotions, and feelings. Study the phases of the moon, and observe how they are caused by the varying angle at which its lighted surface is seen from the earth.

Sensitize yourself to the natural flow of the new moon to the first quarter as you begin to clarify your intent and expectation. This becomes a time for initiating patterns and building your desire. During the time between the first quarter and the full moon, cultivate your carefully selected patterns and peak the energy necessary for their successful completion. On the full moon, feel the climactic and orgasmic energy rushing through you. As you move into the last quarter of the moon, patterns manifest and energy is distributed. You reap the bountiful harvest of the goddess and her consort. During the last quarter to the new moon, explore the deeper meaning and potential of all things while the night luminary prepares for rebirth.

The deeper you merge with the energy of the moon, the greater your comprehension of the affects of lunar positioning. Allow your relationship with the moon to blossom by practicing a technique called *drawing down the moon.* Raise your eyes to the full moon and lift your arms overhead in the traditional goddess position. Create a chalice or cup out of your body. Taking a deep breath, receive the moon's energy and light. Filled with the powerful moon flow, purposefully direct this accumulated energy towards positive patterns and relationships.

Explore those mysterious hidden places you can only glimpse by moonlight. On the first High Moon after Yule, The Warrior Queen Medb shows you qualities of unity and purity. Commanding a vast army of heroines and heros, she represents a goddess of the land's sovereignty, meaning that kingship could only come through marrying her.

As the Wolf Queen, the goddess Medb embodies the intense sexuality of her totem, enjoying numerous lovers. She is intoxicating, and her name means "mead." Appearing with flame red hair and emerald green eyes, the beautiful goddess wears orange-red and honey-colored robes. Every man that looks upon the splendid queen Medb is overcome by desire. Just to be in her presence deprives her opponents of two-thirds of their courage and will.

Goddess of Tara, The Good Queen Medb acts as the Faery Queen and Queen of Connaught. She is known to be the most generous of all of her sisters in pledges and bestowing gifts. Magnificent and powerful, the goddess Medb runs faster than the quickest horse. Holding her magical spear and shield, she carries animals and birds on her shoulders and arms as she speeds across the land.

Wedded to the land, The Good Father, King Nuada embraces the formidable goddess Medb. He bestows wealth, and acts as a god of war, kingship, carpenters, and smiths. A Celtic Jupiter, the consort Nuada parallels the god Nodens, who is also associated with water and its healing properties, as well as wolves and dogs.

The chieftain god Nuada carries one of the Tuatha De Dannan's four great treasures, the sword from Findias. In a victorious battle on the summer solstice, King Nuada loses his hand while fighting the Fir Boig champion Sreng. A disfigured king cannot rule the Tuatha, so Nuada hands his kingship to Bres. Bres proves unworthy of the task, and thus Lugh takes his place. Lugh excels as ruler. Making him whole again, Nuada's hand is replaced by a perfectly functioning silver hand created by the physician to the gods Diancecht. But even after this, King Nuada allows young Lugh to rule for thirteen days of battle before the elder king meets his death on Samhain.

Also called Llud of the Silver Hand, the handsome consort Nuada appears with grayish white hair and a beard. His silver-gray eyes remind you of storm clouds, and his body feels hard and muscular. He wears a very short brown or charcoal colored tunic, and is good-natured with a prodigious appetite. His magical symbols are a magic spear, the sound of thunder, and lightning bolts.

Rapport with the formidable Warrior Queen and the wise king empowers you in all aspects of your life. Follow the goddess Medb and the consort Nuada as they ascend and descend into other dimensions of awareness. Acquire a taste for new adventures as you travel on the path of the moon. Choices are made moment by moment, so use all of the resources available to you, and enjoy the positive patterns you create in your life. Activate and actualize your dreams as you merge with the goddess and her consort.

Practical Knowledge and Useful Information— Dreaming on the Path of the Moon

Four-tenths of the surface of the moon remains forever hidden from the Earth. This is because the moon shows relatively the same face to the Earth, due to both of their rotational patterns. Moonlight is light from the sun reflected off the Earth and moon, and we see a certain percent of that light, depending upon the Earth's relative position to the sun and moon. Accordingly, the Earth and moon are mirrors of the sun, which is a star.

Like the moon and Earth, you are a reflection of all things, and all things are reflected in you. Also like the moon, certain aspects of yourself remain hidden from the world. Dreaming becomes a way to access those hidden treasures within your being. Using your dreaming experiences as a map to new perceptions, leave your doubts and fears behind, and travel to that place where creative and scientific inspiration walk hand in hand.

Dreaming is one way for the conscious mind to actively participate in processes that are normally considered unconscious. Dreaming becomes an ongoing process you engage in at all times, while awake and while sleeping. There is only oneness. Your conditioned mind creates separation as a practical construct. Cognizant of this unity of being, you create your dream experiences just as you create your life experiences. You act as producer of your own dreams, and writer of your own dream screenplays. You become the director of your dream shows, starring in the leading roles. You start to realize the dreams you craft have personal meaning, purpose, and a message.

Dreaming links you directly to oneness, much like a deep merge. This opens up and evokes the symbolic dimensions of experience, and expands your view of reality. You find yourself in the midst of functioning in your waking world as you simultaneously move within energetic and symbolic dream worlds. Use dreaming to access the boundless, propelling you to that place of pure knowing, and gaining personal insight.

Pay close attention to your dreaming process. Notice the direction and movement of the dream experience, and any transformation or change therein. Adopt an open-ended approach to dreaming, and use your dream key to unlock the vast storehouse of knowledge within and without. Avoid intellectualizing your dream experience. Instead, multi-sense your expanded view, detecting new thoughts, sensations, emotions, and tones. Add these perceptions to your inner landscape, and watch how they play out in your personal reality.

Indigenous healers feel the quality of life depends upon body sensations which are linked to dreams and to the surrounding environment. Dreaming incorporates these unusual experiences and these altered states of consciousness that reach your awareness through signals, such as body symptoms, synchronistic action, movement impulses, and messages from the environment.

Dreams act as snapshots of possible body experiences. Following your body's sensations and movements, you begin to comprehend your contribution to the larger picture. Suddenly you realize you are living and creating life as a moment by moment choice. You feel your dreams, and your dreaming process matures as you notice sensations such as dizziness, aches and pains, and feelings of elation and anger. Multi-sense the appearance and structure of your dreams, flowing with the sensations that arise from them.

15

Your ongoing dreaming process becomes a tool for solving problems in your life and for enriching your experience. The therapeutic and inspirational applications of dreaming are infinite. Use dreaming to release emotions, to move past addictions, and to cope with grief, as well as to improve both your physical and psychosexual health. Expand your dreamscape, learning the healing aspects of dream work where spiritual, psychological, and physical perceptions are confronted and modified, thus reducing negativity, illness, and disease.

Actively participating in dream work through tape recording, journal writing, drawing, painting, and dream incubation promotes growth and positive change. Personal metaphor becomes a viable method for studying your dream images. Remember, your dreams are your own creation, and only you can recognize and tune into their meanings and messages. Openly explore the depth of your dreams, and dare to venture into a realm of enhanced personal development.

Guided Journey

He holds his wand, pointing its giant crystal tip towards the full moon. The moon's light weaves through the facets of the crystal, sliding her way down to the base of the wand. The wand stands quivering in his hands as liquid white light splatters everywhere. His fingers reach up to caress the white light, and he feels her petals open into a beautiful moonflower. The softness of his tongue reaches into the warmth of her stamen, tasting her sweet nectar.

Her petals tingle as she guides him slowly inside of her, his fingers stroking the tips of her breasts. Their bodies pulse together to a primal beat that drums and echoes deep inside. Both of their hearts beat in syncopation, moving into the bliss of oneness.

The energy heightens as she moves him under her, thrusting her full moon upon his wand, his blade into her sweet wine. The cycle renews itself in rapturous harmony. Each petal of the moonflower unfolds like waves crashing over and over again, onto a rocky beach. Energy moves from the unmanifested to the manifested, like shooting stars piercing the night sky, finally bursting into a super nova, propelling itself across galaxies. Together their bodies run like liquid wildfire, melting across the icy winter's night.

Outside the dormer window, snowflakes glisten in the moonlight, falling soft, like white feathers floating effortlessly towards the ground. As she and her lover begin to reach the point of climax, she becomes one of the white snowy feathers flowing through a bright vortex of energy. She feels completely surrounded by white light. The lovers' bodies pulse like a quasar until the energy can climb no higher. But still they pulse higher and higher, filling the cauldron to absolute capacity. Finally the lovers release the energy, sending shivers racing down each of their bodies.

18

The lucent white light fills her body like a warm wave, and the top her scalp tingles from the energy enveloping and surging through her. Off in the far distance she hears the faint song of a wolf calling to the full moon. She touches her lover's damp skin as they lie side by side on the feather bed. The brass on the headboard reflects the rays of the moon spilling into the room from the window. A quiet calmness fills her body, mind and spirit, bringing all three harmoniously into one. She relaxes as she drifts down a river of winding light. Once again she becomes the white feather floating effortlessly towards oneness.

As she streams down the river of light, her surroundings begin to change. Colors become florescent, melting into one another, and forming new unusual hues. She flows through the double folds of space between the end of day and the beginning of night, and the end of night and the beginning of day. She moves to the place where time slows down and momentarily stands still.

The scenery rapidly changes and segues from one surrealistic masterpiece to another, like the giant brush of an artist quickly painting a new reality. Her senses are flooded with a new view by which to ponder the meaning and unmeaning of life which seems as fleeting as the elusive white bird. Whenever caught, it becomes nothingness.

"I am the white bird. The white bird is me." She speaks to herself before becoming the snowy white bird, and continuing on her journey, flowing with the river.

She feels her lover take her hand, and she turns, looking into his eyes. Fluorescent pools of silver-blue draw her in like a magnet. She reaches over and strokes his fine brown hair, fingering the streak of white running through it at his forehead. After caressing and softly stroking one another, the lovers continue together, moving onward until they reach a cave filled with white light. They enter the opening of the cave. The stone walls of the cave are covered with clusters of multicolored crystals. The bright moonlight pours through the lip of the cave, and bounces from one facet to another, causing teeming prisms of color to flare out in all directions. Waterfalls of light cascade from several naturally-formed holes in the ceiling. She takes her lover's hand, and they float slowly upward through one of the holes.

Her feet break through the icy crust of cold snow as she runs toward the light of the full moon. The moonlight creates a path reflected in the crystals of the snow, resem-

19

bling a white carpet to the sky. She stops briefly to sniff the scent of the frosty night, using her senses to scan the white expanse around her. She raises her nose and mouth upward, and emits a loud high pitched howl into the night. Her mate stands at her right side. He also lets out a howl, and soon the whole pack joins the call. After everyone has spoken, the frozen night falls silent once again. Only the occasional sound of the wind through the trees remains, whispering as it brushes against the sharp needles of the towering evergreens.

Again, the she-wolf attunes herself to the harsh environment surrounding her. Her senses reach out into the snowy expanse, reading every minute change, any edge on survival that could be provided for herself and her pack of five wolves. The pack depends on her accuracy in both sensing danger and finding food. One slip could mean the end of all.

Her mate, Blade, looks over at her, and she can see his white tufts reflecting the light. His faces wrinkles as he smiles at her, showing his giant canines.

She trots over and playfully bites him on his rear quarters. He retaliates by lightly biting her on the back of the neck. She feels a shiver move up her backbone into her neck as they momentarily tussle in the wet snow. Soon the whole pack is running fervently around in a circle, yipping and dancing playfully. After completion of the courting ritual, they rest before continuing their trek across the brilliant white carpet of the moon.

As she runs, she scans the distant horizon scattered with the giant shadows of pine trees. The brisk air slaps her face with its icy fingers as she moves up to the top of a steep incline. She tastes the cold wet air, and steam rises from her nostrils and mouth as she breathes in and out. At the top of the ridge she stops with the other members of the pack. They gaze out at the forest below and the stars above them. The gleaming moon sits in the evening sky like a white flower in full bloom.

In the distance a single wolf cry breaks the icy silence. She cranes her head to hear the sound more clearly. The first call is soon followed by a host of other calls in the distance. She lets out a long piercing howl, directing her voice into the frozen night in the direction of the other pack. Cued by the she-wolf, the whole pack sings out in unison. Their howls cease as abruptly as they began, and the night again returns to an eerie silence.

To her left she hears a low rumbling growl. She turns in time to see the other male in the pack, a young black wolf named Midnight, beginning to charge her mate, Blade. Blade's snowy white coat stands up as he readies for his attacker. Both wolves walk in a circle, stalking each other and growling with their eyes firmly locked on one another. Each moves purposefully, looking for some advantage over his opponent. Their tails stand straight out like flags as they circle one another.

In an instant, Midnight suddenly rushes toward Blade, who in one single motion, throws Midnight over into the snow onto his back. Blade pins him, and nips the end of his nose with his razor-sharp teeth. The pack leader then moves back, allowing the young black wolf to get back up. Midnight cowers to the alpha male, and moves off with his tail between his legs, and his lips peeled back in an appeasing grin.

The she-wolf watches as Blade again returns to his place at her right side. She turns to him, playfully jumping on his back with her front paws. They lick each other in the mouth, wagging their tails and dancing lightly on their back legs. She feels the wet warmth of his mouth as he nibbles on the nape of her neck. A soft whine from her throat and the increasing speed of her wagging tail encourages him to move closer. Still pressing their bodies together, the two trot away from the rest of the pack, their movement timed as to maintain maximum physical contact. Soon their shadows disappear among the towering trees.

As the two wolves enter the thick forest, a huge white raven descends from the branches onto the ground before them. She and Blade stop to watch the bird as it dances in the snow while cackling the melody of raven song. Silence once again cushions the great white expanse as the raven motions for them to follow. The white bird glides just below the branches of the evergreens, and the two wolves trail the bird, traveling deeper into the forest.

The white raven lands on a weather-bent tree growing beside the opening of a cave. The two wolves yip and softly howl their thanks to the bird for guiding them to the cave. The bird cackles its brief reply, and flies off into the thickness of the wooded forest. As the raven moves, the moonlight gleams off its snowy feathers. The she-wolf turns to the mouth of the cave, and enters the darkness with Blade at her side. She smells the damp earthy scent of the dark cave, sniffing at the faint residue of the previous occupant.

She feels the wetness of her lover's mouth as he moves his tongue from her neck, and slowly down her back. She reaches over and begins moving her hand along his skin, feeling first the softness of his skin, and then the contrasting firmness of his muscles. His body shakes with hunger as he moves his tongue deeper within her cave. Soon both their bodies quiver as he sits up, and gently kisses her lips. The look in her eye calls to something deep inside of him, a primal pounding, beating into oneness.

Through the soft darkness of the cave, he penetrates her chalice of sweet wine with his fiery blade. Faster and faster, the energy reverberates back and forth between the lovers. Their bodies move in a synchronistic weave of flesh and light, pulsating in harmony until the energy streams out like a waterfall running through each of their heads, and flowing in torrents down over their feet. At the moment of ecstasy, they both howl out into the darkness of the night.

As she lies down with the back of her head buried deep in the soft feather pillow, a white raven moves down from the sky and perches on the sill of the dormer window. The bird stares at her through the window before rising up in the air, rapidly flapping its snowy wings. Brilliantly flashing in the moonlight, the raven's wings look like petals, opening up into a beautiful white moonflower.

The Storm Moon

Epona & Taranis

Dreaming with you
licks me like fire
storming through my senses
I wake up
Alive.

The Storm Moon ☍

Epona & Taranis

Full Moon in Leo, Sun in Aquarius
Fixed positive fire and air elements

The Goddess and Her Consort

The Great Goddess commands the powerful sun, and the fiery orb quickly obeys her. She changes the courses of stars, and takes away the light from the luminous moon, only to restore it at her will. She creates rainbows, filling the skies with clouds and thunder. She acts as supreme ruler of the weather and atmospheric changes. As such, the Great Goddess regulates the growth and evolution of the Earth, moon, sun, and stars. Called by many names, her shapeshifting faces are infinite.

As the Mother Goddess Kerridwen, she stirs up the unmanifested, creating manifested form and knowledge from within her magical cauldron. Accordingly, the root of the word storm means to stir. On the Storm Moon, use the vibrancy of a full moon to move and stir up energy in positive ways, creating the life that you choose.

Storms initiate change, both positive and negative. A wealth of folklore arises from the mighty forces of storms.

A halo around the moon points to rain, and if stars appear in the halo's ring, precipitation is likely to continue for many days. If more than five stars appear in the ring, the weather will be cold. If less than five, the temperature will be warm.

Controlling storms through the sound of drums or singing was practiced among ancient people. The goddess Bridget introduced the art of whistling to humankind, and the seafaring Celts would whistle up the wind to travel over the oceans and waterways. Lore suggests stopping a whirlwind by flinging a knife at it, and using a magical sword to bring up the wind. In Chinese Taoism, thunder and storms grow and subside by means of spells and magical symbols.

Taranis represents the Celtic god of storms and thunder. He controls the passing seasons and is associated with the giant oak, which attracts lightning more than any other tree. Taranis portrays the Thunderer, the god of the Wheel of the Seasons and Stars. Paralleling aspects of Zeus, who was also called the Thunderer because he descended to earth in the form of a bull to seduce mortal women, the consort Taranis represents powerful and potent male energy in motion.

Taranis appears tall and strong with long, free-flowing hair and a beard. Wearing an electric white tunic and mantle, he carries a six-spoked or eight-spoked wheel and a thunderbolt. The consort's eyes shine a stormy blue, and his intense gaze penetrates your very being. He embodies several qualities of the Roman god Jupiter as a protector, initiator, and god of knowledge and elemental power.

The Sky Father Taranis acts as consort to the Earth Mother, portrayed by Epona. Worshipped by the ancient Belgae, who were the fifteen Celtic tribes of Northeastern Gaul, she was doubly honored by being the only Celtic goddess included in the Roman pantheon. The fair-skinned goddess Epona represents fertilization by water. She flows like a rushing river. Her eyes seem gray, perhaps blue, green, or hazel, and her hair looks like a beautiful black mane. Best known as the horse goddess, she wears blue and gray robes and sits upon a white mare holding an apple and a bag filled with endless bounty.

The goddess Epona, nicknamed Regina, bestows sovereignty upon the ancient Celtic kings. As the mare, she portrays the marriage of the earth goddess and her consort. Similar to Rhiannon, Macha, and Etain, Epona carries the strength and power of her totem animal, the horse. Her name means "divine horse," and she is the offspring of a mare and a human man. Because of this, Epona takes the form of either a woman or a mare.

As shapeshifter, the goddess protects and guards horses, asses, mules and all those who interact and care for these creatures. Her special province becomes the fecundity of horses. As such, she embodies the aspects of the Mother Goddess. Monuments depict her riding on a mare, surrounded by horses, or feeding foals. The horse represents the supreme symbol of warrior energy, power and fertility; it was on horseback that the martial Indo-Europeans conquered their enemies and increased their domain.

Stir your world up as you gain rapport with the moving energy of the earth goddess Epona and Taranis, the god of the Wheel of the Seasons and Stars. Learn to better understand and know the earthly and spiritual aspects of your being. The powerful sensuality of the storming consort and the swift-riding goddess weave together in passionate union and everlasting change. They lend a dynamic quality to sexual intimacy and dream work, incorporating formidable elemental forces.

29

Your experiences with the goddess Epona and her consort Taranis increase your abilities and skills to manifest positive and strong patterns in all dimensions of experience. Their combined power emphasizes expansion and movement, while the magnitude of their joined energies motivates you to manifest and fulfill your highest dreams.

Practical Knowledge and Useful Information— Dream Magic

The Storm Moon illustrates the polarities of life: "as above, so below." As is the cosmic Mind, so is the human Mind. As is the commonality, so is the unique. As is the waking world, so is the dream world. The whole of creation is oneness communicating with itself. As Krishna said, "Curving back within myself, I create again and again." As you descend, you learn to ascend.

The innate wisdom of the body is supreme. It mirrors the knowledge and intelligence of all things. Your body becomes a reflection of oneness, and a vehicle of communication with the boundless. As your body and brain slow down, your spirit-Mind moves clearer and faster. This often occurs in the meditative or merged state, and has been closely examined by biofeedback and dream researchers. This slowed energetic state characterizes dream. Dreaming creates a particular Mindscape or formation conducive to interacting with the boundless. In this way, dream becomes the road you travel to access and experience oneness, and ultimately connect to the divine aspects within yourself.

The seeds of oneness reside within each one of us. The Storm Moon reminds us of the polarities of germination, and of the dynamic and continuous changeability within ourselves, nature, and in all things. This dynamic energy unleashes and frees our desires and dreams, increasing our ability to move far beyond our imagination. When you place no bounds on your Mind, you move into oneness, to other worlds and other perspectives. Dream magic comes into play as you utilize your magical skills to pattern and set up your dreams. You can pattern your dreams much like you learned to pattern your world in *Greenfire: Making Love With the Goddess*.

If you dream or imagine an event, that action becomes real or formed in an energetic way. Dream becomes your base reality, which in turn dreams up your ordinary world, in an effort to realize itself. Remember, dream is your road to oneness. In some ways it is like driving your car while looking through the rearview mirror. Stated plainly, you are responsible for manifesting and patterning your personal reality. You explore what you choose to explore through your intention, your deep personal desires and your connection to oneness. Your dreams are your own because you have selected them. On this premise, learning to guide the energy of your dreams into viable patterns becomes a natural progression and a useful skill.

Approach dreaming with complete awareness, deliberately deciding how you want to work with your dreams and the images therein. Learning to dream becomes an active and intentional undertaking. As you become adept at orchestrating your dream experience, the energy and action necessary to manifest particular dreams seem easier and easier to access. Everything falls into place as your dream patterns transform into waking patterns and vice versa.

Dream patterning follows a basic formula. There exist three steps or factors in the frame of every magical work and pattern. In Gwyddonic Druid Tradition, these steps, referred to as The Three Eyes of Kerridwen, are expectation, desire, and merging. First, expectation is the nature, quality, and circumstances of the thing you want. Second, desire becomes how much you crave, wish for, and long for what you want. You gather motivation to create patterns through your cumulative desire, including emotions and sensations. The stronger your desire becomes, the stronger the pattern. The third step, merging, is simply becoming aware of the fact that you are one with all things.

Merging enables you to reach a level of synchronicity with the Ground of Being. The infinite potential of Mind, which describes a larger, more comprehensive concept of mind, and moving Mind can be tapped through merging. By merging, you experience oneness firsthand, storing the information and building your patterning resources. As you merge deeply and purely with the goddess and god, you strengthen your rapport with the many female and male energies within and without you. Allow yourself to explore and integrate these polarities. The relationship you cultivate with the goddess and her consort empowers you in every aspect of your life.

The likely success of any dream pattern or magical work depends upon the clarity of your intention and expectation, as well as the strength of your desire, and the depth of your merge. When you use The Three Eyes of Kerridwen in dream patterning, dreaming becomes the foundation of your reality. Dream dreams, and then do precisely what it takes to manifest those dreams, through patterning and magical works. Follow that which you love, and do whatever you desire most at the deepest level of your being, for that is your commitment in this lifetime. It is wise to be very specific, and to focus on creating positive patterns.

Magical dream patterning uses right and left brain synchronicity. This balancing of the hemispheres indicates the optimal operating condition for the human brain. By using dream magic, you see yourself in a certain way, and this vision overlaps with your manifest reality. When you merge deep enough, you generate the actual event. You create a Mindscape, an energetic landscape or formation that acts as the seed thought for the actual pattern. Mind plays an ever-growing multitude of future oriented landscapes or movies, waiting for you to make your selection. In this way, dream manifests reality. To accomplish something, first know how to dream it.

Dream patterning enhances your world. Dreaming specific patterns, systematically and repeatedly, facilitates a predictable transfer from dream imagery and experience into tangible reality. Images and symbols in dream magic act as powerful tools with numerous applications. For example, the symbol of infinity, a figure eight, can be used in dream as a simple triggering device to move to another world, or it might be used to gain rapport with a goddess or god. You could also employ the figure eight symbol to stretch your mind beyond its normal awareness. Instantly, you become aware of the symbolic Threefold contained within; one that is constructing, one that is taking away, and one that is doing either and/or nothing.

33

Other helpful dream magic devices include the use of seeing your hands or feet while dreaming as a means of directing your dreamscape. Also using cuing words such as, "Perfect Love and Perfect Peace," trigger sensual exploration and experience within your dream. With a clear intention, you can purposefully send and receive messages through dream magic, pattern future events, and change the energetic pictures of the past through the dream medium. Time and space fold and flex as you, the practitioner, become adept at magical dreaming.

Time travel is a fascinating dream method for manifesting and for determining personal choice. Time travel operates by permitting knowledge of description to become knowledge of experience. In other words, you dream yourself into certain situations where you try on a specific behavior, experience, relationship, environment, or even wardrobe, and see if it fits. Dream becomes the dressing room of oneness.

Learn to develop your dreaming skills so they reflect your total being. Move past your barriers of natural resistance and conditioning, and allow yourself to go beyond the definitions of reason. Merge and dream with oneness as you reach out to the unmanifested, to She Who is Nameless. From this ever-changing resource, you experience other worlds and dimensions as you discover vast wells of knowledge and wisdom, consequently establishing new relationships and patterns of being.

In dreaming, it becomes crucial to notice what is happening, and to sustain the view of your experience. Waking dream enables you to notice minuscule subtleties within yourself and your environment. This ongoing process accelerates your pattern tuning skills, and thus affects your magical ability exponentially.

In dream, as well as in other states, pay close attention to spontaneous and synchronistic events. Select experiences and events according to the energy contained in them. Make an effort to carefully observe the energetic structure and flow as well as the pattern of the particular experience. Often events that seem the most bizarre and most distant from your awareness become especially useful in your personal development. Unusual dreams and a feeling of the uncanny sometimes cause you to remember the sorcerer, magician, and wise person within yourself and others. Awareness and amplification assist you as you study the details of energetic patterns, and begin to actively read patterns. As you let go of your ordinary way of viewing reality, you start seeing through the Mind's eye, what Arnold Mindell calls "the dreamingbody."

Mind springs from oneness and constitutes a never-beginning never-ending, ever-flowing life principle. Oneness acts as the source, and must be sustained and renewed by energy and activity.

Aboriginal dreamtime parallels oneness, linking time, dream, and ancestors together. Dreamtime, created at the beginning of things by mythical beings, organizes time and space. Knowledge of the world depends on dreamtime just as wisdom is relative to your merging depth and purity with oneness. Knowledge and wisdom reflect one another.

Remember, as a magical dreamer, you travel through and beyond both time and space. The goddess and her consort will travel with you at your bidding. If you desire, they will act as guardians in your dream journeys. Allow yourself to make an honest effort to use and develop your personal dream skills. As you dream, continue to flow toward perfect love and perfect peace.

Guided Journey

Sitting next to the light and warmth of the fire, the young woman carefully works the string with the needles held in her hands, in and out, in and out. Very slowly, a piece of white lace emerges from her efforts.

Her mother sits close by, concentrating on her own crocheting. The fire light dances on the walls, across her mother's face, and over the lace pattern in her hands. She can hear the wind sounding through the tied reeds of the alder trees by the front door. The strange whistling grows louder and louder with the strength of the stirring wind. The young woman stands, setting her handiwork on the small wooden table next to her. She moves quietly to the window. Her legs are stiff from sitting, and she stretches them out as she walks, feeling a tingling sensation from her feet to her knees.

She lifts the ivory lace curtain, and slowly looks out into the night. She sees the faint outline of the full disk of the moon against the bright crescent new moon. She knows that the old moon in the arms of the new moon means a storm is coming in. She can see the dark clouds moving swiftly across the night sky.

"The moon agrees with the wind, it seems," the young woman speaks softly to her mother.

"They generally do," the older woman replies, smiling and looking up at her daughter. She stands, stretching slowly and putting her needlework on the soft velvet chair. She moves to the window and looks outside at the trees swaying and bending in the powerful wind. The darkness grows as the clouds cover the light of the moon.

Rain begins to fall, hitting the glass panes of the window with a steady ticking sound. The water droplets clinging to the window reflect the inner firelight and form nebulous patterns on the glass, the patterns constantly changing with the pounding wind.

Silently, the woman and her mother watch the powerful storm. Giant fir and pine trees sway in the increasing gale. The wind howls, echoes, and fades rhythmically through the small crevices and cracks of the house. The storm breathes stronger, and the wind slaps against the window, causing the glass to shudder and flex slightly. The young woman places her hand against the cool pane, and feels the pulse of the storm outside.

"Did you know that you can learn to control the wind by tying it up?" the older woman asks, her voice melding with the tones of the storm. The sound of the dripping rain matches the cadence of her words.

"What do you mean?" The young woman's eyes shine with interest as she turns from the window and faces her mother.

Her mother smiles at her daughter's curiosity and continues, "The old wise women practice the ancient ways and rule the storms. They know the art of tying up the wind in three knots. Seafaring people buy the wind from these women in the shape of knotted rope, handkerchiefs, and thread. When they loosen a knot, the wind blows their sails, and moves them along on their journey. So, the more knots they untie, the stronger the wind."

"Do you know how to tie up the wind, mother?" the young woman asks quietly.

"That is something I have yet to master, but your grandmother is very good at it. Though, she rarely uses that particular talent as it is much more wise to let the elements flow on their natural course."

"Do you think I could learn how to tie up the wind?"

"I'm sure you, like your grandmother, will gain great skill with all of the elements. You seem to have a genuine inclination toward the ancient ways."

The older woman reaches out and touches her daughter's arm and says, "Come and sit with me by the fire, and I will show you the art of string magic. Your grandmother mentioned just yesterday that it is time to teach you. String magic is a method for harnessing energy."

The movement of the storm outside echoes in the room as the women sit down in front of the flickering fire. The young woman feels the warmth of the flames against her face and through the soft fabric of her robe. Shadows play with the flames on the walls of the room.

"Have you ever noticed the patterns of this lace—I mean really noticed?" her mother begins, picking up the handiwork from the small table.

"What do you mean?" the young woman asks.

The older woman smiles and adds, "String magic parallels making lace. Here, let me show you."

As the older woman continues, her daughter settles back into her chair, concentrating on her mother's words and actions.

"First like any magical work, choose a location where you can completely focus on the work. Remember to thoroughly clear and calm your mind. You should have a positive intention and a clear expectation of what it is you want. Here, let's do the procedure together."

Her mother cuts two yard-long lengths of lace thread, and gives one of them to her daughter. "Just sit back for a few moments and get a clear and strong image of what you would like to tie into your life. Use your imagination."

The room is completely silent for a few moments. Suddenly, the wind breaks against the house, and sings oddly through the walls and windows, disrupting the momentary stillness. The young woman looks into the fire, and she sees the image of an intense young man staring back at her. She has seen him before. She sees him each morning in her dreams, just before she awakens. For several weeks his face has puzzled her, his piercing eyes filling a corner of her every thought. She smiles to herself. She will tie this dream man into her life, so she can know him, touch him, and love him.

Her mother watches her daughter's face. "Let's begin. Start by tying the ends of your string together in a firm knot. Then loop and slide the thread in and out of your fingers. That's right, use both hands."

The young woman cradles the silky white thread in her hands as she slides its length in and out of her fingers. The rhythm of her motions matches the pounding of the storm. Her hands weave the thread in deliberate and stylized shapes as if sculpting a face in clay.

"Now, turn your Mind completely to what it is you want, what you truly desire. Your fingers, hands, and the thread tell the story of what you want, and form a link with the energy of your expectation. Become totally absorbed in your task as you merge with the boundless. The movement of the thread, your hands, and fingers become one with your intention, expectation, and desire. Everything becomes connected and joined in light. Weave the energy together."

Her mother's words trail off in her mind as she works with the silky white thread, in and out, sliding it back and forth. She merges with oneness and becomes the thread. She becomes the movement of her hands and becomes the intensity of the man's eyes staring back at her.

Her mother taps her gently on the knee, startling her. "After you have finished your work, offer the thread to the fire and thank the boundless for its gift. Next time when you work the thread, try to hum or whistle a special melody to enhance the effect. If you make a mistake, simply use slip-knot magic to untie it or delete it."

40

"Slip-knot magic, what is that?" The young woman focuses on her mother's face, her curiosity again piquing.

"You take the same size thread, and instead of tying the ends together, you make a slip-knot in the middle. Then you take an end in each hand and pull, but don't pull the knot out yet. Fully engage your mind with the energy of what it is you want to be rid of, and transfer this energy completely to the slip-knot. Finally, pull the knot out firmly, with the knowledge that the untying of the knot represents the deletion of the unwanted energy. Burn the string and thank the boundless." Her mother stops speaking and yawns slowly.

"Time for dreaming," the older woman says as she moves over to hug her daughter. "No, don't get up. Goodnight, and have sweet dreams."

The young woman watches her mother walk out of the room. The light and shadows of the fire dance around her. She hears the sound of her mother's footsteps up the stairs. The sound fades as the wind picks up, and slaps the rain solidly against the house. A brilliant light sweeps across the windows and into the room. A few moments later, the house shudders as the thunder sounds in a loud resonating boom. Over and over again, lightning streaks across the walls, followed by loud drumming thunder.

The young woman holds her lacework up to the firelight and looks at the patterns of circles and squares. She sets her handiwork on her lap as she looks steadily at the flaring shapes of light within the burning fire. She thinks about the young man, his intense gaze and her desire for his love.

The woman yawns and sighs deeply, her tired eyes quietly examining the patterns in the lacework, and then finally closing. Her breathing deepens as she moves her dream body into the lacework. The patterns become an infinite sphere, filled with a starry expanse of silver webbing, like the latticework of constellations. She moves along the silky webbing into the night, and finds herself riding across the moonlit sky upon a magnificent white mare. She becomes one with the horse as the storm rages around her. Ahead of her, lightning flashes and arcs on the horizon.

"I am called Whitewind," she hears the soft delicate voice say in her dreaming mind. "I can foretell the future, and outrun any divine or mortal steed. We will ride to the stars and moon, and travel to a place beyond your dreams."

The young woman questions, "Where is this place you speak of?"

"Just below us now. Look down. Do you see the clearing in the trees?" They leave the storm behind them as the magical horse descends slowly through a milky fog. Without a sound, Whitewind deftly lights upon the earth, and ambles toward a large raised mound on one side of the clearing.

Wherever the woman looks, moonlight reflects off of the trees. The shadows dodge and play through the twisted branches. "How can that be? The moon looks full now, but it was just a crescent earlier."

"Many things are other that what they seem to be," replies the divine mare as she continues to walk. Whitewind enters a hidden opening in the large mound. A short tunnel takes them to a small earthen sun house, open to the elements and the night air. At the far end of the structure, the woman sees a large wooden door. As they approach the doorway, she notices a golden horse-shoe hanging above the threshold, pointed upward and gleaming in the moonlight.

The horse stops. "Your future awaits you." With those words, the beautiful white mare vanishes, leaving the woman standing in front of the heavy wooden door. The curious stillness of dream time cloaks her while she studies the gold inlaid runes on the face of the massive door. The door handle and keyhole are also made of gold.

The young woman bends over gracefully, and examines the handle and then peers carefully through the keyhole. She sees something move across her vision, and suddenly she dissolves into light. Instantaneously, she is sucked through the keyhole opening into the mysterious room.

He waits for her. The dream man with the stormy grey-blue eyes stares at her intently. In their depths, she sees shapes of light, the forms of a stag, a golden dragon, a great cat, a silver wolf, and a kestrel. He stands close to her, and she feels the heat of his breath on her face.

"I am the Shapeshifter," the man answers her silent question.

"As you can see, I am reborn in many shapes. You could even say that I shift creation." He gently takes her arm, and leads her deeper into the fire-warmed room. The spicy scent of him fills her senses as they walk.

Immersed in the sight and feel of him, the young woman studies the man. He holds himself like a tall powerful stallion, his body firm and sleek. His clean shaven face looks chiseled out of stone, complete with high cheek bones and a full inviting mouth. She stares at where his hand touches her arm. The fine hair on the surface of his hand shimmers golden in the reflected firelight. Her gaze travels up his arm, and for the first time she notices he wears a pure white poets shirt, open at the neck. The shirt is tucked into tight black velvet pants. Following the length of his legs, she notices his feet rest in open leather slippers.

"Please sit down." He gestures toward a carved oak chair by the warm glowing fire. His curling hair flows around his shoulders like a lion's mane as he sits across from her in an identical chair. Above the wooden mantel hang a golden spear and a large eight-spoked wheel. The walls are carved with runes. Between the two of them rests an oak game table inlaid with milky quartz and obsidian. Intricately designed chess pieces stand upon the light and dark squares. Two candelabras, lit with five white candles each, sit on either side of the fireplace mantel. Their smoke smells of bayberry and beeswax.

She studies the chessboard briefly and then stares at the man. "I know you. Your face appears in my dreams every morning," the young woman says suddenly.

He smiles and hands her a golden chalice filled with liquid. He holds up his chalice and makes a toast, "Perfect Love and Perfect Peace." He gently clicks his cup on hers, and brings the lip of the chalice slowly to his mouth. The sensuous movement excites the young woman. She drinks from her cup, tasting the dry sweet wine in the back of her throat.

She looks away from the man's intent gaze, and sees her reflection in a mirror on the far wall. Her ivory lace dress drapes the ample curves of her body. Her long black hair lays tied behind her neck with lace. As she looks down at her dress, she sees patterns of stars and spirals, and notices her skin looks whiter than the dress fabric. Her white satin shoes gleam faintly. Her flashing grey eyes move back to the man sitting opposite her.

"You and I are the same," the Shapeshifter speaks, his voice resonate and familiar. "Know you are the boundless, and that you are all things. Open your mind and remember you were once a dragon, once an ocean, and many times a flowing river. You are a mountain and a thick green forest. You are the white mare, the marriage of light and darkness."

As he continues, she feels a shiver of recognition move through her body. "I, like you, was once a dragon, once a wooded forest, once a sun, and now I am the wheel of the stars."

She ponders his words in her mind as he takes a ripe golden apple from a small bowl on the table. He rubs the skin of the fruit on his sleeve, methodically, as he continues to study her face.

"You are the boundless at all times." The man picks up a small jewel-encrusted athame, and slices the apple into four equal parts. He continues, "The question becomes: Do you have the courage to experience all things simultaneously, from the common to the cosmic?" He gives her a section of the apple, and its flesh is cool and sweet on her tongue.

The intensity of his gaze penetrates her as he says, "Your mind feels ready to take the journey. The choice is yours, and yours alone." He sensually bites into the apple piece.

"Yes, I am ready." The young woman directs her attention completely upon the man, fascinated by her immediate heated response to him.

"Excellent! First, we will play a game of chess. It will be a magical game. If I win, you must do my bidding. And if you defeat me, I will do yours," the Shapeshifter says with a brilliant smile. He holds his closed fists in front of him and says, "Pick one."

The woman softly fingers his left hand and says, "This one."

The man opens his fist and hands her the white pawn. "Ladies first."

She sets the pawn back on its square, and studies the board. The candlelight flickers across the table, and the chess pieces seem to move and dance about in the shadow play. The fire whispers, spitting and crackling now and again. She feels warmed by its heat, and by the man's steady gaze.

45

Sitting up and leaning towards the table, she makes her first move. Her king's pawn advances forward two squares. Looking closer at the chess pieces, the young woman notices an uncanny resemblance of the king and queen pieces, to herself and the Shapeshifter.

Her opponent counters and mirrors her move. His voice flows into her awareness like warm water. "Have you ever considered what the game of chess represents? The forces of darkness and light rise and do battle within these sixty-four squares." He waves his hand over the table.

"Why sixty-four? Four times sixteen, and sixteen pieces on each side. Sixteen is four times four, corresponding to the four elements. Numbers fascinate me," the woman says enthusiastically.

Her eyes shine as she looks at the man opposite her. All the while, her fingers delicately stroke her king's knight. He watches the small movements of her strong hand. As she looks down at the chess piece, she notices the exquisite detail. The knight rides on a magnificent white mare, his tabard painted over him, cloaking him with the insignia of a red dragon.

He speaks to her quietly, "Besides the numerical pattern, did you ever notice how the bishops, knights, and rooks are named for the queen or king, according to their position at the start of the game? The pawns become namesakes for the pieces they stand in front of." His words help him to momentarily focus on the game, instead of on the beautiful woman sitting across the table from him.

She captures his attention once again as she moves her king's knight to protect her pawn.

He traps her hand in his just as she releases the knight. He dreamily lifts her fingers to his lips and kisses each one, slowly and deliberately.

She watches him, mesmerized by his actions and the softness of his mouth. Her own mouth waters in anticipation and eagerness.

The Shapeshifter stands like a proud stallion. He moves to the woman, and guides her over to the soft velvet cushions at the side of the fireplace. His golden mane grazes her face and throat as he lays her back on the cushions. His hair smells of fire smoke and thunder, and she breathes him in. Laying there, the man and woman look like an extension of the chess board, all vested in black and white.

As the man cradles her in his strong arms, his fingers loosen the lace tie in her ebony hair, freeing and weaving its silkiness through his long fingers. His hands find the buttons down the front of her ivory dress, and he slowly begins to unfasten each one. His stormy blue eyes swallow hers as the fabric falls to either side of her full breasts and willing thighs. Her smooth skin contrasts with the lacy fabric as the man runs his fingers down her body.

She quivers and moans softly as he dips and plunges his hand over her natural valleys and rising hills. She sits up on the cushions and helps him off with his shirt. She strokes his chest and stomach, and slides her hands over the muscles in his arms. She likes the familiar feel of him as she helps him off with his pants.

She leans back, pulling him to her. She kisses him softly and sensuously, her tongue playing over the front of his teeth. Her breathing grows faster as his mouth finds her supple breast, teasing the nipple into a firm flowering bud.

She smells like the rain, the stars and the moon as he kisses her neck and throat. His voice is husky as he speaks to the woman, "I concede the game."

She smiles and replies, "Checkmate." She stands, pulling her dress over her shoulders and arms, and letting it fall to the floor.

She reaches over to the chessboard, and takes the white queen and caresses his chest and lips with the piece, moving her hand down lower to his firm and potent desire.

Firelight pours out from the granite stone fireplace, flooding the lovers in a soft golden glow. The warmth of the flames licks the woman's skin, melting her senses.

The man stands next to her, his maleness stirring against her. He leans over and picks up the black king off the board. He gently rubs the chess piece over her lips, down her ivory throat and softly over each waiting breast.

She embraces him tightly and whispers in his ear, "White to play and mate in two moves." Her hand runs over the length of his hard muscular body, and her palm feels damp from his sweat. She kisses him deliberately, and then invites him to take her as she presses against the game table.

The Shapeshifter mates with her like a mighty stallion, and the chess pieces scatter and fall on the table. She breathes in their passion and the heat from his body. She arches her back, and feels the cool surface of the game table pressing against her breasts and palms.

He moves faster, his free flowing hair dancing around his shoulders and streaming across his damp cheek. He pauses and moves out of her, and then guides the young woman back over to the velvet cushions. The fabric feels cool as she lays back on the soft expanse.

48 The man comes to her like a dream, flowing over her, and carrying her through the night sky in stellar flight. The silky cushions transform into billowing clouds, drifting in the lucent darkness. The fullness of the moon lights the lovers' pathway. Climbing higher and higher, the Shapeshifter flies the woman through the night fire, across moonbeams and flickering stars.

His tongue moves in circles like the wind, swirling into her mouth and over her sensitive nipples. Storming her senses, the man proceeds onward. Like a great cat, he licks her skin, circling her belly button, and then moves down lower, stirring her at her very core.

She moans in her need and desire as she slowly studies the man of her dreams. He becomes a luminous being, and light radiates from his face and hands.

Her body absorbs his light, bathing in its power and vibration. Sensation soars beyond feeling as she rolls over the Shapeshifter, and eagerly mounts his stiff and solid manhood. She rides him through the night, faster and faster.

Their breathing comes in gasps and catches as the man spins and swirls his maleness up into the ivory-skinned woman. The storm rages inside of her as he presses deeper and stronger. Gales of pleasure blow through her, and sweep her into a pure white light. The lovers stare at one another, captivated by the power of their passion. The man's stormy blue-grey eyes lock onto hers.

His intense and compelling gaze drives her deeper into the light, and farther into the night fire. She welcomes his totality, and all of his forms, desires and energies.

He pleads with her to swallow him completely as he thrusts deep within her, "Now together, swallow the boundless."

"Yes, now," she sings out. Her body shudders and contracts as she spins into the night on a wheel of stars.

49

The man moves swiftly in and out of her like lightning as he quickly joins the woman in her release. His voice booms out like thunder, and they travel joined as one. The lovers rise through the roof of the room, transforming into beautiful white birds. They fly together into the boundless night.

Awakening in the soft morning light, the young woman opens her eyes, and carefully studies the sleeping man next to her. His flowing hair fans out across the golden feather bed. She touches her dream man, and his stormy blue eyes slowly open. He smiles at his mate, and softly touches her cheek.

CHAPTER THREE

The Chaste Moon

Arianrhod & Nwyvre

There is a part of me
unspeakable, universal and all-knowing
She moves through time like water
night swimming and day dreaming
mastering Mind and changing with the weather.

The Chaste Moon ☽

Arianrhod & Nwyvre

Full Moon in Virgo, Sun in Pisces
Mutable negative earth and water elements

The Goddess and Her Consort

Virgins act as storehouses of energy. The wise consort Math keeps his feet resting in the lap of a virgin during the times between wars. The virgin makes love with Math's nephew, and she becomes defused, making it necessary for the consort to find another virgin to act as his source of energy and power. Virgins hold similar places of honor in numerous cultures. For example, in her temple at Ephesus, the Greek goddess Artemis is served by chaste priestesses called Melissae or bees.

All sexual experience involves the transmission of energy. Women expend energy, giving it to men. In return, men give energy to women. We all constantly absorb and emit light and energy. In relationship, learn to use this creative sexual energy to manifest patterns in your life. Creating a child is one such pattern. In this way, the exchange of energy ensures the perpetuation of the life force. Creation and fertilization require energy.

☽
53

Through rapport with the goddess and her consort, you begin to understand the continuous exchange and flow of energy within and without. Just as the goddess Morrigan makes love with the Dagda near the river Unius as a way to transmit her warrior energies, you learn to build and focus your energies in your primary relationship. The stronger and purer the connection with your mate, the deeper you connect with these energies.

The Chaste Moon symbolizes purity. Chaste derives its meaning from the root word *castus,* or pure. Virtuous words matched with actions, joined with clean and clear intent, represent the polarity of this High Moon. Pureness in character and quality create a positive polarity in all patterns. Purity indicates a state clean and free from anything that might weaken, impair or hinder that state. In this sense, purity equates with energetic strength.

Purity in relationship includes qualities of genuineness, potency, honest intention, and positivity. Chastity in relationship becomes a natural extension of this purity. As always, sexual preference becomes a matter of individual choice. Choosing one mate, and then focussing your energy and attention on the growing partnership, stems from ancient tradition.

As the third full moon of the cycle, the Chaste Moon represents the energy of the Trinity. The Threefold carries many meanings. Trinity embraces the union of three parts or elements into one. The new, waxing, and waning phases of the moon reflect the triplicity of creation, destruction, and regeneration within nature.

The Goddess Tradition uses the Threefold One to describe the trinity of energy. The All Mother Kerridwen has two faces, one bright and one dark. The Bright One reflects three aspects, as does the Dark One. Because of this, all things, whether bright or dark, have a beginning, middle and end; youth, middle age, and old; positive, neutral, and negative; birth, life, and death. The goddess directs all things in this manner; dormant, the greening, and harvest.

The goddess reflects the faces of the Daughter, Mother, and Grandmother. The Daughter embodies the maiden as a virgin whose powers gather and build. As Mother, she grows fertile, releasing her stored energies, and exchanging energy with her sexual partners. The third aspect of Grandmother depicts a hag or crone, who often acts as the dissipator of energy. *Hag* stems from the Greek *hagia,* which means "holy one." As Grandmother, you become holy and wise when you no longer shed the lunar wise blood, but instead keep it inside.

The goddess Triana represents the Threefold One. As Sun-Ana, she embodies the Daughter goddess of healing, knowledge, and mental arts. She portrays the Mother Goddess of nature, life, and death as Earth-Ana. Becoming Moon-Ana, she acts as the Grandmother Goddess of higher love and wisdom. Accordingly, the Threefold trinity of Daughter, Mother and Grandmother branches out into the Ninefold One; three aspects of each.

Similar to Triana, the goddess Arianrhod personifies the Chaste Moon. As a goddess of higher love and wisdom, she represents the elements air of water. Famous for her beauty, Arianrhod acts as a star and moon goddess, appearing fair, gentle, and powerful. Her skin glows translucent like starlight, and her midnight blue robes shimmer silver. The fabric looks transparent, decorated with star-like jewels and celestial designs.

Daughter of Danu and sister to the powerful gods, Gwydion, Gobannon, and Amaethon, the fertile goddess Arianrhod is associated with sacred kingship, Threefold Death, and reincarnation. In myth, she claims to be a virgin, but when the consort Math tests her, she gives birth to two magical twin sons, Lleu Llaw Gyffes and Dylan Eil Ton.

Her name still carries power as Corona Borealis is called Caer Arianrhod, also known as the Northern Crown. *Arian* means "silver," and *rhod* translates as "wheel" or "disc," so she portrays the noble queen of the wheel or silver wheel. Akin to the mythical Ariadne, who unravels the solar system, Arianrhod acts as a stellar goddess of time, space, and energy. She is the Keeper of the Silver Wheel of stars which symbolizes time.

Carrying her magical tools of stars, moonbeams, and crescent moons, Arianrhod travels on a silver eight-spoked wheel across the night sky to meet her lover and consort, Nwyvre. His appearance parallels hers, with fair, almost translucent skin, and robes of dark blue and silver. The consort is a strong gentle god of the ethers and space, with bright clear eyes that shine like star sapphires. In his hands he holds the nine-pointed star, the sky, and firmament.

As a god of celestial sciences, astronomy and astrology, rapport with the consort Nwyvre gives you knowledge of the universe and the infinite patterns of all celestial bodies. He helps you learn the flow of the galaxies, while exploring the source pattern. With a quiet strength, Nwyvre guides you through layers of time and space to other worlds.

The beautiful goddess Arianrhod, and her cosmic mate Nwyvre, impart the wisdom of the flowing cycle. Together they bring stellar secrets to those willing to adventure with them through the night sky, touching upon the meanings of each celestial body. Begin to envision your primary partner and relationship in the shape of stars, planets, constellations, and galaxies. Immerse yourself into the cosmic union of the goddess Arianrhod and her consort Nwyvre as you learn to shape and assemble energy into manifest form.

Practical Knowledge and Useful Information—
Dreaming Through Time and Space

As you merge deeply with oneness, notice that the boundless takes infinite form. It shifts shape depending upon your view and the depth of your merge. As a practitioner, you realize merging is conducive to all states of mind, and can lead you on adventures that defy normal time and space parameters. Through merging, and through your strengthening relationship with oneness, begin to move in and out of time and space. As you dream and travel with the goddess and her consort, you become aware that time and space exist, as agreed upon illusionary separations and limitations constructed by the conditioned mind.

These constructs enable you to function in the ordinary world. Everything happens on its own accord. Primarily, time and space serve as practical structuring devices. When the practitioner learns to fill space with something larger than space, and begins to see time as horizontal, vertical, or even empty, real growth occurs. Dreaming facilitates this experience.

Events and experience remain unique. In all of time and space, neither can be truly duplicated. In dream, the uniqueness of experience, and the bending of time and space seems commonplace. While dreaming, you explore other times and spaces, moving to other dimensions of sensation and expression. Learn to send your mind into another time, away from ordinary time-space relativity. By doing this, you discover your true self and your totality of being. Dreaming can help you access past, future and parallel experiences that form your personal identity.

Merge with great depth and purity, and make an effort to remember all of your lives and experiences simultaneously. At this moment, you become the goddess and her

57

consort, flowing with the stream of nature. You know that time and reality are how you choose them, and how you view them. You are the boundless. Keep this in mind as you observe yourself integrating several worlds and views into one.

The Threefold pattern of energy plays into the merging process, just as it permeates the many layers of spiritual tradition. Merging with the manifested universe in time and space gives you the patterns leading up to the answer. Merging with the unmanifested equips you with the answer, but not patterns. Merge with both the manifested and the unmanifested to see the beginning, middle, and end of patterns, and all of the correlations therein.

Merging acts as the gateway to all freedoms. As you connect more and more with the goddess and god energies, you respond rather than react to those around you and to your environment. Simply stated, merging with the boundless changes your reactive nature, and is the primary key to modifying all patterns and perceptions. This natural, non-reactive evolution brings the realization that Mind is cellular. In other words, Mind is mobile and no matter where you go, it moves with you.

You are responsible for moving your Mind, and creating your personal views, whether or not you are willing to be a connoisseur of the process. You are what you eat— the summation of your experiences. Allow yourself to harness this knowledge, and grab hold of the reins. Dare to review your past, present, and future without valence, in their pure form.

Travel into the many worlds created and discovered by your imagination and mind. One mind opening experience used by Neuro-Linguistic Programming practitioners is to learn the language and culture of another country. Gaining knowledge about the ways people live becomes a tool to help understand our conditioning. Try this exercise with a dream world or another time, or perhaps a distant universe. Actually be in this "other" place over and over again, until you gain mastery over its form and essence.

Plan ahead to make a big leap in the way you view reality. Make an effort to do a thorough job. Timing becomes everything. By now, you have noticed that patterning energetic concepts and manifesting reality are based on time frames. Purity and clarity of intent act as the main ingredients in modeling energetic concepts into time sequences and forms. As you familiarize yourself with the flexibility of time and space, you begin to understand how to intentionally shape and form, and even change, patterns within these parameters.

Comprehending the flow of all things, including the fluidity of time and space, moves you from belief and speculation to knowing. Mind shifts and your view alters to accommodate new information and experience. The larger picture looms up before you. For example, during a dream or magical journey, a rash, mark, or bruise may occur. Sometimes this marking remains with you when you awake. Other times, a watch, ring, coin, or crystal may travel with you from dream into "waking" reality. These types of happenings stir you up and send you into a deeper level of awareness. In turn, this deeper awareness strengthens your magical potential, patterning skill, and dreaming capacity. Allow yourself to flow with the ever-changing stream of energy and oneness.

As you flex your constructs of time and space, oddly enough, your own mortality becomes obvious. You understand that you are only here for a moment. A beautiful white heron carries a grain of sand every year to a certain spot, and eventually creates a mountain. Creation is

59

merely a flicker of an instant in the whole of eternity, and when taken in context of the longer view, becomes just a little story.

Fully engage your mind, and use your life time wisely. Let the ardor and union of the energies of the goddess and her consort arise in you and in your relationships. Join together and fly to the moon and stars. Journey to dream time, through space, and to the infinite possibilities beyond.

Guided Journey

You sail your sleek vessel in the warm light of the evening sun. You take the sails down swiftly as you reach your destination, a point midway between two lush islands, resting close together in the blue expanse of the sea. Protected by reefs on all sides, the ocean looks as smooth as glass. You wait, securing the anchor, looking toward the shoreline of the smaller of the two islands.

Just as the sun sinks into its watery chamber, you catch the glimmer of three white towers. You have been told by others who have sailed these waters that there are no towers; that they only exist in your mind. You know otherwise.

In the twilight, you hear the faint tinkling of bells carried on the warm and sticky ocean breeze. At the same time, you hear a soft splashing in the water, and see me swimming steadily toward your vessel.

I swim like a sea creature, swift and strong. A strange light streaks through the twilight, casting a blue-green tint upon the water. The odd blue-green glow reflects off my skin as I flow out to you. The water feels warm and silky rolling off my body, and I firmly stroke the texture of the still, tropical sea, moving ever closer to you.

Two large painted eyes at the prow of your wooden boat watch me silently. As I reach your vessel, you help me aboard. I can feel the strength in your arms and shoulders, as you lift me easily from the ocean's embrace.

You seem startled as you look into my eyes, holding me. For a moment you see an old wrinkled crone with shining eyes looking directly back at you. Suddenly you smile as I transform into a young and beautiful woman.

You cover me with a shimmering, silver cloak lined with dark blue silk. At the same time, the twilight slips into the dark of night. Time and space shift.

We find ourselves floating in a sea of starlight. I touch your face softly with my fingertips, and lean toward you and kiss you deep and long. As our salty lips meet, a shower of stars falls on us from the night sky. They land on my cape, and tangle in our hair, sparkling like jewels all around us.

The moon awakens to watch the lovers. The White Lady rises over the crystal-like water, and the Mother of the Seas lights the starry expanse with moon fire. She waxes boldly, and illuminates the darkness.

I stand back from you slightly and say, "I am glad you are here."

Your eyes smile with delight. Your voice sounds deep and smooth as you reply, "Every moment I am with you.

Every moment I want you. I feel you, breathe you, and dream you." Your body looks firm and eager, and your charcoal swimming trunks hug your hips and thighs, plainly outlining your desire. Your chest lays bare, with dark hair curling across your glistening skin. You watch my eyes travel over, and then down the dark curls. You begin trailing your hand over my damp hair, under the shimmering cloak, slowly and deliberately touching every part of me. You ask, "Why can't I visit you on the island?"

I moan softly as your hand continues to travel under my cloak methodically. "Remember what I told you. When you land on the island, time changes. It actually speeds up. So when you return home, several hundred years will have passed."

You wear the same puzzled frown as you do every other time you ask this same question. You reply, "Then leave the island, and come with me." You words fade on the stirring breeze.

"You know I cannot do that. I still have much to learn from the Ladies of the Towers of the Wind. They can show me how to become the sea and how to direct the weather. The Great Ladies know how to change into any animal shape. They can cure all illness, and foretell the future."

I take your hands in mine, and stare into your glowing eyes, "Let us enjoy all of the time we have tonight, and every night we share. Always know whenever you come to me, I will come to you."

You hold me to you roughly, and then move away slightly. "I packed bread, fruit, and wine," you say as you gesture to the wicker basket on the bench next to my feet. "I'll get the sails up, while you lay out our feast. It's a perfect night for sailing around the island."

I watch your hands grip the length of the wet thick chain as you quickly lift the anchor. You move to the sails,

63

working the ropes and gently teasing the breeze with the porcelain white sailcloth. You join with the elements and forces as they greet you. Instinct edges out reason as you connect with the hot moist wind. You allow it to sweep us along on a sensual odyssey. The sails bow and flap in the breeze as we dance on moonbeams, weaving through constellations painted on the water. The mast creaks as if answering the increasing wind.

I sit on the slatted wooden bench, and unpack the basket of food. The wine is already uncorked, and I pour it carefully into two deep silver cups. The vessel bobs up and down in the waves. The wine mirrors the rhythmic movement as I slowly glide toward you, handing you one of the filled cups.

"To the White Lady." You raise your cup and call out to the moon and stars. At the same instant, a shooting star, glowing red, orange, then gold to blue-green streaks across the horizon. It resembles a fiery red dragon with wings of multicolored feathers.

"When the red dragon flies, oneness will return to the land." My voice carries on the surface of the glistening watery expanse. The vessel lifts lightly on the soft waves in response to my words. I lift my silver chalice, "To oneness."

We drink the dry full-bodied wine, toasting the goddess and her consort, and toasting the water and the wind. We nibble on hunks of rye bread, and on dripping slices of pineapple and mango.

As we feast, the seaworthy vessel circles the isle, gliding under the silver, wheeling incandescence of the stars. Now and then, a group of sleek and shiny dolphins joins us in our voyage, leaping and diving gracefully alongside the boat. Their skin sparkles in the cascading moonlight.

You sit at your place by the tiller, holding it as you would the stock of a crossbow. You steer the vessel as it slowly dips on the gentle sea. The sail riggings gleam in the moonlight, and stars spring from the mast heads. We sit together, our bodies touching, gazing up and around at the astral river flowing into the night sky. In this river, the mother of the moons washes her radiant children before they run and play in the firmament.

"Star levels are beyond our imagination, but so close it seems I can reach out and pull them to me. Star worlds are where we began, that place of dreams where we all return one day." I speak, my voice sounding against the low swells slapping at the sides of the vessel.

Clasping you to me, I smile and continue, "Did you know that *desire* means 'from a star?'" Your damp skin feels hot and slick beneath my touch. The moonlight shines in your eyes like a huge silver and white flower as I trace my finger over your lips and down your jawline.

Without answering, you take my hands in your free hand, and lower them both to your rising desire, like sails cupping the wind. You voice your growing pleasure as the vessel slides into the familiar bay, locked between the two lush isles.

The breeze quiets and becomes a faint breath from the north. After securing the tiller, you stand up and begin to take down the sails. The moonlight blinds me momentarily as I look in your direction. I watch your every movement, focusing on your eager and pulsing arousal outlined in the full moon. I notice the thick muscles in your shoulders and arms flexing and knotting. You drop anchor, and its heavy bulk splashes down, breaking through the still, glassy water.

I move over to you effortlessly, and we sink into the bottom of the boat. I help you slide off your trunks, and you sweep back my silver cloak, spreading it over the folded sails behind us. Your body gleams in the night light like a candle flame.

You drink in my shape and desire as I lay naked, looking over at you. I wear the jewels of the stars and moon, gifts from the Ladies. At my throat hangs a small amulet in the shape of a crescent moon, set with a star sapphire. On my left hand, a dragon ring winds around my middle finger, a moonstone gripped firmly in its talons.

Your hands are as hungry as your admiring eyes. They feel slightly rough as you softly cup my full breasts in your palms, stroking your thumbs over their hardening buds. Your mouth is as willing as your hands, and you kiss me on the forehead and lips. Your tongue and mouth cover my skin like moon dust, tickling and licking me as we drift on a mirror in the stars.

My heart thuds harder, and my breath catches. Every time you touch me with your tongue, you carry me away in a current of ecstasy to other worlds and times. I taste like the salty sea as you dive down the length of my body. You savor me as you would a feast, consuming me in your desire.

The vessel rocks softly. You lay back as I run my lips over the dark hair on your stomach and downward. Your hardness tastes of the moon and stars, stirred by the sea. You groan and pull my head down, encouraging me to continue.

The ocean air, edged with an earthy scent, fills my senses. We kiss eagerly, and your hips ease against me, inviting me. The gentle rolling of the boat guides us as my body instinctively unites with yours in an ancient ritual.

We ride on the chariot of the moon, and ascend the silver tide to another world. As we fly between the stars and the sea in our golden-white vessel, every motion and sensation becomes stronger and more acute. We breathe and float, fluid and boundless through the windless air, and you feel like a river of light weaving through me as we make love.

You steer my body with your weaver's beam, like you guide your vessel. Ever so slowly, you slide in, and then almost out of me, shifting your hips underneath me.

As you fill me with loving light, I transform into the star weaver, holding a weaver's sword of white bronze with seven beadings of red and green on its ends. A translucent, jewel-covered cloak drapes across my shoulders, clasped at my throat with a silver broach hammered in an interwoven circle. My sword exudes bright beams of silver white light, and becomes a bridge of radiant brilliance leading us through the myriads of eternity. Whirling and keening like the wind, the power of our love fills the ethers.

I shift into myself as our lovemaking lifts yet another veil of sensation. Ever-changing, ever-flowing, I slide off of you gently. Standing up, I lead you to the mast. Leaning back against the rigging, I spread my arms over my head and feel the solid pole behind me.

First you kiss my lips tenderly, and then tease and taste my breasts. I feel the tumble of my hair on my back as I arch and moan my response. Your breathing is hard and fast, and finally you lift me against the wide mast. Your eyes lock onto mine as you enter me completely. The soft waves slap against the anchored vessel, echoing the sound of our bodies sliding together, again and again.

Like the rising wind, you whirl inside of me. I churn around you like a raging sea, totally surrounding you. Under us, the boat dips softly in the sea, rocking to the rhythmic motion of our moist bodies. I become your wise and crafty vessel as we ride on through the starry night. Our spirits dance on the glassy surface of the moonlit sea, without leaving a trace of our presence.

You thrust your power into me, and I moan your name in the moon-filled silence. We become vessels of light, transmitting streams of spiraling liquid brilliance toward the stars. Giant waves of pleasure crash inside my body as I move wildly with you. I surrender to you, falling over the edge of abandon.

You fly, half hidden in my open gateway to the stars. The quiet sea rises up in the twinkling of an eye, and carries us to the source. The wind suddenly blows its hot breath across our faces as we cry out in the night fire. Our voices sound like great seabirds, louder and louder, calling out to the stars.

Staring into your eyes, our climax creates moons, stars and the sleeping sun. You become every man and every lover, and my spirit entwines with yours. As we sing in harmony with the spheres, becoming all things, we turn with the Silver Wheel of the Stars. We exist without name and without form, waiting to be shaped by the White Lady. Light shoots out from our union, and together we balance the elements of the sea and sky.

You hold me to you for a few minutes, and your hand brushes back my damp hair as you tangle it through your fingers. The sea is silent. Only when it moves against the vessel does it whisper a little.

Our breathing slows as we lie among the daughters and sons of the moon, the shining stars. You close your eyes, and fall into a dreamy sleep. I watch you for a time, then kiss you lightly on the forehead, and move quietly to the side of the boat.

The still water's surface seems like a mirror, oddly reflecting my shape as I gaze downward. I look into my own mirrored face, and into the boundless as I dive into the warm tropical sea.

I swim swiftly toward the isle. As I reach the sandy shoreline, I look back at the vessel. It rests in the still water like a bright star in the night sky.

CHAPTER FOUR

❧ The Seed Moon ☙

Coventina & Dumiatis

The stars pour out like moonflowers
across the warm night sky
as your love cascades over my spirit
blossoming into brightness.

CHAPTER FOUR

The Seed Moon ♌

Coventina & Dumiatis

Full Moon in Libra, Sun in Aries
Cardinal positive air and fire elements

The Goddess and Her Consort

"As for creation, I was created from nine forms of elements; From the fruit of fruits, from the fruit of God at the beginning; From primroses and flowers of the hill, from blooms of woods and trees; From the essence of soils, I was made; From the bloom of nettles, from the water of the ninth wave." I invite you to discover all of my amazing qualities in *The Book of Taliesin*.

As a seed of the goddess, I dance with the elements. I travel through the wind, sprouting wings, and soaring over treetops on silky parachutes before finally falling down upon the fertile ground. Animals bury me and carry me in their fur. People drop and plant me seasonally, and I pass through birds like the wind through the trees. Rainwater washes over me, and quite often, I ride in rivers and streams, carried by the rushing current. The powerful sun draws me upward in its awesome light. Warmed in the womb of the earth, I germinate, take root, and grow. I am harvested and consumed every year, only to be reborn again in the spring.

On the Seed Moon, learn to weave the elements into viable personal patterns. As you interlace the energies of oneness, notice that the initiation and seeding of your patterns are crucial to their successful outcome. Within the small seed lies the ancestry, and the infinite potential of all things, the manifest and the unmanifest.

Seeds are ovules from which all things spring. From the fountain of oneness, stems the perpetuation of life. The seed contains the combined energies of oneness. The development of the species and the development of the individual depends upon the harmony of the quality and environment of the seed; i.e., the genotype and the phenotype. Gauge the quality of a seed by the quality of its husk, and notice how nature continuously exemplifies simple truths.

The Seed Moon is the time to plant seeds. Begin by selecting something you really want. Select the finest seeds, and plant them with positivity and light. Take active steps to sow and cultivate them with love and care. Build a strong desire into the energetic pattern for these magical seeds to grow to fruition. Fully engage your awareness, and merge deeply with oneness.

You choose and select the seeds of your own personal development. Learn to discern the qualities of a healthy seed in your patterns and relationships. Holistically view and examine the qualities of whom and what you interact with. Cultivating viable patterns requires self-honesty, self-responsibility, wisdom, and love. When you apply these four keys, your efforts will reap a plentiful harvest.

Know the properties of your personally selected seeds, and the nature of what it is you are planting. For example, some seeds need light to germinate and thus require no covering, while others need a covering of soil three times their width. Plant root crops during the dark of the moon, and above-ground crops in the light of the moon.

Each seed, each pattern, and each moment becomes unique, and imprints oneness in its own way—as does each of us. Remember to always replenish the soil in preparation of the next cycle and pattern. Through your ever-growing connection with the goddess and her consort, you continually restore the energetic flow of oneness with bright feelings, thoughts, words, and actions.

The Seed Moon reminds us that each woman and man carries the seeds for the future of humankind. In sexual union, fertile seeds lie awaiting the penetration of potent sperm. Children grow from this union, and from the source as testament to our creative ability. Cultivate your relationship with your children with feelings of positivity and love, and they will develop accordingly.

We are all star seeds arising from the cosmic fabric. We have the ability to choose whether to sow the seeds of creativity, cultivating positive change, or to sow the seeds of negativity, fear, and our own destruction. On this fourth High Moon, allow the goddess and her consort to show you how to grow your magical garden, and reap the rich fertile harvest of the Great Mother.

The goddess Coventina resides in this magical garden of oneness. She peacefully lays on water weeds, and pours the waters of infinity over the fertile ground from an urn she carries. Her sacred well represents the unmanifested, the womb of the earth. From her well issues the patterns of all things. As a water goddess of inspiration and poetry, the gentle Lady Coventina of the Carrawburgh rules childbirth and the renewal of the ever-growing, never-ending cycle of life.

The goddess appears young and vigorous with a supple and eager body. Her brown hair and fawn-like eyes shine with the colors of the earth. Vested in deep shades of rich brown, Coventina waits next to healing springs in lush, wooded forests, and in deep hidden valleys. In Northumberland, England, she greets you with a smile, granting you a wish as you cast a small white pebble into her sacred well.

Dumiatis embraces the progeny of Coventina. He portrays a god of creative thought, and acts as a protector of children. Similar to the consort Lugh, Dumiatis depicts a Celtic Mercury. The master teacher appears tall and slender, with dark curling hair and golden eyes. He flashes a brilliant smile as he sits on a grassy knoll or under a shady tree surrounded by children. They listen intently to his teaching tales.

The patient consort Dumiatis seems quietly intense when he visits you. His gentleness spreads out through infinity, and his touch feels light and feathery. He often takes long walks, or spends his time talking with children. The loving consort carries his magical symbols of the quill pen and ink well, writing staves and the Books of Knowledge. His mind is full, and his heart is open.

Together, Coventina and Dumiatis blend their energies into one. The seed springs from the well of the goddess, cultivated with love and positivity by Dumiatis. As you develop your rapport with the goddess and god, remember the seeds of the future rest within each of us. Make an effort to be mindful in their planting, so we may all reap an abundant and flavorful harvest.

Practical Knowledge and Useful Information— Full Moon Healing Using the Four Elements

Dreaming occurs in your relationship with oneness, acting as a natural pathway to new adventures. Your ability to dream, and to create energetic patterns depends upon the strength and clarity of your intention and desire, and on your personal connection with oneness. The energy of oneness permeates all things. When you engage in healing work, you tap into this flow of energy, directing its beneficial effects toward a specific purpose and end result.

In shamanic tradition, the power to heal is intimately tied to the energy of the healer's surroundings, i.e., the people and environment. African shamans honor this connection by respecting the bush, and by giving each child who crosses their path a penny. They feel the children form the source of their healing ability. When the children are healthy and happy, the shaman's medicine is at its strongest.

Energy forms the foundation of each healing work. Everything is energy. Whether you work alone or with others, notice the tone and cadence of energy of those involved. Healing involves moving energy and power through oneness, and directing it through expectation, desire, and merging, into manifestation. You become the magician, the fifth element. You shape patterns from the source, gaining mastery and rapport with the energies of the goddess and god. The strength of your rapport reflects in your healing ability, and proportionately, in all other aspects of your life.

75

Become keenly aware of your intent. Discover and observe your personal intent as part of an ongoing personal journey. Intent is everything. As a practitioner, your interest in metaphysical traditions reflects your intent to explore and direct the four elements of nature. Initiation into the Gwyddonic Druid Tradition gives the seeker clues to the mastery of these elements.

The fertile Seed Moon represents the solidity of the four elements of manifestation; earth, air, fire, and water. All patterns contain combinations of these four elements, assembled and fashioned by you, the practitioner, into tangible reality. You act as the fifth element, and as the conduit and cultivator of the boundless.

Follow me now, as we step into the earthen North Gate. It opens to the Castle of Glass where you learn the secret of control over all material and physical things. The watery West Gate opens to the Castle of the Lady of the Lake. She teaches the secret of control over all desires, emotions, and feelings. As we arrive at the Castle of Fire at the South Gate, learn the secret of control over all forms of energy and power. Finally at the breezy East Gate, enter the Castle of the Winds, and learn the Great Wisdom. This Wisdom gives control over all things, whatsoever they may be.

The Children of Danu, the Tuatha De Danann, brought four magical objects with them. These objects represent the four elements and the balance therein. Moving in a clockwise direction, The Stone of Fal rests in the North Point, and The Spear of Lugh thrusts out from the East Point. Cutting through the South Point is the Sword of Nuada, while the ever-flowing Cauldron of the Dagda sits at the West Point.

The symbolic representations of the elements within myth and folklore, point to their relevance and esteemed presence within magical traditions. In Tarot, the pentacle embodies the element earth at the North Point, acting as a shield or mirror, and symbolizing abundance and prosperity. The five-pointed star, the five senses, and the five extremities characterize the pentacle.

The East Point represents the air element as you magically pattern and transform energy. The wand in Tarot depicts this mastery point. Animation, energy, enterprise, and growth stem from the rod or wand. The unmanifest passes through the wand, and becomes patterned or manifest. Ideas, hope, and renewal of the cycle blow through our awareness from the East Point.

Fire fills the South Point, symbolized by the sword in Tarot. The magician's athame fills with power and strength as it informs and cuts through oneness. Bold and intelligent action, courage in the face of adversity, and the destruction of negativity all lie within the athame or sword at the South Point.

The symbolism of the West Point, embodied by the cup in Tarot, includes emotions and feelings of love, pleasure and beauty. Instinct, fertility, well-being, and sensuality fill this watery point. All things of a fluid nature are ruled by the moon.

Flowing with the full moon's energy, healing work illustrates the uses of the elements. North, earth, gives you a foundation from which to work. East, air, grants you freedom, while south, fire, gives you strength and power. Finally, the direction west, representing water, shows you how to flow. In that fluidity, you learn to stay afloat, and finally swim gracefully with the goddess and her consort.

Colors also correspond to the elemental circle. North is green or black. East is gold or red. South shines in red or white while West is depicted by blue or gray. Red symbolizes the rising sun, and white signifies high noon, as gray represents twilight, and black denotes midnight.

Learn to move with the tides and rhythms of oneness as you gain insight into the elemental nature of all things. Remember, whenever you engage in energy patterning, constantly refer to the four keys or Wynds: wisdom, self-honesty, self-responsibility, and love. These keys form a structure or format from which to work.

Traditionally, High Moon rituals and healing begin after dark. Start by setting up your arena. Place your magical tools in their positions upon the altar. Smell the incense burning. Watch the flames dance on the candle tops, and listen to the soft harp music playing in the background. Consider the timeliness of the healing work, in light of the energy of the particular full moon. For example, the Chaste Moon sets the stage for healing the different aspects of yourself, whereas the Blood Moon is conducive to healings of a circulatory nature.

Clear out your arena with cobalt-blue light, saying, "May all evil and foulness be gone from this place. I ask this in the Lady's name. Be gone, now and forevermore." Do this three times, turning in a sunwise circle and sweeping the area with your hands and mind.

Next, draw a clockwise circle with your athame, seeing the blue-white flame flaring out of the blade. Purify the four corners with salt, starting at the North Point and chanting, "Ayea, Ayea Kerridwen! Ayea, Ayea Kernunnos! Ayea, Ayea, Ayea!"

As you face the altar after moving around the four corners of the circle, say in a firm voice, "Blessed Be! Blessed Be the Gods! Blessed Be all who are gathered here."

Merge with the goddess, and knock nine times on the altar with the handle of your athame or wand, in three series of three. Be creative. If you are without your tools, outdoors or traveling, use your hand to rap nine times on a tree nearby, or on whatever is convenient.

At this point in the Ritual of the Full Moon Circle, call in the Four Wards. Bring the four elements into the center of the circle. If you are working with a group of people, the woman and man representing the goddess and god are the only ones in the circle at this time. The man takes the athame and draws a circle of sacred fire on the already laid circle. He stands at the North Point. The woman hands him the bowl with earth (salt can also be used), and he sprinkles it three times before handing it back. He holds his arms up, and with his athame in his right hand says, "Oh Great and Mighty One, Ruler of the North March, come, I pray you. Protect the Gate of the North Ward. Come! I summon you!"

The man moves clockwise to each of the three other points in the circle, repeating the same words, inserting the appropriate directional point at each corner where needed, i.e., east, south, and west. The woman hands him the elements one by one, and he waves the incense three times, carefully waves the lighted candle three times and sprinkles water three times, accordingly, depending upon his position in the circle. Everyone present merges deeply with the elemental energy of each of the Four Wards as they are called in to stand watch over the circle.

Traditionally the man performs the preliminaries, and also calls in the Four Wards. The woman, representing the Great Goddess, gives him the elements of energy. These elements symbolize the tools of infinite potential. She bestows these gifts of oneness to the consort, and in turn, he willingly gives his strength and power in the ever-changing, ever-renewing cycle of life.

Woman holds the power, and man wields the light. Woman and man represent polarities of energy, aspects that are blended within each of us. Always keep oneness in mind. Everything is connected. Separation is an illusion. For example, if you are working alone, you play the parts of both the woman and man in ritual, goddess and god. Feel free to make up your own guidelines.

After the Four Wards are called into the circle, the man traditionally cuts a gate, just below the East Point. The woman removes the four elements. If you are working with a group, the others now enter the circle through this energetic gate. The man then closes the gate with his athame, and hands it back to the woman, who places the athame back upon the altar.

Whether you work alone or with a group, the process of healing remains the same. First, examine your intention for doing the healing work. What is your expectation? If the person to be healed is present, then that person must desire to be healed.

Ask her or him, "Do you want this healing? Do you accept this healing energy?" Continue with the healing work, only after you receive a strong confirmation or indication from the person that they want to participate fully in the healing experience. If you meet with a less-than-positive response, move on to another healing or magical work.

Next, choose the sponsors for the healing work. Select goddesses and gods based upon your rapport, and their attributes. Every goddess and consort emits and absorbs certain types of energies, elemental and otherwise. Match these energies as closely as you can to the healing work. For example, if a malady can be remedied by application of wet heat, ask Borvo to be one of your sponsors in the healing.

Utilize the magical symbols and tools, as well as other correspondences, like color, stones, sounds, and scents associated with the particular sponsor you have selected. Generally, three sponsors are selected for each healing work. Chose the same, or different goddess and god energies for each healing work. Remember, healing is a pleasurable and positive experience.

Join hands with your mate and/or the group members. Energy flows more efficiently in an alternating current, so make an effort to link your healing circle in an alternating pattern; woman, man, woman, man, woman. You are manipulating powerful polarities of energy when you do a magical work, moving into other dimensions of light. Build your desire for the success of the healing work and merge with the flow of oneness. Pay attention to the qualities and types of energies you encounter as you merge. Notice the nuance and subtlety of energy, its shapes and movements, and the feel of oneness. Within every cell of your being, know that you are the boundless.

Traditionally, blue, green, and gold light are employed in healing work. Blue cleans out and washes the existing pattern. Green sets up the new healthy pattern, while gold fuels the new positive pattern. Ultraviolet is used carefully to destroy negativity or burn up disease within the body. White helps in healing spiritual pain, and motivates patterns. Visualize, feel, taste, touch and smell the colors of light you use in healing. Be the light. Be the energy of each color.

Begin to chant the names of the sponsors you have chosen. Traditionally the goddess or god name is chanted three times or nine times. Again use alternating female and male energies in your chanting pattern. For example, if you chose Kerridwen, Dagda, and Danu to be your sponsors, you would chant, "Kerridwen, Kerridwen, Kerridwen! Dagda, Dagda, Dagda! Danu, Danu, Danu! Ayea, Ayea, Ayea!"

Merge deeply with oneness, and peak the energy within and without you. As you chant the names of the goddess and her consort, run your arms out and upward, hands joined. Allow the healing energy to move through you, and outward towards your selected destination. In a firm and focussed voice, chant the final triplet, "Ayea, Ayea, Ayea!," and let go of the hands of those next to you. Release the healing energy out into the manifest universe, and direct it to its recipient. If you are working on your mate or yourself, or someone who is physically present, actually lay your hands on the person, and run the healing energy directly into them. Remember, you are the conduit of oneness.

Mirror a new healthy image back to the person being healed. Give them an opportunity to see a new vision of themselves by reflecting a new positive image back to them. This facilitates the healing experience, and adds to the cohesion and success rate of the healing work. Know the healing is complete. Turn your Mind to this result. When you are finished with each healing work, clear the area thoroughly.

Swaying, toning, texture, and general environment all enhance the healing experience. When you sway back and forth, you pattern the energy around you. Toning and chanting likewise pattern the energy. How you set up your circle and perform the preliminaries all figure into the healing experience. Each time you interact with energy and with oneness, it interacts with you.

A healing works through patterning energy. Mind moves. As energy moves Mind, Mind moves energy. To more deeply understand the properties of energy, Gwyddonic Tradition teaches several simple techniques. You can either work with your partner or in a group. Face your partner, if there are two of you. Be aware of which directional or elemental points you are standing on. How do the sensations you feel when you stand on the North Point differ from those you feel when standing at the East Point?

Experiment with elemental positioning. How does it affect your energy and the flow of everything around you? At large gatherings, work in groups of five, with each person standing at each of the four directions—North, East, South, and West—with the fifth person waiting outside of the circle. Make an effort to match the energy of the person to the direction. A certain person may seem more earthy, while another may radiate a fiery energy.

Next, face your palms up toward your partner; in this case, the person across from you. Run as much energy as you can from oneness through your body and out your hands. Choose a particular color of light to run, and practice changing the color. The usual pattern for this technique begins with bright blue, changing to green and then moving to gold. Build the light and energy through your intent, expectation, desire, and depth of merge. When you work in groups of five, the fifth person then steps into the center of the circle and receives the positive benefits of this healing energy. Add clear quartz crystals in each person's hands to enhance the energetic field and vortex of light. Also try toning, OM-ing or chanting to magnify and direct the field effect. This technique parallels the Tibetan art of Tumo which generates massive amounts of body heat.

As you become adept at healing and patterning energy, you learn to flex and bend conditioned time and space, in new and innovative ways. Distance healing acts as just one example of these new time-space continua. Notice the subtle differences and similarities between healing someone who is present, as opposed to sending healing energy several miles or light years away. Move beyond your imagination, and explore the infinite patterns of energy.

Dreaming serves as fertile ground for healing work. Set up your dreams with the appropriate intention, expectation, desire, and merge as a way to pattern healing energy for yourself or someone else. Healing relationships, memories, and the energy of events is done by accessing oneness through dreaming. Use dream images to heal stress and psychosomatic disorders and to balance energies. Try using color, light, warmth and heaviness to enhance the process. Dreaming of another view or world can also assist in the healing experience.

83

Learn to heal through dream stories or teaching tales. Dream stories reach into oneness and reshape it. Consider asking Dumiatis to help you create a unique dream story for yourself, or for your children. As you tell your child a dream story at bedtime, be aware of your tone, pitch, and body gestures. Adults as well as children respond to stories relevant to issues in their lives. Shape your dream stories in such a way as to capture your full attention, leading you on a healing and magical adventure.

Guided Journey

John-Michael races out of the bathroom, still wet from his bath. He runs out into the middle of the living room and jumps up and down three times before leaping on to the couch, just beyond his mother's grasp.

"John-Michael, come here and let me dry you off," she pleads while holding the towel out toward the naked child jumping on the couch. "Sometimes, you sure act your age...three."

She laughs while bounding over to the couch. She moves the towel over John-Michael's wet body as he giggles and squirms off the couch. She chases him into his room and after much pursuit, puts his night clothes on him.

"Come on, John-Michael, it's time for bed," she calls to her young son.

"Aw Momma, do I have to go to bed?" he asks sweetly. "I'm not tired yet."

She looks into his blue gray eyes, and watches as he gives her his most innocent and endearing smile.

"Please, Momma?"

"I'll tell you what," she counters. "What if I tell you a bedtime story."

John-Michael responds by screaming with delight and jumping up and down.

"Come on, you have to get into bed before I begin the story." She turns down the covers, and John-Michael leaps into bed.

"What story are you going to tell me, Momma?" he asks as he looks up at her with anticipation.

"I'm going to tell you the story of the Seed Woman." She smiles.

"Who is the Seed Woman?" he asks with an enthusiastic glee.

"Listen and I'll tell you," she answers while stroking his soft, light brown hair.

"Long ago when the world was young, there lived a group of people known as the tribe of Una. For many suns and moons, the great hunter Esus had always provided for the peoples of Una. Many times, the men of the tribe had returned from the hunt with their heads high and their pouches full. And many times, they gave their thanks to the great hunter god Esus." She pauses long enough to catch her breath, and once again looks down into her son's anxious eyes.

"Tell me more," he smiles at her, feasting on her words.

"This hunting way of life went on for many years for the tribe of Una, until one horribly cold winter. The snow storms were many, and the winter was unusually long. The tribe sought refuge from the freezing cold in the caves of Adu, on the south side of Ellenglen. To survive the winter, the tribe was forced to use what food they had saved from the previous summer. This was not very much because the people of Una had never wanted for anything before. Everything had always been provided for them by Esus. As the cold spell continued, they prayed more and more to the great hunter god.

"Finally spring came, the rivers thawed, the snows melted and things seemed to look up for the tribe of Una. The people came down from the caves, and into the valley below as they had every spring before. The men gathered, and after praying to Esus, they left on the first hunt.

"Fourteen days passed, and the men still had not returned to the village. The women began to worry something terrible had happened to the hunting party. On the eighteenth day, the men finally returned to the village, but their heads were hung low, and their pouches were empty. 'There was no game to be found anywhere,' they exclaimed in desperation.

"Other hunting parties followed, but they also came back empty-handed, and the people of Una began to feel the gnawing pangs of hunger creeping closer and closer. Each hunting party went out farther than the one before it. East, west, north, and south, but their efforts were to no avail.

"Just as it looked like the tribe would starve, an old woman came before the Council of Elders. Her name was Coventina, the crazy woman. They called her the crazy woman because she talked to plants, and was never very interested in the hunting ways of the rest of the tribe. She spoke to the Council about how plants and food could be grown and harvested. She said the tribe would never have to hunt again. Many in the Council Chambers whispered to each other that it couldn't be done, while others openly ridiculed the strange old woman.

"Coventina would not let their doubts stop her, and she reached into one her deep pockets and pulled out a handful of seeds. She called to the four winds of harmony, and as she moved her hand across the land, little dots of light sprang forth. Soon the earth was alive with different types of plants.

"The people of Una watched in awe as different fruits and vegetables began appearing on the branches of the trees and plants. Coventina picked an apricot from a nearby tree, and gave the ripe, juicy fruit to Bridget, head of the Council. Bridget held the orange ball in her hand, surveying it with amazement before biting into the apricot's sweet flesh. With a smile of jubilation, she held the piece of fruit, with one bite taken from it, high in the air for all to see.

"'From this day on, the people of Una will become one with the Earth Mother, and in turn she will provide us with food.'

"Bridget turned to face Coventina and declared, 'Also, from this day forward, Coventina will be known as the Seed Woman.'

"The tribe rejoiced, and a great feast was enjoyed by all."

John-Michael looks up into his mother's eyes with an innocent clarity that she often finds startling. "I liked that story, Momma," he says softly while touching her hand with his. "It reminds me of you and your flower garden."

She smiles at the young boy. "Before you go to sleep, I'd like to do a healing for the Earth Mother."

"You mean a healing like we did last week for Grandma?" he asks in his excited voice.

"Kind of like that," she responds with a chuckle.

"Why are we doing a healing? Is the Earth Mother sick like Grandma?"

"Well not quite like Grandma, but sort of the same. Right now, the Earth Mother needs all of the energy people can give to her. Just like the tribe of Una, people must become aware of the Earth Mother's needs and cycles, or she won't provide for us anymore."

She feels the boy's small, soft hands grab hers, and a warm energy begins to fill her body. With her mind she draws a blue-white circle of light around the room, bringing in the Great Wards to stand at the four corners.

"Let's use the energies of Esus, Coventina, and Anu while imagining an ocean-blue, and then a forest-green color in our minds," she says to him as she presses her fingers against his.

Together they chant, "Esus, Esus, Esus! Coventina, Coventina, Coventina! Anu, Anu, Anu! Ayea, Ayea, Ayea!"

The room becomes silent as mother and son hold their joined hands up in the air, finally releasing the healing energy toward the Earth Mother.

"Now goodnight," she says softly, while bending over to kiss his forehead.

"Goodnight Momma," he responds with a tired yawn. She closes the light, and looks up at the stars painted on the ceiling with phosphorescent paint. Their glow stays in her mind, even after she leaves her son's room and moves to her own room.

Through the bedroom window, she sees the fullness of the moon as it fills the horizon, like a giant, fluorescent, golden sphere suspended in the sky. "I don't think I've ever seen it so big," she whispers to herself before sliding her body into the soft over-stuffed chair in front of the window. Lying back in the chair, she feels herself drawn to the moon. She pulls its light to her. The milky-orange golden light escapes the luminous orb, spiraling toward the earth and flowing into her.

The spirals of light weave through her body like fingers, caressing the top of her head, and then easing down to touch her face. All around her lips, the moonlight strokes and kisses her. Moving down the soft curves of her neck like a warm tongue, she shivers slightly as the spiraling moonbeams surround, then climb, her breasts.

Waves of ecstasy cascade through her body as the moonlight glides from her breasts, like mountains, and then down through her canyons. The spirals climb through the trees, and passionately caress the earth below. Her body quivers and quakes, with each aftershock greater than the one before it. The sensation intensifies until she feels a river of light busting open like a dam. A sudden torrential rush sends ripples running down every inch of her body.

From the doorway her mate watches as she strokes the soft earthiness of her body. With eyes closed, she lightly caresses her soft skin. In the pale moonlight and against the backdrop of the light blue chair, her dark skin seems even darker. Her hands move to her long, dark brown hair, and then down her shoulders to her supple breasts.

He watches each movement intently before moving closer to the chair. He can hear her breath as it becomes deeper, and more pronounced with each passing sensation. Soon he stands above her, still watching as she increases the intensity of her stroking motion. He watches the moonlight dipping down her breasts, and drinking in the darkness of her thighs. Her legs and feet move back and forth against one another.

From within her pleasure, she feels a hand caressing her hand. She opens her eyes, and sees the man's golden eyes staring into hers. His dark brown, curly hair falls down around his face as she reaches up to grab his arms, and pulls him toward her. His hungry lips devour her neck. His warm tongue sends chills down her spine, and she grabs a handful of his soft hair and gently tugs. His mouth now feels like liquid fire as he moves his tongue between her thighs. His hands stroke the contours of her rounded bottom as he grips her softness, and pulls her ever closer to him.

He pauses and then joins her on the chair, gently pulling her on top of him. As she mounts him, he stares deeply into her dark doe-like eyes. Pushing deep within her well, the rhythmic movement of their bodies becomes synchronous, moving faster and faster.

He touches his lips to her soft skin, and tastes the saltiness of her sweat, and the sweetness of her perfume. Her warm, moist breath grazes against the inside of his ear, sending waves of burning desire crashing through her like the ocean breaking against the shore. She is the earth, bearer of life, and Mother of All Things. He is the sun, sower of the seed, and Father of All Things. Together they form a star child, symbol of their union of perfect love and perfect peace.

She feels a hot final rush of light and sensation as his body begins to tremble. A river of potent liquid moves down Coventina's well, planting a new kernel. Life anew; life renewed.

The Hare Moon

Danu & Math

We ride together through the starry night
Dragons leading us to light
We breathe and dream as one alone
And as one becomes two becomes three.

The Hare Moon ☽

Danu & Math

Full Moon in Scorpio, Sun in Taurus
Fixed negative water and earth elements

The Goddess and Her Consort

Venture into Wonderland like Alice, as you follow the hare down through the magical passageway, leading to personal self-discovery. At moonrise on the fifth High Moon, glean the transformative secrets of the quick and agile hare. From this knowledge learn to master your control of self and physical manifestation.

The word "hare" stems from the Old English word *hara*. Hara in Eastern thought means "the belly" or "the seat of power." Hara represents the point of origin and potentiality of energy. In concurrence with this concept, Eastern North American Algonquian tribes credit the hare with forming the earth, then ordering and enlarging it. In trickster tales, a human-like hare plays the main character. Called Great Hare or White Hare, he acts as a masterful magician.

Popular throughout European folklore, you find the fertile hare concealed in Queen Boudicca's cloak. The powerful Iceni warrior queen unleashed the hare when she defended her land from Roman Invasion. The formidable Mary Queen of Scots used the animal as her personal emblem as well. Folklore suggests that practitioners of magic change into hares and cats more than any other animals. By doing so, these adepts acquire the particular animal's characteristics and qualities.

Just as the Wolf Moon mirrors the face of the predator and hunter, the Hare Moon expresses the qualities of the prey and the gatherer. Hares quietly feed at night in the light of the moon. They possess an affinity for water and are extremely strong swimmers. Timid yet curious, hares adapt quickly to changes in their environment. In fact, they even alter the color of their coat depending upon the season.

In Gwyddonic Druid Tradition, the hare serves as the emblematic badge for the first stage of learning. The badge is a reminder of the goals of this particular level of instruction. As a hare, you have large ears, large eyes, and learn to listen. In fact, as a hare, you are born with your eyes open, and accordingly you learn to look and see. Above all, as a hare, you are especially fertile with boundless potential.

The goddess embodies the fertility of the hare. Danu is the Mother of the Tuatha De Danann, which translates as the Children or Family of Danu. The Tuatha are the divine race of people in Old Irish mythology who became learned and powerful in the Northern Isles of Greece. Motivated by their birthright, the Tuatha De Dannan returned to and conquered what is now called Britain. Gwyddonic Druidism stems from the Old Religion, and from the sacred knowledge of the Tuatha.

Representing the elements air of air, the goddess Danu possesses wisdom and control over all things, whatsoever they may be. In addition to being a goddess of the people, she is also the goddess of complete abundance. Her name stems from the Old Celtic *dan* which means "art, knowledge, and poetry."

Originating from the North, the people of the Mother Goddess Danu possess the gifts of magic, and understand the energies and forces of the Otherworld. Symbolically then, the goddess Danu becomes the vessel of the forces of oneness, in the shape of planets, patterns of stars, and in solar systems and universes. Rooted in stellar mythology, the constellation Cassiopeia honors the goddess in its name, Llys Don, meaning Danu's House.

Appearing as an elderly plump woman with silver hair, the Mother of the Gods glances at you with deep piecing gray eyes. She wears robes of silver and grey. In the blink of an eye, the image of the goddess Danu changes into her other face, that of a young beautiful woman. She wears bright green or white robes, and wherever she travels, a green cast of light follows her like a trail of abundance and growing prosperity. The Lady Danu carries a magical staff as she floats across universes.

Consort and sometimes symbolic brother to the goddess Danu, Math portrays a Welsh god of sorcery, magic and enchantment. As master druid and teacher, he portrays the seasonal king, and represents the cycle of life, death and rebirth. The consort dies and is reborn every year, moving from one dimension to the other. Thus, he serves as king of the empire of the domain, with ready access to great wealth and knowledge.

Math generally appears as a mature, virile man, with white or silver streaks in his hair. The wise and powerful consort feels protective, and has a spirited sense of humor. Math is all knowing, and nothing escapes the attention of his deep blue eyes. Loving and kind, he appears in light blue or white colored vestments.

An active participant in Celtic Mythology, Math acts as uncle and teacher to Gwydion. He helps his young student and shapeshifter to create Blodenwedd, the flower goddess. The consort Math also tests Arianrhod for virginity. On a practical vein, Math brings the swine to Ireland, and is closely linked with the pig, representing the Underworld and transformative powers. He weaves his will through his magical symbol, the Fabric of Life.

Merge with the consort Math and with the goddess Danu to gain control over self and physical manifestation. The consort shows you how to create all patterns from oneness, and the giving goddess brings you abundance and prosperity as you gain deeper rapport with her many faces. Allow yourself to openly receive the wisdom and power of the Mother of the Gods and her wise and noble consort.

Practical Knowledge and Useful Information— Control of Self and Physical Manifestation

Gwyddonic Druid Tradition bases its teaching on three stages or degrees of learning. As a First Degree Hare, you start upon your adventure into the boundless with your eyes and ears open. As a Second Degree Raven, you sprout wings and are finally freed from past concepts and conditioning. As a Second Degree Raven, you can be taught to talk and can learn wisdom. As a Third Degree Owl, you sit on the shoulder of the goddess, and have learned to merge at will.

Ancient tradition teaches you to follow your spirit energy and listen to the messages of animals and plants, as well as to your body and to your dreams. Listen to the boundless while looking deeply into oneness. Merge with the knowledge that you have the power to move beyond your conditioning, and the illusionary limitations of culture and consensus society. Allow your individuality and creativity to grow and flourish.

Adventure on a journey of personal self-development and control of self by acquainting yourself with totem animals. The word *totem* means "from kin, my kin, her kin, his kin." As Lord of the Animals, Kernunnos serves as an example of totem mastery. He often appears with antlers growing from his head, and he rules and protects all living creatures. The attributes of the consort embrace the qualities of totem energy.

As sacred animals, totems are regarded as mythical ancestors, protectors and friends. Taboos against hunting and eating totem animals are common. On the other hand, the ritual killing and eating is also practiced. Totemism mirrors itself and seeks to balance. Often a sacred totem animal is selected primarily on the basis that it serves as the main food source.

Obviously, food plays the leading role in survival. Totemism directly results from this relationship in nature. The raven leads the wolf to food, and the wolf leaves plenty for the raven. Learn to mirror nature. People gain knowledge about the energy and patterns of nature through a special relationship with animals and plants. They frequently take the names of animals as their own.

By cultivating rapport with the energy of a totem, the wisdom of the sacred animal or plant passes into you. You marvel as you flow into all shapes, all animals, and all energies. Totem animals in Gwyddonic Druid Tradition include the salmon, hawk, owl, bear, hare, eagle, raven, deer, cat, horse, cow, ram, pig, duck, swan, fox, wolf, dolphin, whale, manta ray, hound, serpent, and dragon.

All animals stand as totems. Any animal you encounter in your world, in dream or in a merged state, can act as your totem animal. Modern totem animals appear on T-shirts and belt buckles, picturing cats, dogs, wolves, ducks, dinosaurs, and horses. Choose a favorite animal for your totem, or create your own unique animal. Anything you image in your mind can serve as your totem. While moving through the totem experience, remember the elemental and astrological qualities of the animal. For example, the scorpion and eagle generally relate to the West Point and water, whereas the bull is associated with the North Point and earth.

One practical exercise using the totem is projecting the double. The double arises from the primary through merging deeply and projecting your Mind energy outward into another energetic shape. Take the form of any animal as you energetically shape and pattern it in your Mind. The double returns into oneness. Remember to carefully pattern your totem experiences through positive intention, expectation, desire and a deep merge.

Set the stage for this experience just as you would any other magical work. As you move freely into whatever form you choose, you become the shapeshifter. Practice shifting and assembling energy into the shapes you turn your Mind to. Begin to understand you are your own totem. You are the human animal. What is your energy form? How does it differ from the energy of other animals? How is human energy configured, shaped, recycled and renewed? What is its pattern? How connected are you to human energy?

Gain insight into people and the human experience by taking time to watch people. Accumulative skill comes from noticing the similarities and differences of people and patterns. Consider watching your hand until you slowly move it. Explore simple movements, and notice their natural structure and complexity, paying attention to subtle changes. Learn to read body language, body movements, and subvocal speech. Move to a world beyond labels as you begin to see things as they are, without connotation. Understand the flow of the boundless as you become more deeply aware of your body sensations.

Allow these sensations and impressions to guide you in your personal self-development and exploration. Mastery often lies in tracing and knowing your dreams, fantasies, impressions, double signals, and incongruities.

Learning control of self requires your constant participation. The inner motivation in the form of desire must be present. Your intention should be as clear as possible, given the information and knowledge you have at that particular time. The more you comprehend and work with body energy, the more control you will have in your daily world.

Your body harbors many secrets, waiting for you to rediscover them. Your connection to the sensations of your body increases your vitality and sense of presence. Body awareness acts as a key element to living in the moment. Your creativity thrives as you live more closely to your flowing body energy and to your dreams. Know yourself and understand the harmony of all things as you merge deeper and deeper with oneness. Expand your awareness, viewing and relating, as you begin to multi-sense your every perception and impression.

Relationship creates opportunities for you to learn control of self. Anyone or anything you have a relationship to, or relate to, should strengthen you. In turn, you strengthen anyone and anything you relate to. We are constantly absorbing and emitting light, and this holds true in relationships. Learning to balance energy in relationship comes through practice and effort. Control of self and self-awareness walk hand in hand.

Sexual experience becomes a viable mode for gaining control of self, and for increasing personal rapport. Abandon and control play roles in sexual expression. Moving between these polarities gives you a means for accessing knowledge about your body energy. Draw your attention to each sensation as you travel through your sexual adventures. Merge deeply with your total being, with your partner, and with oneness. Allow yourself to experience all things.

Control of self springs from controlling what you move your Mind toward. There is great power in this one concept. Mind creates, and Mind patterns. Mind stems from oneness. You can direct Mind. Cultivating the impersonal observer becomes a necessary prerequisite in the control of self. Ego becomes a movie-like filter or overlay as you watch your reactions and responses. You begin to adopt another view as a way beyond reaction, so you can better respond to your world. Detach yourself from your ego, and watch yourself mirror your world as your world mirrors you. A key to developing rapport is by observing and creatively mirroring people's behavior and responses. Very few individuals reach this plateau of total non-reactiveness. To do so is to become a God.

Always apply the four keys of wisdom, self-responsibility, self-honesty, and love as you tap into the collective storehouse of knowledge that lies within. Merge with oneness and realize that within you are the resources for the totality of creation. Learn to acknowledge and use these natural powers and energies.

Your bright self outshines any negativity you encounter. Your bright self resides within you as a natural healthy core, and you maintain this bright center through turning your Mind toward positivity. Trust and understand your inner self and oneness as you gain control of your personal energies. Intend your bright self to grow and prosper.

The root of all physical manifestation stems from one-ness. There exist boundless shapes and forms of energy, manifest and unmanifest. As you become more adept, you learn to know and direct these energies into tangible patterns. Control of self facilitates physical manifestation. You become who you choose to become, and do what you choose to do. You manifest the energies in your life accordingly. You begin to shape and form energy in seemingly magical ways.

Recognize your own life pattern. Develop an awareness of change as you see the fabric of life. Energy moves in a fluid form, where every action has an effect. Every thought, movement, feeling, and sensation affects the whole, changing the face of oneness. The Upanishads fully understand this concept, writing it into their philosophy, much like the aboriginal people.

Anything you dream, merge with, or otherwise imagine can be used to pattern. Allow ideas and sensations to unfold through all the channels of your awareness. Mirror and mimic their characteristics and qualities. Follow your patterns forward, backward, and crosswise to better understand their ever-changing location and their shape in the flow of oneness.

Mastering skills, creative ability, and other forms of personal self-improvement can be obtained through merging deeply with oneness, and taking action steps to fulfill your patterns. Dream your own dreams. Use your intention to direct the energy in your dreams and personal patterns. Follow that which you love, for that is your true commitment in this life.

Merge with the boundless and travel to new vistas and worlds as you learn control of self. Allow the goddess and god to teach you novel ways to view and perceive your life adventure. Dream of infinite possibilities as you voyage into a world of light.

Guided Journey

She stares intently at the computer screen and her eyes feel sore and tired. She rubs them, and then smoothes her hair back from her face, weaving its length through her open fingers. She sits up slightly, trying to build up enough energy to continue her writing. She looks out the picture window at her left toward the deep shadows of the tall pine trees. The dusky twilight turns swiftly into night as she shifts her focus back to the screen.

The only audible sound is the quiet hum of the computer. Her eyes close again, then open, then close again. She sighs and gives in to her exhaustion. She flips off the computer switch, and stares at the empty screen. Her eyelids grow heavy, and they finally close as she leans back in the overstuffed chair. Her head falls back, and she breathes deeply. She clears her mind and merges intentionally into dream. She shifts.

The boundless flows before her, as her body becomes supple and warm in her restive state. She looks luminous in the darkened room. A golden spiral of energy suddenly streams out of her left wrist and twirls in the air. Cascading sparks of light jump off the swirling energy stream. A brilliant green-blue spiral of energy pours out from her right wrist.

Her body shifts slightly, as a red spiral of energy boldly leaps from her left ankle. The red light weaves its essence into the shape of a giant dragon. The great red beast fills the room and spills into the darkness of the night. A pure white light, larger than the others, spirals out from her right ankle and joins the other energies dancing before the dreaming woman. The colors of spiraling light weave their way around her, lifting her upward on wings of rainbow beams, like massive dragons. They move her through the dream door, where there is no door.

The swirling beasts carry her purposefully forward, flying her to another world, to a familiar place in oneness she travels to willingly in her dreams. The colorful dragon-shaped energies move her slowly and deliberately through the portal, acting as intermediaries between the manifest universe and the unmanifest.

The spiraling lights reverse positions on her body, mirroring themselves in dream. Their light colors weave together like a double helix as they move her faster and faster to a reality somewhere beyond her waking world.

She sees realms of energy flash by, worlds arranged and layered like the petals of a rosebud. As clusters of these consecutive realms peel back against the dark void, the woman feels herself unfold as well.

The spiraling dragon lights soar away from her, and she floats into a world of pure energy. She transforms into a sphere of fluid green light and feels herself being sucked through a bright gaping hole. She is pulled into a radiant universe that is tied together with multicolored threads of light. The threads of energy form web-like lattices of shining energy that crisscross, filling the space in all directions.

She flows like green fire. As she moves with intention across the endless fabric of light, the brilliant threads seem energized and strengthened by her action. The glistening filaments stretch out infinitely before her. Each motion of her spherical light seems to trigger a response from the threads of the fabric, like an impression or perception of pure, direct energy. She melds herself to the expansive labyrinth of light and traverses great distances instantly.

She knows where she is going. Flowing over strands of shining color, she dips into a soft tunnel-like opening. Rivers of white and gold light cascade through her as she plunges into a vortex of teeming brilliance. She merges with the source, and spins out of the vortex, feeling dizzy and excited.

Fleeting perceptions and momentary sensations of boundless shapes of energy pass over her. She rolls smoothly off the tresses of gold and white light, and splashes into a cup of soft white liquid energy.

Suddenly, a shard of crimson light flashes down next to her, settling into a sphere of red pulsating liquid energy.

She turns her glow of awareness toward the magnificent red sphere. Her green light swims towards it, and rolls off the outpouring of warm red light. She senses the flow of coursing energy. Its current, differing from hers, runs more strongly male.

He spirals toward her in the shape of a figure six. She winds around him, interweaving green liquid light with the contrasting red. She bounds away, forming a figure nine of green radiance around him, shooting through him and mirroring his pattern of pure energy. They dance and join into a figure eight briefly, and then flow slightly away from each other, their light humming and throbbing.

He quickly showers her with white pearl-like beads of light. The exquisite beads touch her perception like snowflakes, tickling her, flooding her sphere with swirling pulses of soft radiance.

She tempers her response to match his energy pattern. She flows to him and then away, wavering and spinning her liquid green light into a vast rainbow of colors. They travel together out of the radiant cup of white energy, and flow along the colored lattice of pure bright light. They move in every direction at once, flowing and floating effortlessly.

The motion fills her awareness as she swims through the air. She plunges and dives through liquid fields of pure light. Now and again, she joins her vibrant green field of energy to his flaming red radiance, as they traverse the intricate pattern of the luminous fabric. Energy flows as energy. Swimming balls of beautiful color move together, creating myriads of gleaming light. She dives even more deeply into oneness, gently pulling him with her.

He follows her as if she were a energetic map, gliding along her sleek lines of brilliance, down through her glowing valleys, rolling over her cascading rivers and pulsating mountains.

In a pure energy world without filters, the green and red balls of light connect and completely flow into one another. Their energy bodies melt into one multifaceted rainbow, casting tiny bubbles of colored energy into the fabric around them. The radiant threads caress the liquid balls of energy, softly weaving the spheres into a braid of vibrant white, green and red.

Her awareness fills with lightning-red light, piercing her spherical field. She sustains her perception as she surrounds his fiery energy in circles of soft green ringlets. They blend into one another, and wheel even faster along the fabric of light.

Ever-flowing and ever-renewing, the balls of light flow swiftly into a powerful place of wonder and bliss. Their combined radiance forms a massive cone of light, and the brilliant cone speeds into a world beyond worlds, and then directly into the boundless. Small loat bubbles of energy float freely, circling, spiraling, clustering, and leaping in every direction in a never-beginning, never-ending dance. Their motion creates a strange, low, humming tone.

The ever-growing cone of rising energy thrusts itself through the gateway of infinity, looping back through the fabric and spiraling out beyond. The fertile cone splits into two, then three shapes, then four and five, and then in countless balls of fluorescent multicolored light. Awareness and perception flow to and from the shores of the source, and she feels the pure energy flood her being. She circles and spins as she drifts in the pure liquid radiance.

Joined together, he moves with her, and they whirl and blossom into arching white light.

She calls her intermediaries of dragon light. White, gold, blue-green, and red spirals of light lift her gently from the threads of brilliant energy, and wing her slowly back to the overstuffed chair. She intentionally moves her perception to a coherent position, and stretches her body slightly.

She shifts.

Her eyelids flutter, and then her eyes open slowly. She awakens and looks out the picture window to her left at the evening sun, casting its last beams through the branches of the pine trees. She flips the computer switch on, and listens to the faint whine and ping of the machine as it boots up. Her fingers stroke the smooth keys of the computer keyboard. They move gracefully, as she brings up the file "Moonflow," and continues her writing.

The Dyad Moon

Mei & Gwydion

Your eyes blaze like liquid wildfire
across galaxies of heated memory
A passion play in a dream filled night
A memory so ancient, it stands in stone.

CHAPTER SIX

The Dyad Moon ☽♃

Mei & Gwydion

Full Moon in Sagittarius, Sun in Gemini
Mutable positive fire and air elements

The Goddess and Her Consort

The Dyad Moon serves as the next landmark on our journey along the path of the moon. The sixth full moon lies
approximately halfway along the path of the moon, where
the energies of light and darkness meet. Symbolic of time
and union, this moon is also called the Boon Moon in
Gwyddonic Druid Tradition. Signifying the time of year
when the goddess grants you a gift or a boon, your appreciation of this full moon directly correlates to your positive actions of the previous year.

The concept of the boon, which is a divine gift from
the goddess, reminds the practitioner to stay positive and
bright. From the boon you learn you alone make and
break your own patterns. You learn about timing as you
create your world and the gifts within it. Notice how it
behooves you to direct your attention toward the positive
mating of energies as you orchestrate your magical works
on this High Moon.

The word *dyad* stems from the Greek and Latin word *dyas*, meaning "the number two." The Dyad Moon represents the strengthening force of two. A dyad is defined as an element, atom or radical that has a combining power of two—that which is doubled or paired. Paired relationships create infinite possibilities. For example, chromosomes are paired, creating new life. Also, much of modern technology, for instance the digital computer, is based on binary or paired systems.

The pairing of energies reflects in nature by the multitude of ways energies mate and intertwine. The twining moonflower vine, a type of morning glory, embodies the combining energies of two. From the mating and twining of energies, nature moves through the cycle, seeking a ever-renewing balance that never ends, never begins, ever flows, and ever grows.

Reproduction in humankind springs from the relationship of two, woman and man. In sexual experience, the exchange of energy between lovers strengthens each partner. Harmonious partnership, reflected in the mating powers of female and male energy, serves as a huge resource of energy. Positivity engenders positivity. Hence, the more energy you bring into your primary relationship, the stronger the union and the cumulative power of you and your partner.

The young and beautiful goddess Mei, pronounced May, combines the power of two, representing the earth and the sun. Similar to Rosemerta, Mei symbolizes wealth and prosperity, seen in the natural abundance and richness of the land. She smells of sweet meadow grass and wildflowers. Mother to the consort Gwalchmei, the goddess of the greening reigns as the queen of the flowers.

The Lady Mei moves like the warm sun over a grassy meadow, and wears silky sky blue or leaf green robes that seem to float and ripple as she moves. Appearing with long lustrous, wavy, golden-brown hair, her eyes shine the brilliant blue of spring skies. When the goddess touches you, she feels like a soft flame brushing against your cheek.

May Day celebrations are held in honor of the goddess Mei. Akin to the Roman fire goddess Maia, she embodies the natural fertility cycle of the seasons. Allow the beautiful Mei to share her secrets of warmth and thriving abundance. Her embrace feels like pure energy stroking your deep inner fire. The radiant Mei represents sexual heat and growth, bringing with her all the vigor and vibrancy of spring and early summer.

The great bard and enchanter Gwydion acts as consort to the lovely and fertile Mei. His shapeshifting ways entice and lure the sweet goddess as he courts the Lady with the delicate sound of his magical harp. Appearing young and handsome, the eloquent Gwydion has curling blonde and brown hair and brilliant blue eyes. He carries a staff of enchantment as he travels across universes. Usually he wears a blue robe or tunic, but at midnight he dresses all in gray.

113

The wizard Gwydion is the son of Don, or Danu, the Mother of the Tuatha De Dannan. Math, the all-knowing wizard, handed on his infinite skills and wisdom to his student and nephew, the god Gwydion. Brother to Arianrhod, Amaethon and Gobannon, Gwydion was one of the twelve that brought the swine to his people, supplying an everlasting source of food. The helpful consort gave his son Llew, his name, his right to bear arms, and created Llew's bride for him.

As Prince of the Powers of the Air, Gwydion acts as a master of illusion and fantasy. He touches you softly with his kindness and healing energy while showing you the divine majesty of the boundless. His long artistic fingers weave magical patterns over your skin as he plays you like well-strung harp. When Gwydion smiles at you, magical melodies seem to float through the air. You feel uplifted as his steady gaze transforms you into a powerful eagle, winging over tall rocky mountains and deep river canyons.

The combining energies of the lovely goddess Mei and the talented consort Gwydion represent the endless strengths and possibilities of union. In their joining, creativity and artistry blend with the vibrancy and fertility of the greening cycle. Rapport with Gwydion expands your perception of all things, while Mei gives you the energy and stamina for personal exploration through these new dimensions. As you integrate the qualities of the goddess and god, allow yourself to move into alternative realms of being, and into brave new worlds of dreaming.

Practical Knowledge and Useful Information— Realms of Dreaming and Doubling Out

Other worlds and realities that seemingly defy time and space commonly appear when you are in a merged state, especially in dream. Tibetans dwell in many worlds at once, and the third degree Indian Brahman achieves command over time, space, and even death. Move past your energetic conditioning, and go beyond your primary world. Begin to understand that your rational conception of the universe has its practical purposes, yet in the long run, serves as a somewhat distorted data base. Your true powers of perception lie in seeing all things as one, without connotation.

Carl Jung states, "Our unconscious existence is the real one and our conscious world is a kind of illusion, an apparent reality constructed for a specific purpose, like a dream which seems a reality as long as we are in it.... Unconscious wholeness therefore seems to me the true spiritus rector of all biological and psychic events." He was obviously aware of the oneness of energy.

You are your own magician. Use your Mind to move beyond time and space, and learn to access infinite worlds and resources of information. Allow yourself to merge and know the boundless. Dreaming acts as your vehicle on this avenue of self-exploration into other realms of being.

Discover that oneness is all things. As you merge deeper and deeper, the seeming separation between waking and dreaming becomes an illusion. When you are dreaming, Mind shifts and you realize that you actually live your dreams. With your eyes open, independent worlds of energy become available to you and your awareness increases proportionately. You begin to experience several worlds at one time, moving freely through the doorway of infinity, and into the flux and flow of oneness.

Use your mind to travel to these other worlds, rather than your body. Gwyddonic Druid Tradition teaches it is possible to take your body with you, but highly inadvisable. If you do take your body and then make even a tiny energetic mistake or error while in this secondary awareness, it is improbable you will return to your primary world in the same shape as you were in when you left.

Begin to perceive a homogeneous new world as you dive into the boundless while sustaining your awareness. See realms of energy and intent arranged like the petals of a rosebud. Every time you experience or touch another realm of existence with your Mind, another petal opens until finally you become a full and fragrant rose. Allow your energetic awareness to blossom and grow, and continue to move toward the light as you travel in the infinite realms of existence.

Information and awareness is encoded on a light level. When your mind expands and your awareness grows, it is because you have had an experience of more light. You constantly emit and absorb light, simultaneously. The more light or energy you have, the greater your capacity for experience. Place no limits on your light, for to do so cuts off your life. Instead, flow forward toward positive intention and expectation, enhancing and enlarging the scope of what you perceive.

With your increased awareness and perception, you begin to make constructive use of your own potential. Permanent changes occur when you merge with oneness and travel to other worlds. New relationships and views begin to form in your mind as you integrate and incorporate merging and dreaming into your daily life. Allow yourself to awaken to the boundless possibilities.

Mind can transport itself to the ends of the universe in a fleeting moment. Merging and dreaming become traditional ways of exercising and tempering your energy as you learn to flow in the ocean of oneness. Sustain images and awareness in a merged state. By doing this, you can directly access the information and knowledge you desire in order to enhance your chosen lifestyle.

Gwyddonic Druid Tradition teaches the process of the double as a means for experiencing other worlds while retaining awareness within your primary self. The primary must exist for the double to exist, and the more experience you have in the primary, the greater the potential for experience in the double.

Doubling out is achieved by merging deeply with oneness, and deliberately projecting your energy outward. Choose a specific destination and energetic shape. Pay close attention to the formulation of your experience. Notice how sound echoes as you double out. As you practice waking dreaming, your awareness moves with the double while still functioning in your primary world.

Learn to appear energetically in two places simultaneously in the primary manifest world as your double becomes more adept at traveling through time and space.

Merge deeply enough so your double can view the past, or actually be seen in the past. Freely change your perspective as you experience lifetimes in the past, present, future and otherwise.

Use the double to create patterns while your physical body is asleep. The implications of actively participating and directing your dreaming awareness are boundless. Enhance your dreaming abilities by making a pooka designed specifically to transport you to realms beyond your imagination.

Once you master the double, try quadrupling out by moving four minds outward. Live in infinite worlds simultaneously, or move from awareness to awareness, one at a time. Personal preference regulates how many doubles you choose to project at one time. Remember, the double is merely another face or view.

Your experience and perception in the double and the primary self move you toward the Concept of Oneness. Merging and dreaming knit energies together in fascinating and empowering ways. Keep in mind every view you adopt or hold is merely an aspect or assembling of oneness. All views reflect the Grand Unification of oneness. Remember to cultivate your impersonal observer as you double out so you do not get caught up in your ego and self-importance.

Begin to gently unwrap the illusionary cocoon of your ordinary existence. Expand and transform your reality, giving yourself a positive sense of personal identity. Set your Mind free. Once you learn to project or dream the double, things reverse and you find that the double dreams the self. You become the dream, and the double dreams you. You just think you have dreamed it. You are your double, the maker of dreams.

117

Guided Journey

"What is thy Name?" commands the voice.

"I am Desiree," comes the reply.

The aroma of stale air penetrates her nostrils as she opens the top of the old black steamer truck. The lid is heavy from both the weight of the metal and the decorative oak trim that lines the edges. Inside, the peach-colored paper covering the sides and bottom looks like a faded image of what was once a colorful floral design. A stack of linens, heavy with the odor of mothballs, sits neatly folded on top. As she holds them up, she notices the intricate embroidery and cutwork that decorates each piece of cloth, an art lost with the passing of her grandmother and great aunts.

"What is thy Name?" commands the voice again.

"I am Lisa," comes the reply.

She slowly surveys the room around her. As she expected, there is no one there, and she resumes her search through the trunk. On the left side, she sees a pouch which seems to hold a small oval object. She lifts the worn velvet pouch from its hiding place, and opens it. Inside she finds a watch. On the face of the watch, delicate designs of white gold combine with small diamonds around the perimeter, projecting the image of a gleaming moonflower. The white gold band glitters silver in the light as she turns the watch over in her hand. She notices the band consists of three strands of white gold woven into one. She wraps it around her left wrist, but when she goes to fasten the clasp she notices it is broken.

"What is thy Name?!" demands the voice, this time with even more authority. Unlike before, now she feels compelled by an unknown force to answer.

"I am May," she says quietly, almost to herself.

"May, I know thee and know thee full well, for I have seen thy comings and goings. May, what dost thou seek?"

She stops, and for a moment seems lost in the question. Suddenly, the room fills with the music of a soft distant harp. The tune sounds familiar, but she can't quite place it. The melody haunts the deep corridors of her being.

"Were you talking to someone?" comes a concerned, but comforting voice. Still kneeling in front of the trunk, she looks up to see her mother's green eyes staring down at her.

Not waiting for a reply, her mother resumes. "I see you have found your grandmother's old trunk. Oh, and I see you've even found her watch," says her mother, stopping for moment to reflect. "I think that was probably the one material thing she treasured most in this world. It held a special meaning for her."

"When I touch it, I can feel a piece of her inside of it," muses the girl, turning the watch over again in her hand. The face of the filigreed watch mirrors her own face.

"Why don't you keep the watch? I know she would have liked for you to have it, as a special remembrance of her."

Her mother's voice trails off at the end, and the girl notices the wetness around those green eyes. She softly takes her mother's hand, and looks knowingly into the older woman's eyes. A smile, a squeeze of the hand, and her mother moves toward the door.

"I'm going to bed. Do you need anything before I do?" the older woman asks in a voice that is once again composed and matronly.

"No; go ahead and get some sleep. I'm fine," she replies. "I'm going to look through this trunk for a little while, and then I'll probably go to bed, too." She listens as her mother descends the steps down from the attic. She slowly resumes her search of the oak-trimmed black steamer trunk.

The next object she pulls from the trunk is a red book, 8½" x 11" in size, with a circular silver inlay on the front cover. She opens it, randomly picking a page. She reads the title at the top, "Ritual of the Granting of a Boon." It is hand printed and done carefully in calligraphy. She stops reading momentarily, thinking to herself, "What is a boon?" She reads further down the page.

"On the sixth full moon after Yule, the High Priestess performs the following ritual. She grants a request or boon to each person as a blessing for their positive works done in the previous year. She can also lay a woe on a person who has done negative works."

She stops suddenly, realizing that the words at the very beginning of the ritual are the same words she had heard spoken by the mysterious and strange voice. As she glances down the page, she finds the place where the voice left off. She begins to read aloud. "Great one, I pray that thou will grant me a boon."

The voice returns, "May, I have said that I know thee well, and have seen thy comings and goings. I have seen thy good works. You gave freely of yourself, and with positivity when your sister became ill earlier this year, and needed someone to take care of her two children. I will grant thy boon! What wilt thou?" asks the mysterious voice.

Without hesitation she blurts out, "I pray great one, thou will grant me the boon of having my own child."

"May, I grant it to thee."

"Praise be to thee, blessed be, blessed be, blessed be." As she speaks each "blessed be," she bows her head slightly. With the last one, the room again falls silent. Clutching her grandmother's watch in her left hand, she descends the stairs to her room.

She feels odd being back in her old room after so many years. Things seem familiar, but foreign. She had come for a brief visit at the invitation of her mother, but now she wonders if her grandmother's energy somehow played a hand in bringing her here. It was just a feeling more than anything else, since her grandmother had passed beyond, when May was only a year and a half. Most of what she knew about her grandmother was from the stories her mother and great aunts used to tell around the table after family dinners at holidays. She knew her grandmother was slightly unconventional, that is, compared to the rest of the family. From the book she found in the trunk, she guesses there may be some truth to the rumor.

The night-light seems to bring the shadows on the white walls to life. In the dim glow, she sees the outline of the Maxfield Parrish print that hangs on the wall across from her bed. Through the darkness, she sees the image of a girl swinging naked in the clouds. She becomes the girl, and she feels the air rushing by her face, blowing her hair wildly in its wake. She thrusts her feet upward into a billowing cloud shaped like a fluffy elephant. For a moment, for eternity, she hangs suspended in the cloud.

Like a dream, the harp begins to weave its chords in and out of dimensions never seen, only heard.

"What is that melody?" she wonders aloud. Instantaneously, she finds herself walking down a path of diamond-like stars that leads to a room of light. As she moves closer to the light, the music grows more resonant.

The handsome young man at the harp smiles at her as she enters the room. He plucks each string, and each tone sounds and then echoes. The music vibrates through her like a wave of energy. Primal rhythms release themselves, as she dances the clockwise dance of the sun around the young man and his exquisite harp. The music draws her in, and diffuses her like a cloud. She feels them both running naked on a soft sandy beach, the ocean spilling up over their naked bodies. The music rushes in, and the water rushes out.

"What is that song that you are playing on your harp so sweetly?" she asks in a voice that harmonizes with the music.

"It is called 'Come Sweet May.' It was written by a friend of mine. Maybe you know him? His name is Wolfgang Mozart." His voice radiates a deep warmth that draws her ever closer.

"Don't I know you?" she inquires with a teasing laugh. "I know, only in my dreams."

His fingers caress each string as he glides his hand down the soft, curved cadence of her body. His mouth blows seductively on her horn, each note opening her body and mind like petals opening on a beautiful white flower. Her porcelain skin is ablaze with moon fire as he strokes her entire body. The blazing flame consumes the room, leaving a burning desire. From one rune, she moves to the next; from one act to another.

She moves on top of him, and he moves on top of her. Over, under, sideways, down—energy moving like a planet revolving in space. Spinning around the light, she is pulled to the source, expanding and contracting like billions of multi-verses. She flows into that which is nameless, becoming the Mother of All Things. As two becomes one, one becomes two again.

The passionate, throbbing desire echoes through the lovers, vibrating each chord in the key of flesh. The sweat beads off her face as she feels him strum her faster and faster. Like the finale of a symphony, they become each instrument building to that final crescendo. The cymbals clash, and the cannons roar. The fireworks explode into a wondrous flash of color, like a rippling field of vibrant wildflowers on a spring day.

She feels him inside of her. He feels like a bull screaming with an ancient need and passion. The room lights with a lucent glow, and primal rhythms and primal needs cascade and decorate the night with wondrous delight. Through a stellar world of tiers, she ascends to the highest plateau, soaring upward through the clouds. He feels like a shooting star from the night sky. Climax! Union! Two into one!

For quite a while the two lovers silently gaze at one another. Cradled in the passion of their union, a soft glow radiates from their bodies.

Before she leaves the room, he hugs her one last time, and says to her, "I have a gift for you to remember me by." On the palm of her hand he sets a small white box topped with an emerald green bow.

She takes the gift, and eagerly opens the box lip, discovering to her surprise that her grandmother's watch lies within. As she picks it up out of the box, she notices the clasp is no longer broken.

He takes the watch from her, and gently secures it around her left wrist. It fits perfectly. The handsome young man kisses her, and then in an instant before she can ask him about the watch, he and the room are gone, vanished into sand.

The morning sun shines through the window with the beckoning call of a new day. She can hear the cuckoo clock in the hallway. Still partially asleep, she slowly walks into the kitchen and sees her mother sitting at the table reading the newspaper, her black reading glasses perched on her nose.

"Oh, you're up. Did you sleep well?" her mother asks, looking up from the top of the newspaper.

"Yes, okay, except for this very odd dream," she mumbles while trying to remember all the details of the dream.

"What kind of dream?" inquires her mother, only half interested as she returns to reading the paper.

"Well, there was this room filled with light, and a golden haired man sat playing the harp. In particular, he was playing 'Come Sweet May' by Mozart." She begins to feel conscious of the fact that she's talking to her mother, so she decides to skip to the end. "And what was really odd, was that before I left the room, the man gave me a box with Grandma's watch in it."

As she looks over at her mother, and she notices the older woman has set aside the paper and is now staring across the table at her. She feels a certain uneasiness. "What's wrong?" she asks.

Her mother stops to take a deep breath before speaking. "I never told you this, but I never knew my real father." She registers her daughter's surprise at the revelation.

"I know you thought Grandpa was my father, but that's only because I never saw the necessity to tell you the truth." Her mother pauses before continuing, "As you know, your grandmother had some very strange ways. They used to call her a little eccentric, well maybe more than a little. Anyway, she always told everyone that she became pregnant with me by a man who made love to her in a dream. She said the man was golden-haired, and summoned her to a bright room by playing 'Come Sweet May' on a beautiful harp. She used to tell everyone I was a gift from the god Gwydion, and that he gave her the watch when they parted company that memorable night."

The young woman stares at her mother for the longest time without saying a word. She reaches in her robe pocket for a tissue, and feels the outline of her grandmother's watch. She pulls it out of her pocket, and caresses it in her hand for a moment before stopping abruptly. The clasp on the band is no longer broken.

The Mead Moon

Cliodna & Angus

Quiet voices whisper in the heated night
calling out the dawn and twilight of souls
singing softly through my body
dreaming something new, yet remembered.

The Mead Moon ☽

Cliodna & Angus

Full Moon in Capricorn, Sun in Cancer
Cardinal negative earth and water elements

The Goddess and Her Consort

Symbolic of etheric harmony, lunar fertility, and lucid dreams, the Mead Moon rises upward into the starry expanse. In Northern England, the seventh full moon shines down upon the Mead Factory at Lindesfarne, on Holy Island where they make an alcoholic mixture of fermented honey and water. Malt, yeast, and spices are also added to create the brew. The Welsh spiced mead called *metheglin,* literally means "healing liquor."

129

Probably the first fermented beverage made by humankind, mead is best known as the heavenly drink of the ancient Teutonic gods. Lakes and rivers of mead flow freely in English and Scottish Ballads. The gift of a continuously replenished supply of mead in return for gestures of goodwill is often referenced in folklore. Mead appears in cultures throughout the world—in Rome, Egypt, Greece, Scandinavia, and Assyria. The Incas and Aztecs also made the sacred drink.

The Baltic people of Rugli used mead in the worship of their magnificent sun god. Every year at harvest time a cup of mead was reverently placed in the hand of the idol. During the rites of seed-time or first fruits, the priest took the cup from the god idol. Studying the contents left in the cup, he predicted the nature of the coming year.

Odin, creator and god of wisdom, has an insatiable thirst for knowledge and almost loses his life while trying to obtain a drink of mead. Odin's mead acts as the mead of poetic inspiration. This special beverage, brewed from the blood of the Kvasir in the Odhroerir kettle, is contained in three vessels. Whoever drinks this magically-imbued liquid at once becomes a poet and great knower of poetic charms.

As a gesture of her sacred and perfect love, daughter of the Chief Druid to Manannan, Cliodna of the Fair Hair serves mead to her lovers and consorts. The goddess takes mortal lovers and is reputed to be a vigorous and sensuous seducer of young, spirited men. Her name means "shapely one." She becomes the most beautiful of all women when she takes human form. Cliodna's body feels full and ripe, and as the bird goddess she moves swiftly and deftly.

When the young goddess of the Otherworld calls to you by the seashore, three brightly-colored birds perch nearby. They sing so sweetly that their song soothes the sick and wounded to sleep. These magical birds feed upon Cliodna's apples as they accompany her to the Land of Promise. She reigns in this Otherworld where there is no death, violence, or decay.

Cliodna manifests at times as a young aspect of the Dark goddess, and at other times as one of the three Faery queens of Munster. She exudes a certain zest and her presence washes over you like the waves of a great ocean. The goddess Cliodna rules the ninth wave of every series, and she transforms into a magnificent white seabird at the blink of an eye.

The youthful goddess appears fair and white like a delicate bird. Changing shapes, Cliodna's dark face looks out from rich brown eyes. Her dark chocolate hair feels fine and soft, and her skin feels velvety like the petals of a summer flower. She wears silver-white or russet-colored robes.

The goddess toasts the Mead Moon with the young and handsome consort, Angus Og. Beautiful and divine son of the Dagda and the river goddess Boann, the well-endowed Angus acts as god of love and intimacy. As brother to Macha, who is the ancestress of the Red Branch, the consort's name means "Angus the Young."

With a natural propensity toward love and pleasure, Angus, often called the Irish Adonis, plays god to youths and maidens. His flashing green eyes lure you as he smiles. His body responds quickly when you stroke his fair skin and finger his thick, curly, red-streaked hair. The loving and charming Angus travels on the wind to his home on the River Boyne. Flying over his head, four bright birds accompany the active consort.

131

Together the goddess Cliodna and her consort Angus fly you to new dimensions of love and sexual pleasure. The sweet song of birds fills the air as you are swept away by the vitality and fertility of the youthful goddess and her consort. Angus teaches you to actively participate in your sexual experience, and to enjoy the natural harmony of each individual sensation. The strength and potency of the warming season rushes through you as the beautiful goddess Cliodna and the virile consort Angus share their dreams and secrets.

Practical Knowledge and Useful Information— Shared Dream, Incubation, and Patterning

Explore shared dream as a pathway to personal self-discovery and development. As you turn your mind to oneness, you begin to perceive that whatever you dream personally is actually part of a whole we all dream together. The unique and the commonality blend into one. Dreaming permeates all things, and shared dream brings unity out of diversity.

Learn to move past the boundaries of the conditioned mind and beyond the illusionary closed doors of your perception. Flow into mutual dream-space, a place in oneness where there are infinite possibilities of personal, global, and universal healing. Shared dream implies a deep level of intimacy between partners or groups of people. This deeper level of communication and understanding spills over into all aspects of your life. You awaken again and again, and find your personal patterns and your connection with oneness strengthening exponentially.

Practice shared dreaming with your mate as a mode of new and exciting communication. Agree to meet in the same dream, and make an effort to remember similar details or impressions within the dream. For example, you both might remember a particular color, emotion, sensation, or word sequence. Keep in mind that shared dreaming is a learned skill and requires a clear expectation, strong desire, and consistent effort.

Intend your shared dreaming experiences to expand your awareness. Reassemble your mind with the newly-found knowledge from your exploration. Try layering other dimensions such as telepathy, clairvoyance, and precognition into the experience to enhance your shared dreaming adventures. Allow your double to emerge, and perceive several shared dreams simultaneously.

As you learn to master dreaming, strengthen your lucidity and awareness, and allow the goddess and god to act as your travel guides. Just ask, and they will gladly take you on wondrous adventures. Openly embrace the probability of experience and perceptions far beyond your imagination. Glide into the arms of the Lady as you caress the boundless potential of energy in motion.

Dreaming, especially shared dreaming, lends you insight into your personal strengths and weaknesses. As you transcend the normal parameters of your daily world, begin to use dreaming to expand your positive patterns. Dreaming gives you a direct entrance to the higher centers of your innermost core. It acts as your invitation to the boundless. Begin to use this great storehouse of oneness to understand your personal history, as well as access information concerning your probable future.

Tap this well of knowledge by learning to incubate your dreams, shared and otherwise. *Incubate* means "to lie on," and "to maintain under conditions favorable to optimum growth and development." The traditional Celtic Dusii or the Greek Incubus are symbolic of this mysterious flow of awareness. They join their light to mortals in order to impart their sacred knowledge.

Penetrate the deeper, ever-changing meanings of your dreams by allowing the energies within you to mate and unite. Begin dream incubation by setting up the dream. Find the most unusual thing happening right now in your life. Focus on it, and then amplify, strengthen, and support the energy surrounding the event or issue in an effort to unfold its significance. Take day-notes to set the stage, looking at the issue or event from all angles. Ask one clear and simple question while focusing on the issue at hand. Repeat the question over and over in your mind.

This method for dream incubation works especially well if you repeat the question out loud to yourself as you awaken, or just before you go to sleep.

Generate a strong desire for resolution in your dream incubation. In other words, pattern your dream so you will receive the knowledge requested. Be specific and pay close attention to the process. Shift into your double, and explore dream incubation from this perspective. Each new dream experience teaches you and guides you further along toward your spiritual center.

Incubate shared dreams with your primary partner and mate your energies with your lover. Select a specific time and space to meet in, and then agree upon a question. Merge together and move into dream, and travel through new realms of sensation and perception. Experiment with grids of programmed clear quartz crystals to enhance your experience. Remember to be mindful of your intent, expectation, desire, and the depth of your merge.

Dream technologies of the future will offer you new ways to explore shared dream and engage in dream incubation. You will learn to control, direct, and pursue specific goals and objectives in dream. You will be able to indulge in entertaining adventures and fantasies. Creative solutions will be found as we explore new Mind frontiers.

As lucid dreaming goes mainstream, the concept of shared dream will alter perceptively. You will virtually be able to relive your dreams, or anyone else's for that matter. The uses and implications are endless, and all point to a deeper level of awareness and continuity of Mind. In this sense, shared dream could very well be the key to creating a more positive future for ourselves and the Earth. As people dream together, they will begin to understand that light and love connect all things in oneness. Be mindful as you cultivate your worldly garden with loving care.

Guided Journey

"The more it changes, the more it stays the same," I whisper quietly as I walk up the winding footpath from the beach toward the sprawling white house. Behind me pine trees cover the rocky coastline. The rhythmic ocean waves seem to reply to my statement in a soft, fading whisper as I walk on.

The earthen path branches into two. A large birch tree rests at the crossroads, the "eyes" of its trunk watching me as I walk. I follow the path lined with gold and orange marigolds, angling away from the house and leading to the rose garden. The warm earth soothes the bare soles of my feet as I pass the huge bird of paradise bushes awash with exotic blooms. Ash and rowan trees protect and shade the pathway on both sides, casting strange shadows in the late afternoon sun.

I smell the fragrant roses as I walk toward the garden gate. I pass under three massive archways covered with climbing pink, white, and velvety-red roses. I can hear the faint buzzing sound of the bees sampling the pungent nectar of the flowers as I move slowly and purposefully to the eight-spoked wheel gate. Lifting the wooden latch, I swing the white wooden gate open. On either side of the gate, ivy weaves wildly through the fence slats, marking the entrance into the aromatic garden.

Stepping through the entrance, I leave the gate ajar. On the bleached fence post just inside the garden hangs a long circular bronze trumpet. Picking it up gently in my hands, I hold the mouthpiece to my lips. I blow three notes, slowly and clearly. Each note seems to echo out over the garden toward the soft pounding waves on the rocky, pine covered beach.

I carefully set the instrument back on the post and notice how its metallic surface glistens bright orange-gold in the evening sun. I glance around me and eagerly wait.

Surrounded by a mighty circle of trees, the rose garden stands like a beautiful woman. Hawthorn trees shield her perimeter, and holly and blackthorn bushes fill the space between the tree trunks. The branches of the trees tangle together like the sharp and thorny bushes below them, as if to reinforce one another. A thick carpet of chamomile caresses the base of the naturally mated trees and bushes. Blue vervain borders the delicate chamomile. Rose bushes and climbers on trellises fill the space. Every kind and color of blooming rose form a shapely image of spellbinding color.

To my left lays a small, curved, wooden bridge that leads into the depths of the lush and perfumed greenery. A tiny brook rushes underneath and the water feeds the thick honeysuckle vines that twist over the rails of the worn bridge. A wren sits on the rail closest to me and sings a rhythmic series of musical notes, trilling, "Chewee, chewee, chewee, chewee."

On my right, a natural rock basin opens into a small garden pool. Like a natural fountain, several tiny streams flow down the rock face on all sides. The constant trickling of water sounds soothing and relaxing. The tiny streams flow into the garden and then out into the ocean below.

The whirling sound of a hummingbird's wings catches my attention, and I turn and see the tiny bird hovering next to me. Twittering and squeaking loudly, the ruby-throated bird dances backward and then over my head.

I follow his flight as he swoops over the soft meadowsweet and red heather spread along the rocks and down over the banks of the clear garden pool. The ruby-throated hummer disappears into the silver fir trees that line the far side of the water in a semi-circle. Breathtaking antique salmon and gold roses climb on trellises in the corner behind them. On the opposite side of the clear pool stands an ancient weeping willow with white impatiens encircling its massive trunk.

137

Two cranes sit toward the top of the willow, resting in its massive branches. One of them utters a loud rattling, "kar-r-r-o-o." Suddenly they both glide down to the ground and face each other. I see the red feathers covering their foreheads as they leap determinedly into the air. Extending their wings, they throw their feet forward in an ancient dance. Croaking loudly, they bow to each other and repeat their movements three times. They bow to the

Mother, and they bow to the Sun. Flapping their wings, the two cranes fly off, their necks outstretched as they stroke the evening air. I watch them as they fade into two tiny dots in the crimson sky.

My eyes continue to feast on the exotic color of the rose garden. Breathing deeply, my senses fill with the heady fragrance of the damask rosebush next to me. I touch the soft buds and as my fingers brush against them, they suddenly spiral open into full-petaled rosettes of glowing pink. My feet tread on wild mint and the scent of the oil blends with the fragrant roses.

I feel you nearby, and turn to watch as you enter through the white wheel-shaped gate. You latch it firmly behind you, and then move slowly toward me. Loose, white drawstring pants ripple against your firm thighs as you walk. Your chest is bare and darkly tanned. A thin covering of blonde-brown hair weaves over your chest in a V-shape, down and across your stomach. My eyes travel down your body, and I feel my growing response and desire. I am always amazed by your incredible beauty.

Your smiling god-like face shines golden in the late afternoon sun as you stand in front of me. The rich tones of your voice roll out, "You called me here. Now, what would you like to do?"

"I have several pleasurable suggestions," I reply, laughing softly, and moving into your strong, embracing arms. I can feel the radiant heat between our bodies, growing hotter and hotter.

"Are you hungry?" you ask, your question thick with double meanings.

"Yes, very hungry," I answer, softly running my tongue over my upper lip.

"I saw some ripe strawberries by the gate," you say as you move away from me. You travel along the last rays of the sun, following them to a laden berry patch. You bend down and feel the plants. Choosing the warmer plants, you pick several ripe red berries. With your two hands full of strawberries, you toss the succulent fruit high into the air, and catch them all as they come down. You complete the task without breaking the flesh of any of the delicate fruit.

"I'll bet that you can't do that standing on one leg, and with one hand tied behind your back."

You laugh and move to my side. We sit down on the mint ground cover. I twist a green fleshy leaf between my fingers and smell the spicy-scented oil. I take a couple of berries from your hands and brush them off, slowly and seductively, on the hem of my cotton tunic. After gently twisting off the green stem, I bite off the very end of the fruit. Dripping juices trickle over my fingertips as I guide the remaining fruit into your waiting mouth.

You take a bright red strawberry and hold it in your teeth while leaning toward me. I bite the ripe fruit in the middle, kiss you, and then finish eating the sweet berry. Your lips are covered with strawberry juice. I move purposefully into your arms, sitting on your lap and kissing the traces of juice from your mouth.

I slide onto the ground next to you, and we sit side by side for a while, watching the sun sink into the horizon. A string of bees stream by, pouring over the low-spreading spindle tree. They finally settle on the thick stand of scotch broom, tasting the sweet nectar of the delicate yellow flowers.

"Ask the wild bee for divine wisdom," I whisper to the soft breeze tickling my face.

"Wisdom before love, for love without wisdom can never grow," you reply, brushing back your thick curling hair as you speak.

You stand up and give me your hand, pulling me to my feet. Leading us over to the pool, you steer me onto a mossy flat rock. I sit down by the reeds at the water's edge, and run my hand through the cool clear water. You sit down next to me on one of the smooth boulders situated at the mouth of the bubbling artisan spring feeding the pool. You pull a penny whistle from your pants pocket, and begin to play a sweet melody.

Hazelnuts hang from the tree branches nearby and swing softly in the gentle ocean breeze. I speak to you as you play your penny whistle,

Quiet voices whisper in the cool water
Light ripples stream through my mind
Flowing into my body
Forming something new, yet remembered.

Quiet voices whisper in the silent wind
Words of lifetimes drift into one
Sweeping through my body
Hearing someone new, yet remembered.

Quiet voices whisper in the heated night
Calling out the dawn and twilight of souls
Singing through my body
Dreaming something new, yet remembered.

Setting down your penny whistle, you take my hands in yours and look deeply into my eyes for a few moments.

You say in a husky voice, "I will always remember you, every lifetime, every dream, with each breath and every moment."

You kiss me soundly, stroking my long silky hair before moving away slightly.

The perfume of the rose garden seems more noticeable in the twilight. At the edge of darkness, shadows deepen and blend into one. I can hear the echo of the pounding waves as they crash against the rocky shoreline nearby. The rhythmic pulsing kindles my growing passion and need. I feel a tide of sensation rush through me and I stand, grasping your hand in mine before pulling you quickly to your feet.

In the darkening twilight, I begin to see soft shining fibers of light crisscrossing the circular garden, tying us to the trees, flowers, and the earth. The natural shapes blaze in the lattice of light. Crickets call out. Their high-pitched voices join and then fade into the silence between the rolling waves in the near distance.

The full moon rises swiftly overhead. As if to turn night into day, the luminous disk fills the sky like a giant mirror reflecting the starry skies. The garden glows in a storm of pure white radiance, ablaze with moon fire.

We stand next to the pool, its surface shining like slick glass. The moonlight floods over us like petals of a lucent white flower as we embrace in the perfumed garden. The elder trees overhead sway gracefully in the gentle breeze. Moon beams weave mysterious shadow patterns through the branches and over the glassy pool. The beautiful luminescent weave covers my hair and tunic.

As I slowly raise my hands, the beams of light seem to flow off my wrists, endlessly weaving out over the garden like fine silver threads. At the same time, bubbles of light dance out from the small artisan spring at the source of the pool.

Your kisses magically transform into small silver birds that carry messages of love. They drop the messages over us like tiny beads of white light. You catch the brilliant beads and throw them up into the sky, creating a new splash of milky stars across the night sky.

I notice a large black raven sitting on a thick branch of the alder tree, next to the rocky outcropping. The bird glows in an unearthly light, and gestures toward the flowing spring with her beak. She speaks to us, "Drink from the source. Drink to the gods, and they will visit you tonight." The strange bird flies toward the ocean.

I lean down and cup my hand into the stream, bringing the water to my lips. It tastes sweet and spicy like mead. You bend down next to me and do the same. We drink several handfuls of the magical liquid before sitting next to the water along the mossy outcropping.

You dip your hand into the cool honeyed stream again, and stroke your damp fingers across my lips and down my cheek, touching my neck. Your mouth tastes like sweet mead as you kiss me.

The perfume of the roses and the night scent of the trees and earth mix with the warm salty breeze drifting in from the sea. Moving apart for a moment, you help me pull my soft cotton tunic up over my head. I untie the drawstring at your waist, and you step out of the loose pants. We drape our clothes over the large, flat, mossy rock.

Your tanned skin shines like porcelain in the moonlight, and my pale skin looks almost translucent. Like the blossoming moonflower vine curving and climbing through the rocks by the pool, we twine together. Your skin feels warm and damp, and you taste intoxicating.

I run my eager hands over your taut and muscular shoulders. Your muscles instinctively respond, flexing and shifting fluidly under the pressure of my fingers. You dip your cupped hand back down into the stream and smooth the magical brew of wetness and light down between my breasts and across my stomach. Your tongue follows the moist pattern of sweetness, sweeping over the tips of my breasts. Circling my stomach, the stroking touch of your tongue moves down deeper between my thighs and into me.

I become the moonflower, fully opening for you in the brilliance of the full moon. I am soft and pliant, and you drink my nectar like a wild bee. Hot desire courses through me.

As you quench your thirst, your hands wander over the supple curves of my breasts, softly kneading and stroking their fullness. Waves of pleasure teem and roll over me as I sing out in the moonlight.

You draw away from me gently, staring into my eyes— through the windows of oneness. Cradling me in your arms, you carry me toward the middle of the rose garden. I can feel your hard arousal rising up against me as you walk.

At the central hub where north, east, south, and west converge, you set me down on the roomy weather-worn wooden bench. Built in a circle, the bench frames the trunk of a mighty apple tree covered with immature fruit. The tree's branches weave the moonlight into mysterious moving patterns on the wooden slats and over our skin before flowing down over the ground.

Underneath and surrounding the bench grow bushes of perfect miniature white roses. I reach down to touch one of the blossoms and notice they have no thorns. The flowers look like tiny pearls gleaming in the night. I lean against the bark of the massive apple tree, and as my flesh touches the tree's skin, the hanging fruit transform into magnificent, ripe golden apples. The large ripe fruit seem to glow with an unearthly light.

I reach up and pluck one of the exquisite apples from the tree. Looking up, I notice three small birds setting on a low branch of the moonlit tree, feasting on the remains of a hanging apple. I smile and take a big bite out of the side of the golden sphere. I hold the apple in front of your mouth, and you fasten your teeth on its juicy flesh, biting off a large piece.

We sit, holding hands and crunching apple in the quiet perfumed garden. The pounding of ocean waves sounds in the distance as the sea breeze begins to gather strength, dancing through the white poplar and evergreen yew trees in front of us. The wind grows in intensity, and then fades just as quickly.

Taking the partially eaten apple, I rub the sweet, juicy white flesh over your cheek and chin. Licking your sticky chin softly, my tongue finds its way between your inviting lips. I slide the dripping apple over your chest, and spread the juice across your stomach. Wrapping my fingers around your velvety hardness, I slowly circle your arousal with the wet sticky fruit.

My tongue deliberately follows the trail of sweet juice from your chest to your stiffening desire. I stroke and lick your pulsing flesh. Moaning your appreciation, you tangle your fingers through my fine hair, and encourage my continued feasting of your taut and potent body.

Shafts of white brilliance seem to beam off of our bodies as beads of sweat glisten and flash in the luminous moonlight. Slowly I draw away from you and take your hand in mine. Gathering up our clothes by the glassy pool, you follow me. Leading you across the curved wooden bridge, I smell the fragrant blossoms on the honeysuckle vine as our footsteps echo over the footbridge.

I guide you to a soft bed of dark heather, edged with wild mint. Spreading our clothes out on the moist natural carpet, I lay down and gesture to you. First, you move over to the honeysuckle vine and pick two flowers. Then moving back, you place one of the blossoms in my hair, over my ear.

144

Biting off the tip of the second flower, you place the end on my lip and whisper in my ear, "Taste the sweetness. Taste the boundless."

The velvety tip of the honeysuckle flower tastes like wild nectar. You take the flower from between my lips and place it carefully on the bed of heather above my head. Your eyes focus on my mouth as you lay down next to me and kiss me.

Like a circle within a circle, a small grove of young oaks surrounds us. Your fingers circle sunwise over each of my breasts as you tease and squeeze each nipple into a perfectly budded rosy peak. I moan and cry out. Your eager mouth tastes one bud, and then the other. You nip and lick the hard peaks as your hands stroke and rub the damp bare length of my back.

As you move over me, the stars begin to spin like a great wheel of light around the luminous full moon. I guide you into me, and I catch your eyes in mine. Pure ecstasy floods through me as you slide in tight, tighter still, and fill me completely. My hips lift upward, drawing you deeper as you move fast and strong. Loats of white and blue light float past my vision.

145

My breathing grows quicker and harder. I feel your generous hands stroke and press against my flaming skin as you thrust into me, again and again. Above us, I see a white stairway made of rose petals and bird feathers leading up to the spinning wheel of the moon and stars.

We move as one up the dreamy stairway. We float on a large white feather, soaring higher and higher, swooping in circles and dipping deeper still. Like great spiral birds of light, we flow and spin through the boundless. Transforming into two beautiful white swans, we fly up out of the heady scented garden, pausing to look at our bodies making love on the ground below. Soaring across tree tops and out over the ocean, we fly higher and higher toward the moon and beyond. We climb out of ourselves and flow as pure white light engaging light.

You move into me faster and faster as part of me rushes out into you. We sing out together, free in the glowing night.

Waves of exquisite sensation shoot through me, and I can feel your fiery release inside of me. I contract around you again and again.

Arms of light cradle us as we rest on the thick fragrant heather. The sweat from my body feeds the soft leaves beneath me. Our breathing slows, and I look up at you. Behind you the stars glisten like a sea of diamonds across black velvet. You smile and move out of me gently. You reach above my head and pick up a white feather lying on the moonlit carpet, in exactly the same spot where the honeysuckle flower had been. Slowly, you tickle my forehead with the feather.

CHAPTER EIGHT

❧ The Wort Moon ☙

Artio & Amaethon

*Slivers of light
the twinkling of stars
pieces of a puzzle
scattered through time.*

The Wort Moon ☽

Artio & Amaethon

Full Moon in Aquarius, Sun in Leo
Fixed positive air and fire elements

(Note: In years with 13 full moons, both the sun and moon signs shift back one sign, usually on the Wort Moon close to Lughnassad. Refer to an ephemeris for exact positioning.)

The Goddess and Her Consort

☽
149

Celebrate the ascendancy of the Wort Moon and flow with its vibrancy as the forces of light and dark converge. Moonrise occurs close to the Great Day Lugnassad, which marks the time when moon energy becomes more prevalent than sun energy. Corresponding to the harvest, the eighth High Moon represents the gifts of personal knowledge and protection gleaned through transformation and rebirth.

The word *wort* stems from the Old English *wyrt*, meaning "root or plant." The wort represents a type of plant or herb, such as liverwort, navelwort, and pennywort. Also, in the brewing of beer the infusion of malted barley combined with hops and other specialty grains produces a wort. This wort, when combined with the yeast organism, ferments and springs to life, beginning a cycle that ends with the magical beverage known as beer. The wort symbolizes the earth, waiting, and wanting to be seeded by the yeast. In this sense, you are the wort awaiting the catalyst of knowledge and experience.

The Wort Moon acknowledges the dynamic, never-ending, ever-renewing yearly cycle. On this summer night observe the movements of the stars, planets, moon, and sun as a means for predicting the seasons and for understanding the natural rhythms within you. From these patterns and flow, you acquire the knowledge to fortify and protect yourself and your patterns.

Protecting the never-ending, ever-renewing cycle of life becomes the responsibility of the bear goddess Artio. Representing the monad of all female bears, Artio parallels the Greek goddess Artemis. As a Mother Goddess of wildlife, she carefully watches over animals and nature. Like Artemis, the powerful Artio shapeshifts into a bear, typifying the ancient personification of natural law.

150

Folklore portrays the bear as a powerful spirit helper from whom you obtain magical powers. King Arthur took his name from the bear goddess in honor of her magnificent power and intimate bond to the land. The goddess Artio's knowledge and wisdom stream both from oneness and her basic instinctual connection with the boundless. Animals often possess this quality, and like the bear, remain one with the goddess. Instinctual awareness is a gift that we all possess. We, as the human animal, need to connect and become one with these innate and sacred gifts of the beloved Great Mother.

Moving quickly and purposefully, the goddess Artio embodies the qualities of the predator. On Bridget's Day, the bear goddess comes out from hibernation. If she sees her shadow, she sleeps for another six weeks. The popular

Groundhog Day is an offshoot of Artio's yearly ritual. When she awakens from her winter slumber, Artio reflects strength, vigor, and fertility as she chooses her mate and moves through the continuous cycle of the seasons.

The consort Amaethon acts as mate to the fertile and beautiful Artio. His name means "plowman," and as a god of agriculture, he is aptly called the Harvest King. Son of Danu and brother to Arianrhod, Gwydion, and Gobannon, the friendly consort Amaethon possesses the skill to till the impossible field. His magical tools are the hoe, the plow, and the sickle, along with the succulent fruits of the harvest.

Vested in robes the color of wheat, corn, and grapes, the handsome consort Amaethon appears with bronze skin. Amaethon's sun-streaked, dark blonde hair streams behind him as he moves formidably through the meadows and fields. His brilliant smile charms those it shines upon, and his blue-green eyes are bright and deep. Amaethon enters from the Otherworld after stealing a magnificent young female dog and a white roebuck. His theft causes the famous Battle of the Trees.

151

The goddess Artio and her consort Amaethon represent the polarities of energy within nature. From the huntress Artio you learn the skills of the predator, understanding the usefulness of protection and knowledge. From the harvest god Amaethon, you gain the skills of the agrarian, learning how to grow and cultivate your patterns and reaping the boundless harvest from your positive efforts. The dynamic polarity within oneness, female and male, positive and negative, perpetuate the never-beginning, ever-growing cycle of life.

Practical Knowledge and Useful Information—
Personal Awareness and Positive Patterns

Oneness unites all things at the source. This innate connection creates what you experience as reality. The Welsh word *Hud* describes oneness as a wider magic which serves as the key to life and matter itself—the awareness that the divine resides in everything around you, in every action, every dream, every thought, every breath, and in all of nature.

Gwyddonic Druid Tradition stems from the Concept of Oneness. The teachings emphasize a deconditioning or reconditioning process of the Mind based on the truths and principles of nature. Doing ritual on each of the Great Days and on the High Moons becomes a method for tuning or centering your spiritual self. You learn to re-align yourself with nature's rhythms and cycles.

Allow yourself to become a blade of grass, a drop of water, or a cool mountain breeze. Begin balancing your awareness and energy by merging with oneness, and turn your mind toward the patterns of nature. In harmony with nature, you begin to perceive the world around you as your partner, or as you would a part of your own body; it sends you messages of positivity and negativity.

Journey through the boundless and know the feeling of being in perfect love with all nature and being at perfect peace with everything. Become all things. Merge with the earth, the ocean, a seed, the moon, and another person, and begin to truly comprehend the never-ending, never-beginning, ever-changing cycle of oneness.

As you merge with the boundless, allow your light and energy to flow and grow. The brighter you become, the easier you move through the many levels of spiritual self-development. Pattern your experience with light and

152

know you are on the path you have chosen. Always make an effort to move toward your bright self and mirror that positive face to others.

Be aware of how you assemble or construct yourself in your daily world. What are the qualities you carry with you when you dream or merge into other realms of perception? Asian philosophy states that how you make tea is indicative of how you live your life. How do you make tea? Pay close attention to your words and your actions, and observe the congruence therein. The manner in which you move through the world parallels your inner potential and expectation.

You imprint your energy on everyone with whom you interact, and on everything you touch. For example, when you talk on the phone, energetic residue remains on the phone. When you walk in the woods, you imprint the ground you walk upon. Predators use this imprinting of energy to hunt and track their prey. It behooves you of learn to be aware to these useful forms of energy.

153

Likewise, if you love someone or have a pleasant experience, you impart loving energy and positive light. If you strongly dislike a particular situation or person, you will most likely fill the energetic space with negative energy.

The Rishis feel human consciousness is one single awareness that is shared by everyone. From this perspective, the advantages and benefits of positivity are shared by all. This also means that the disadvantages and destructiveness of negativity are shared by everyone.

Aboriginal people of Australia feel successful when their relationships with others are in balance and their community is well. They recognize that who you interact with builds the foundation of your life. Who are the people with whom you relate, work, and exchange energy? Your interaction with these people defines the polarity in which you exist, whether it be positive, neutral, or negative.

Be mindful that relationship is cyclic and so becomes ever-changing and ever-renewing, paralleling the waxing and waning of the moon. Make an effort to be flexible and remain current with the changes in yourself and your relationships. What are the emerging patterns in your connections with others? By observing the flow, relationship becomes an empowering transformational tool.

The four keys to positive awareness and patterning are wisdom, self-honesty, self-responsibility, and love. As you apply these simple concepts, you begin to let go of rigid personal constructs. Allow yourself to know that you are all things. Identifying with your ego only limits your experience and perception. Avoid struggling with your world. Decondition and then recondition your Mind, and begin to travel beyond ordinary reality.

Clear expectation and clean intention, mated with a strong desire and a deep merge with oneness, creates positive patterns. Use your previous patterns as a gauge to understand and improve your present and future. Study and learn from the past and from what has gone before. Pay close attention to all the steps along the way, keeping in mind that you are responsible for where you find yourself. Celebrate the freedom of personal choice.

Taking responsibility implies accepting all that you say, feel, do, perceive, write, see, hear, and communicate as a part of you. Responsibility means knowing your connection with oneness, and becoming aware of all the events around you and within you.

You begin to cultivate an appreciation of life, discovering every experience is potentially valuable to your patterns and self-development. As you take responsibility for your world, you find synchronicity and harmony everywhere. You start to truly notice the unusual, and seemingly strange events become a normal and enjoyable part of your life.

Perceive the harmony of oneness in all things, and flow with the goddess and her consort between the boundaries of consensus reality. Plunge through the socially constructed walls of illusion as you awaken to new possibilities. Discipline your awareness to recognize subtlety and nuance. These skills will assist you on your adventure.

Notice that there is no separation or duality. These are conditioned constructs of your Mind. Everything is oneness. All things are fluid and flow into one another on a basic energetic awareness. Like an inexhaustible cauldron, you have constant access to this boundless river of light and knowledge.

Learn to live your dreams, and to move past doubt and hesitation, taking responsibility for what you perceive and know. Begin to view and multi-sense your own self. Self-awareness leads to knowledge and spiritual development. Notice that mindful positive images create a positive self-image, whereas self-destructive images create a negative self-image. Thoughts, intuitions, sensations, and perceptions combine together to form your picture of reality. Be aware of what you turn your mind to.

The powerful energy of thought has long been recognized. Positive thoughts heal and engender positivity, strengthening you. Negative thoughts break and injure, creating havoc and disruption, and eventually weaken your life pattern. The word *positive* means "to place" whereas the word *negative* means "to deny."

Perfect your patterns by valuing your perceptions and what you sense and experience. Empower yourself by enhancing the positive and bright aspects of yourself. Free your mind from the unnecessary limitations of conditioning and develop your personal power and awareness.

Know the perfect love of knowledge and perfect peace of wisdom.

As your bright face begins to emerge and fully awaken, you learn to manifest your dreams. You live your dreams proportional to your alignment with your bright self. Campaign for the Bright One. As you allow your mind to travel into the boundless, begin to build viable patterns through positive action and dreaming.

Guided Journey

Reaching for the next divot in the rock, she tries not to look down at the abyss below. Finding a handhold, she grabs the rock and begins to move horizontally along the face of the cliff. Above lies the top with its sacred earth she so desperately needs, and down below a drop of ten thousand feet. She continues the arduous climb until the top of the mountain rests only six feet away.

Suddenly her foot slips, and for a moment she falls through the air, clouds whipping across her face. Her hands once again find the stability of the rock, and she pulls herself up to the top of the mountain. As she walks along the edge of Table Top Mountain, she looks below her to see the tops of the clouds. Reaching down, she grabs a handful of earth and stuffs the soil into a small pouch. She carefully places the pouch into the dark green pack she wears on her back.

"That's one down, three to go," she mumbles to herself, happy that the first step of her quest is complete, but realizing she still has a long way to go until her father is free once again.

"Three more steps," she thinks to herself. "A wand carved from a branch of the Apple Tree of Amaethon, the Blade of Borum, and water from the Crystal Springs."

These three tools along with the earth from the mountain will be used to draw the circle that will break the spell of the Dark Wizard. The Dark Wizard came nightly into her father's dreams until alas, her father was slowly going insane. All the wise and learned healers in the kingdom had been called, but to no avail as her father slipped farther into insanity. It was at that time when a strange old man showed up in the square one day, waving his ancient book in the air, saying he had the solution for breaking the spell that hung like a shadow over her father. That was the day her quest began, and the reason she now found herself on the high mountaintop.

Once back down at the bottom of the steep mountain, she begins her journey eastward along the red path leading to the Forest of Time and to the Apple Tree of Amaethon. She begins to feel a tugging at the back of her head while walking. The closer she moves toward the forest, the more the tugging increases until she can go no further. She sits down beneath a large oak tree and falls immediately to sleep.

"Wake up," the voice calls out through the foggy expanse. "Wake up. You must wake up."

She feels a hand plucking at her sleeve, and she looks up to see the beautiful face of a young girl. The girl has bear-like features, long jet-black hair, and a body that is strong, quick, and agile.

"You fell under the spell of the Dark Wizard, and would have continued sleeping through eternity if I hadn't come along." The girl stops speaking, and looks at her pensively for a moment as if deciding something. "How would you like to learn a bit of magic that will prevent the Dark Wizard from casting his spell over you ever again?"

The woman quickly nods her head in agreement.

The young girl continues, "Good, then let me show how to find your Secret Name. I will teach you how to use this special name for protection from those people who wish to do you harm."

"Can this Secret Name you speak of truly protect me?" the woman asks eagerly,

"Yes. The Name is a magical and powerful tool. Let's begin, shall we? First search within the weaves and fabric of your inner self to find your true Name," the young girl says in a voice flowing like the wind. "Look for your Name within the Eternal Now, the point where you can see anything and find everything. When you discover it, you will know without hesitation or doubt that it is your Secret Name."

As the girl speaks to her, the woman can feel the tentacles of her mind reaching out into oneness. Deeper and deeper, she feels them probe the inner reaches of her self. She sees a white raven fly effortlessly across the sky in broken motion like light moving through a strobe. Each image ignites like the flash of a camera going off in her mind. In an instant, a sense of warm knowing covers her being like a wool blanket on a cold winter's night. She knows her Secret Name.

The girl watches her face transform and continues, "Now that you know your Secret Name, recite this chant over and over to yourself, using your true Name. 'The wind calls me White Raven, for that is my true name and the essence of me. No one can do any negative work of magic against me unless they know my true name, White Raven. If my true name is discovered, it cannot be used against me until the person has counted every atom in the universe, consecutively in sequential time, over and again, forever and a day.'"

As the woman chants the words, she feels the sticky energy that had attached itself to her, move off and away from her. The sleepiness also begins to fade, and she picks herself up off the ground. She feels fresh and filled with renewed life. She looks around, but the young girl has gone, disappearing without a trace. Oddly she now knows the Dark Wizard can no longer use his sleep magic to stop her from completing her quest. Once again she walks on the red path, moving closer to the Forest of Time.

160

The branches of the trees look like the many arms of a giant octopus, reaching ever higher toward the sunlit sky. A green covering drapes itself around the branches, blocking the sunlight from the forest floor. As she travels deeper into the forest, the light grows so dim that day turns into night.

Glancing to her left, the woman sees scattered rays of light coming from what appears to be a candle shining in a large dark room. She moves closer to the source of light, discovering the brilliance emanates from a small clearing in the thick trees. Approximately fifty feet across, the clearing looks like a perfect circle neatly cut out from the forest. The woman notices the only tree in the clearing is medium sized, gnarled and tangled with age. As she walks closer, she sees the bright red fruit hanging on the trees branches. She suddenly realizes that she has found the Apple Tree of Amaethon.

She jumps abruptly in the air when a hand touches her on the back. For a moment, her breathing is ragged and heavy, and her heart pounds like a hammer in her chest. She turns to look at a handsome and virile man with deep blue eyes, blonde hair and a sun-bronzed face.

"I didn't mean to scare you," he says apologetically, but with a huge grin on his face. "Are you lost?"

"Ah, no," she fumbles with her words until once again her brain and mouth synchronize. Collecting her wits about her, she addresses the mysterious man, "I was looking for the Apple Tree of Amaethon, and it looks like I've found it." As she speaks, she casts her eyes on the tree sitting in the clearing.

"You have at that," he sings merrily, but then with a note of hesitation he questions her further, "What do you want it for? You don't mean to bring it harm, do you?"

He eyes her closely as if drinking in every drop of her essence with a single look. "No, I don't think you would hurt the apple tree, would you?" he teases her while his penetrating blue eyes beam with a bright smile. His radiance seems both blinding and illuminating at the same time.

"No, of course I won't harm the apple tree," she admonishes him. "I only need a small branch, so I can make a wand to aid me in my quest."

"And what quest might that be?" he questions with interest.

"Why, the quest to free my father from the spell of the Dark Wizard. The wand is essential in drawing the circle of light, so darkness will no longer be able to consume my father's dreams." Her voice raises and her body tightens visibly when she thinks about the Dark One. She feels him

161

in her, building anger, still trying to weave his dark energy around her like a python constricting its prey.

Quietly to herself, she again speaks the Secret Name chant. The sticky darkness leaves like a shadow scurrying swiftly off through the forest undergrowth.

"I can help you," the man says assuredly. She watches as he touches the base of the tree, and for a moment man and tree become one. A small foot-long branch descends into her hands from the apple tree. She looks at the branch with astonishment as the man smiles at her.

"Thank you, you are very kind," she says, her words full of genuine appreciation.

"You are very welcome, my Lady. Now I will make you a wand that will be truly enchanted," he chuckles while taking the stick from her hands.

She watches as he takes his athame from his belt and begins to peel the bark off the branch. He carefully gathers up the shavings and distributes them clockwise around the base of the apple tree. From his pocket, he extracts a clear crystal point and carves three runes on the wand face with the sharp tool. Then he fastens the shining stone to the end of the wand with a strip of red leather.

When he is finished, the bronze-skinned man holds the wand up toward the sky. Suddenly to her amazement, the sky turns dark.

The full moon pours out over the horizon and descends down to the earth to dance in the crystal tip, coyly playing with every facet. Abruptly, the whole wand begins to glow with the lucent white light of the full moon.

As he hands her the wand, she can feel it pulsating with spirals of energy. She watches as a bright light shoots out the tip. She moves the intent to heal into the body of the wand.

The man begins to chant in a language that sounds foreign yet familiar. His voice has a soothing strangeness that calls the energy of the gods into the wand. As he finishes his chant, the sun returns to its previous position in the sky. The wand is complete.

After thanking him for his and the apple tree's wonderful gift, she travels on with the precious wand tucked snugly in her pack, right next to the pouch filled with earth from the mountain. Her path now leads her South, into the heart of the sun and the Blade of Borum.

The famous Blade of Borum and its magical powers were legendary. She had heard many a *shanachie,* or storyteller, tell the tale of how the Blade had been forged by the god Lugh himself, out of pieces of the sun. The mighty Blade had the power to cut portals into other worlds such as Tir-nan-Og, home of the gods.

The Blade, once complete, was entrusted by Lugh to an ancient people who called themselves the Borum. The Borum lived in the highlands overlooking the Forest of Time. They were farmers famous for the brewing of fine liquid concoctions, as well as for possessing the magical Blade.

163

A young man with soft brown eyes and dark, wavy brown hair greets her as she reaches the outskirts of the Village of Borum. He holds his hand outstretched toward her. "Welcome to our beautiful village, fair Lady," he calls out eloquently.

He smiles and she smiles back. They both feel the jolt, a flash of intimate knowing. Seizing the moment, a divine hand of light clasps the woman to the man. They stare into each other's eyes as if in a hypnotic trance. For a few moments, time completely stops.

"Why have you come to Borum?" he asks, his voice sounding dreamy and distant.

She brings herself forcibly back to the present. "I seek the Blade of Borum, so that I might free my father from the spell of the Dark Wizard," she says, surprised a bit that her words are so coherent. "Can you tell me where I might find it?"

"Of course, the Blade is kept by the Weaver who is also known as the Brew Master. If you follow me, I will take you to him." The young man then turns, motioning her to follow.

The footpath winds around several buildings. Toward the center of the busy village, an old man sits in the shade of a mighty oak tree. She sits across from him, and the young man sits down beside her.

The old man scratches his beard while looking deep within her eyes. His mind knows no bounds, and she loses herself in the enveloping grey cloud of his eyes. He is all-seeing and all-knowing, enticing and inviting the energies of the universe into one single point of light.

He listens intently to her tale of the Dark Wizard, nodding his head as she tells him of her quest to save her father. She finishes speaking and he continues to stare intently into her eyes. A wave of self-consciousness splashes across her mind. She looks nervously over at the young man sitting at her side. He smiles at her.

"I will allow you to use the Blade of Borum in order to complete your quest and free your father," the old man's voice commands, in a tone that is not loud, but strangely reverberates throughout the small village. "My son will accompany you, to assure the safe return of the Blade." He motions toward the handsome young man next to her.

The woman flashes the younger man a quizzical look, silently asking, "Why didn't you tell me you were his son?"

The young man smiles and defers to his father. The old man gestures for a tray of golden cups. The vessels are filled with a rich, brown liquid. The old man hands a cup to the young woman and then one to his son before taking one for himself.

"Before you go, let us toast the gods," the old man says, as he holds his golden cup high in the air.

They drink the syrupy dark brew mixed with light amber ale. Each goddess and god is toasted aloud until the woman's head fills with a warm glow.

"The quality of the brew lies in the quality of the wort and the strength of the yeast," the old man says, motioning at his cup. "Once the yeast is added to the wort, life springs forth, completing the cycle, and the brew transforms into a fine concoction like this." He holds his cup up and takes another drink, saying clearly, "Ayea gods!"

The old man sets his cup down. He reaches into the folds of his blue robe and takes the Blade of Borum out and solemnly hands it to his son. "Make sure you return the Blade when the woman's quest has been completed. Our ancestors go with you." The old man stands slowly, gesturing toward the West path leading out of the Village of Borum. "May you be successful in your quest." The Brew Master bids them, "Farewell for now."

The woman and young man follow the winding path out of the village, moving westward. As they journey closer to the Crystal Springs, she notices the breeze smells clean and fresh, with a slight dampness. As the Springs come into view, the splendor captivates her senses.

Crystals everywhere, all shapes, sizes and colors, circle the Springs, and move infinitely into their depths. Light seems to dance from one form to another, up and down, in and out, spiraling endlessly through the water in a kaleidoscope of streaming radiance and color. In the pool below the flowing Springs, she sees the reflection of herself and the handsome young man standing next to her. She takes a flask from her bag, reaches down, and fills it full of water from the crystal well.

He draws the circle of light with the Blade, and she calls the goddess and her consort with nine strokes of the wand. They both grab handfuls of the special earth from Table Top Mountain out of the pouch, and move to the North Point of the magical circle. Casting the handfuls of soil back to the earth, they begin to call in the Four Great Wards. Her arms stretch out over her head.

With both hands held high, she feels his body next to her. His muscles bulge like formations of rock as she strokes his shoulders and chest. His hands flow down the length of her hair to her breasts, which loom like two mountain peaks demanding to be climbed, upward and upward until his fingers reach the top.

The circle of light pulses around them, flowing in long silky rivers to the source. She senses his every movement magnified across larger dimensions of awareness. He caresses her skin, its smooth suppleness driving his desire to new heights until the air around them liquifies and swirls and the lovers dance in dizzy passion.

She takes him in her arms, kissing his neck before moving up to his ear. He feels her hot breath penetrating the lobe. Hot flashes of Light ignite and flame as their bodies move together in rhythmic unity. Sweat glistens across his face as she looks up into his eyes. An immense blue ocean floods her senses. Ascending higher up the staircase into the stars, the white light beckons the lovers to a place beyond the darkness—a place where the Dark One dares not enter, and the Loving Light knows no bounds.

He takes her into his arms, and his hands dive down the middle of her back. He lifts her gently, placing her on top of him. Her movements start slow and exaggerated, but soon heat to a point of rapid boiling.

His moist tongue slides across her skin, moving up to her apex. Her body shakes as she raises the upper half of her torso to move closer and deeper. Faster and faster, the rhythmic meter increases, building up for the last poetic crescendo. A bolt of liquid energy launches out into the cosmic well of the universe.

Her awareness shifts dramatically, as she feels herself being pulled out of her dream. "Momma! Wake up!" the high voice whines in her left ear. She feels small hands shaking her shoulder, and opens one eye to see the bright smiling face of her son. His eyes are blue like the sky, and bright as the morning sun.

"Get up, momma! No more sleep!" he demands while tugging at her hand, trying to pull her out bed.

"Honey, are you awake?" she asks while reaching her hand out across the bed. She feels her husband's naked body. "Honey? Our son wants us to get up," she says playfully, grabbing her mate under his arms and tickling him until suddenly he sits up with a sleepy smile.

The young boy jumps up on the bed, laughing happily. His mother tickles him and he screams with delight while squirming on his back. The little boy demands, "Tickle, tickle me more!"

His father laughs and joins in briefly. Still half asleep, he takes a deep breath and lays back down on the bed.

She yawns and says to her husband, "I had the strangest dream last night." Before she starts to tell him the details, she hears the phone ring.

She sleepily stumbles into the kitchen with her young son bouncing and giggling behind her. As she picks up the receiver, the anxious voice of her sister greets her.

"Oh I'm glad I caught you at home," her sister says sounding tired and strained. "It's Dad. He had a heart attack late last night."

The words reverberate through her head. "What happened? Is he alright?" she cries, fighting the wave of emotion that threatens to drown her.

"Yes, he's doing better this morning. Things were touch-and-go all night, and at one point, we didn't know if he was going to make it." Her sister's voice pauses momentarily. "I don't know. Suddenly it felt like there was this divine energy watching over and protecting him. After that his condition improved and this morning, he sat up in bed looking like nothing ever happened. It's the oddest thing," her sister's voice trails off. "I've never seen anything like it."

The woman thinks momentarily about telling her sister about the dream before deciding against it. "She'd just think I'm crazy, they always do," she says to herself. She talks to her sister for a few moments, says good-bye and returns the telephone receiver to its cradle.

She walks over to the refrigerator for a glass of milk, and notices the handle of a piece of wood protruding from a stack of papers on the kitchen counter. She grasps the end of the stick, pulling it into view. On the other end sits a clear quartz crystal, bound to the wood with a red leather strip. A short way down from the crystal point, she sees the runes etched into the wood.

A wave sweeps across her consciousness, breaking into tiny droplets that spray across infinity. She feels another veil lifted from her senses like one reality fading into the next reality, one view leading to another.

CHAPTER NINE

❧ The Barley Moon ☙

Fliodhas & Robur

*You sing me into a silent sleep
when you whisper my name and smile.
Like water flowing into the earth
your voice embraces me
in a stream of wonder.*

CHAPTER NINE

The Barley Moon ☙

Fliodhas & Robur

Full Moon in Pisces, Sun in Virgo
Mutable negative water and earth elements

The Goddess and Her Consort

According to Pliny the Elder, a Roman scholar who lived
in the first century AD, barley with its triple spikelettes is
the oldest of foods. As the first cereal cultivated by
humankind, barley served as a staple for many people,
transforming hunting cultures into agrarian societies.
Women directed the planting of the barley seeds. Cultivated with care, the barley was harvested and dried. The
grain was then stored or used in bread making, used med-
icinally for healing, and malted for brewing beer.

Common in religious rituals, barley was honored at
initiations, weddings, births, and funerals. The Greek goddess Demeter is associated with the grain, as is the Barley
Bride of the Berbers near Tangier. Likewise, the lake-
dwellers of the Stone Age in Europe recognized the fertil-
izing power of the goddess in the form of the Barley
Mother.

Like the Corn Mother, the Barley Mother symbolizes the never-ending and continually renewing cyclic aspects of nature. The Barley Moon represents the magical balance of nature, and the aspects of birth, growing, maturing, and rebirth. The goddess marries death and in doing so, renews herself.

Magic, healing, and wisdom prevail on the night of the Barley Moon. The full moon ritual on this night gives you the energy to influence the course and nature of your life just as the ancient rituals influenced the course of nature in the past. Learn to produce the results you desire and begin to reap the harvests of your efforts.

Flowing with the seasonal cycles and rhythms, the goddess Fliodhas teaches you how to commune with and positively influence nature. As protectress of the woodlands and animals, the ancient and shy goddess appears as the Stag Mistress who roams the earth in a chariot drawn by deer from the Otherworld. Calling all the wild animals her cattle, Fliodhas is associated with the deer goddess Sadv.

Smiling brightly, the beautiful Fliodhas wears robes of woodland green or an earth-brown tunic and breeches. Crowning her long honey-colored hair are headbands woven of ferns, seeds, and flowers. When you meet her in the lush green grass near woodland springs, her sunny personality shines through. A large fertile doe often accompanies Fliodhas as she walks in the forest or in open meadows.

Robur acts as consort to the lovely and gentle Fliodhas. He protects the animals of the forests and represents the monad of all oaks. Called the Forest King, the god Robur appears with bright gray-brown eyes, an unruly beard, silver-streaked hair, and a moustache. Often seen walking nude through the woods, the consort's skin is the color of tree bark. When clothed, he dresses in a short leather tunic.

Rapport with Robur expands your wisdom of nature and the ever-renewing cycle. With mistletoe tangled in his wild hair and beard, the consort reaches into the depths of the earth and pulls the knowledge of the Mother out into the open for all to see. Wisdom travels up his roots through his trunk, into his limbs, and flows out into the perfect majesty of his lush green leaves and fertile acorns.

Journey through the woodlands, across mountain streams and over warm grassy meadows with the goddess and her consort. Come to know the innate strength and the natural pattern of all things by observing the boundless facets of oneness. Wander through the forest of dreams and traverse the boundless river. As you look below at the watery ravine, find a certain stone. Perhaps you will find a quartz crystal. Work with the facets of the stone, and begin to discover the faces and reflections of yourself.

Practical Knowledge and Useful Information— Crystal Healing

From that which has no name issues She who is the Mother of All Things. She is the sun, the Earth, and the moon. She awakens to become all nature, waiting for you to discover her secrets written in the stones. In particular, clear quartz crystals amplify and transduce the boundless energy of oneness, giving you access to beneficial currents of light.

Crystal healing serves as a useful method in breaking unhealthy patterns. People heal themselves; i.e., the desire and potential for healthiness lies within the individual. You are the conduit of the healing energy. When you do any healing work, set aside your ego during the procedure and access the healing energy of oneness.

The light of the full moon is the optimum time to do

healing works. We respond to light, especially moonlight. As living creatures we are in a constant state of flux, absorbing and emitting light. When you perceive or experience pain or hurt at any level of awareness, including spiritual, emotional, and physical pain, you suffer a loss of light. The absorption process becomes blocked and a dimming ensues. Healing requires restoring your energy by building up your light. In the healing process, crystals act as transducers and amplifiers of light. The stones facilitate energetic balancing.

In Gwyddonic Druid Tradition, the use of specific color wavelengths of light enhance all healing work. Start with the blue wavelength. Use a vibrant cobalt hue to clean out negativity and to wash away the old unhealthy energetic pattern. Green represents the DNA structure. Use it to create or re-establish healthy patterns as you proceed with the healing work. Add gold to fuel the new healthy pattern. Depending on the type of blockage, use ultraviolet to break up unhealthy patterns on a cellular level. Use this powerful color wavelength to remove or destroy the growth of unhealthy cells or to break up congestion. Apply ultraviolet before you use the blue cleansing light. Be particularly careful when using ultraviolet energy, as it breaks up and destroys whatever energetic pattern that is in place. White light motivates the new patterns you build, and vitalizes the healing centers of the body. Rose color strengthens the desire for healing and gives you a sense of love and balance. The color red gives strength and vitality as its wavelength heats up the body. Finally, orange is used as a clarifier.

Structure your healing work using stones and crystals as you would all other magical works. Be mindful of your expectation, desire, and depth of your merge. Be sure to clean all of the stones you use. To do so, breathe deeply and as you hold your breath, move your intention into the stone. Intend for the crystal to be clear and clean as you pulse your breath out. You may choose to see a single point of white light permeating the stone. Become aware of and use whatever sensation means clear or clean to you, passing this feeling into the crystal.

Enhance your healing work by laying out a grid within your magical circle. Use four clear quartz crystals pointing in, one at each of the four directions, and place the energy of the corresponding element within each crystal. Move the quality of water into the stone used for the West Point. In fact, the stone you select for the West Point might actually look more wet or water-like than the other crystals. Be mindful. Study and question all of the subtleties of the stones and the nuances of your healing pattern.

The following crystal healing process was taught to me by Marcel Vogel, an individual who exemplified remarkable spiritual awareness and the healing power of love. This particular procedure requires you work one-on-one with your partner. Healing work implies a form of shared intimacy because you are there for the other person. They trust you to help them in their healing experience. Simply modify the techniques if you work with a group.

Choose a large pointed clear quartz crystal as a healing tool, one that fits comfortably in the palm of your hand. Structure the crystal for healing using your intention and breath. Hold the crystal in your hands and breathe in through your mouth. Firmly fixing your intention in your mind's eye, pulse your breath out through your nose, transferring your intention to the crystal. Do this procedure several times until you master it. Merge with the crystal as you move your intention inside of it. Become the crystal. Eventually as you grow more accustomed to working with crystals and stones, learn to structure or program them by gazing at them or by simply turning your awareness to the stone or crystal.

Always call in the goddess and god energies to assist you in your work. Ask those with whom you have the greatest rapport, and select those goddess and god qualities most appropriate to the work. Merge with the goddess and her consort, filling your awareness with their light, love, and boundless strength.

The instructions that follow are from a woman's view, working with a male partner. Begin by suggesting your partner sit down comfortably. Be sure to ask him whether he wants to be healed. After definite confirmation, hand him the crystal healing tool and begin working. Have him breathe deeply in and out, with the intention of slowly filling the crystal in his hands with his awareness. Match his breathing pattern with yours and merge with oneness.

Quietly ask him to return the crystal tool to you. Feel the energy in the crystal, and merge your awareness into the crystal, joining to his awareness. Ask him what needs to be healed. The more specific he is, the better you can hone in on the blockage. Make an effort to multi-sense the energetic dimness or blockage.

Hold the crystal healing tool in your right hand, with the stone pointing out. Move it over the thymus area, or witness area, which is about three to five inches below the throat chakra. Do not touch the body with the crystal at this time. Take a deep breath and hold it. While using a counter-clockwise twist of your right wrist, energetically enter your partner's subtle energy body with the crystal tool. This is the only widdershins motion you will use in the healing work.

Start moving the crystal tool in small up and down motions and in small clockwise circles. You and your partner will feel a tugging sensation as you connect into his energy field. Keep matching your breathing patterns. Use your left hand as an anchor on your partner's back. This left hand placement also completes the energetic circuit, promoting the transference of light.

With your right hand, move the crystal over the blockage or pain to be worked on. Breathe together, all the while asking your partner about his sensations and impressions in the problem area. Ask him what color and what texture the area is, and if there are any feelings, sounds or images contained therein. Place the crystal healing tool on his body, and have him fill the stone with his awareness of his illness or pain.

As your partner moves these impressions into the crystal, it will begin to build up with the unwanted energy. The more he participates in the healing, the better the results. Shake the build-up of unwanted energy off the healing tool. Use your intention and breath. In your own way, image or multi-sense a clear cobalt blue light washing out the stone. Move out the blockage with your intention. As you hold the crystal tool over the troubled area, begin using clockwise motions to fill the dimmed area with bright light using the succession of colors; blue, green, and then gold. This builds a new healthy pattern of energy.

As you and your partner merge with the new healthy image, know that the healing is successful with your entire being. Join together and visualize your partner in a perfect state of health and oneness. Use your right and left hands in tandem, and begin wide, sweeping motions. Do this at least three times as you continue to match his breathing. As you breathe and sweep his energy field,

177

make an effort to amplify the light and healing energy moving through you. Direct this vital energy through your hands, the crystal, and then into your partner.

End the healing work by moving the crystal back over to the witness area. With a clockwise twist of your right wrist, exit your partner's energy body at the same place you entered. Set the crystal down carefully and stand him up slowly. Smile and give him a warm hug. Suggest your partner relax for the rest of the evening and that he drink plenty of fluids. Toast the goddess and her consort and thank them in your own way for their helpful assistance.

Clean your crystal healing tool out after the healing by using your intention. Then pull up your circle and energetically clean the area thoroughly. Be creative and make an effort to remain loving when you do any healing work. Feel free to turn your mind toward oneness as you let the light flow through you.

Guided Journey

Wizards dream their own way. This is the story of two such wizards in the Kingdom of Anu, on a small island called Belit.

She lies back on the cushioned chaise and looks up at the azure blue sky. All around her, oaks, madrones, and pines dance gracefully in the late afternoon breeze. The scent of the woods drifts over her. She watches as a swift and agile grey squirrel dashes, leaps and scurries through the thick green foliage.

As the evening sun sinks into the horizon, she notices patterns of golden orange light flowing in slow motion like a giant hand sweeping across the forest. The occasional sound of a crested blue jay breaks the natural silence of the evening. She focuses on the sound of the mountain jay's call.

Instantly she moves her mind to another dimension, to an island called Belit in the Kingdom of Anu. The island is a special place she visits often. She belongs on the lush isle and always feels welcome by the people there. Several island nations make up the Kingdom of Anu, where the wizard scientists use crystal technology and the science of mind to shape and change their world. On Belit she is a young wizard called Hara. In a flicker of light, she finds herself in the City of the Sun. It is here that she continues to expand her awareness and her perception of all things.

Hara looks out over the city's free-form domes, to the brilliant expanse of cobalt blue water surrounding the island. Toward the far shoreline at the edge of the city stands the circular Dream Tower. She covers the distance with her mind, moving up the bleached stone walkway to the Tower door. The hard stone surface feels warm and slightly rough on the bottoms of her bare feet. Tethered in a braid, her golden hair swings behind her as she walks, and she feels the bulk of the braid touch her naked back.

Woven along the outside of the Dream Tower are the dense branches of nine massive broad-leafed trees. The trees encircle the building, standing tall like natural guardians. Hara pauses and fingers a bright green leaf with her mind, spinning rose and gold light over its surface. She moves the light over the branch and across the mighty sentinels. She sweeps the gentle light over their limbs like a soothing lover's touch, and the trees bend and sway toward her in response. She continues walking.

As she reaches the entrance to the Dream Tower, the carved wooden door opens suddenly. The young man called Telyn greets her with a powerful embrace. First he weaves his mind through hers in a flash of warm white light, and then takes her in his hard and muscular arms and kisses her soundly. The feel of his skin on hers excites her as she weaves and spins small circles of blue water light over his solid body.

He is her lover, friend, and spiritual mate on the Island of Belit. He speaks to her silently with his mind, his thoughts clear and pronounced, "We have been expecting you."

"I know. I came as soon as I felt the need," Hara mind-speaks to the handsome man holding her, twisting his curling golden hair between her long, thin fingers.

He seems both young and ancient as his brilliant blue eyes fix upon hers. "The others are waiting for us in the central hub," Telyn says silently as he guides her to the inner chamber. The hallway glows in an orange-gold light that bathes the walls. Small stones placed at determined points create the flame-like illumination.

Hara moves sensuously, flowing like a mountain stream across the stone floor. As she enters the central hub, the floor under her feet changes to a deep green malachite. The swirling patterns of the polished stone floor resemble a fluid green meadow, and for a moment she actually feels the soft grass under her feet. Looking up, she notices the ceiling is shaped like a large dome, intricately patterned with punched copper plates. Large copper cables extend and drape down from the metal ceiling and connect to four directionally-placed pillars of milky white quartz.

At the North Point stands Ognar the dream wizard, and at the East Point stands her teacher Achren. The Lady Melwren waits patiently at the West Point as Telyn moves to his place at the South Point. Each of them holds a large nine-sided quartz generator crystal, specially grown and tuned for dreaming.

In the middle of the domed room stands a wheel-like hub. A large white quartz platform holds the dreaming chair. The platform is surrounded by twelve equally-spaced, waist-high black tourmaline pillars. These waist-high pillars are perfectly aligned with the four directional pillars. The entire Dream Tower, consisting of the crystals, pillars, dome, and people, creates an exquisite pattern specially designed to promote a deeper kind of dreaming.

Hara moves her mind to the central area. She takes her body and sits carefully in the dreaming chair. The chair, fashioned from a huge amethyst geode, rests in a channel of clear warm running water that flows out of the Dream Tower and into the calm azure sea nearby. To either side of the smooth natural chair sit large cavities of tiny purple lilac crystals which spill out and drip down onto the milky quartz platform, cascading out across the swirling malachite floor. The lilac crystals look like tiny purple flowers resting on a grassy meadow.

Hara can feel her awareness shift and amplify as she sits down. She moves her intention into the stone chair beneath her and then out into the room. The warm water stokes her naked skin, relaxing her more and more. Her eyes close slowly and in the far corner of her mind, Hara sees Telyn sitting before her.

His mind flies out like a swift arrow and clasps a golden bow-shaped harp from out of the ethers. His fingers tune the instrument with its jeweled tuning key. He begins to sing sweetly to her, a song about a beautiful woman who visits him in his dreams. His song lulls her quickly into a sound and silent sleep.

The four people standing at the directional pillars turn their minds and point the generator crystals toward Hara. Each intends a tone. Together, their combined energy and sound starts the wheel of black tourmaline pillars spinning clockwise. It spins rapidly, faster and faster around the quartz platform, moving around the woman resting in the dreaming chair.

Hara's mind travels across a gleaming lattice of light as warm water flows over her soft and supple skin. A portal of light opens and she empties into it like a mighty river into a sea of radiance and pure energy. Infinite threads weave together, creating a strange checkerboard configuration of light and color, moving out in all directions.

"Marissa," a deep voice whispers in her mind. "Marissa," the voice continues, this time much louder. She knows the name. It is one of her many names. Cutting through etheric space, she follows the voice into a dimensional realm of stones and trees. The voice transforms into the Crystal Seer, a male being shaped by her intention.

The Seer stands a foot taller than her and moves like fluid stone. His shape changes and shifts as she looks at the different facets of his being. He gently touches her throat. As the Crystal Seer removes his hand, a small gold circular disk inlaid with petrified wood hangs from her neck on a golden chain.

183

"Use the golden circle to enter the continuum," he mindspeaks with thoughts that feel like cool water splashing on her face.

He guides Marissa to a massive oak tree growing on a slight incline. The tree rests next to three large granite boulders. In front of the giant oak stand two lion-sized cats carved from single stones. Falcons sit on their shoulders, motionlessly watching her. She moves between the cats, through a natural door and into the center of the mighty tree.

Inside the tree rests a round mirror-like stone surface surrounded by thirteen chairs. The table and chairs have no visible means of support and they seem to be suspended in space. Each chair has an occupant except for the chair nearest Marissa.

She sits in the empty chair and turns her mind to the others seated around the table. As she takes a deep breath in, she notices her fingers skate over the slick mirrored table surface as if it were made of reflective ice. As she breathes out, the bottoms of her hands seem to stick to the top of the odd circular table.

Beginning at her left, she gazes, one at a time, at the others seated, moving clockwise. The first three beings are very human-like. A young man, a young woman, and an older smiling man watch her carefully. Suddenly the young woman speaks. Her voice feels rhythmic, like ocean waves. "We are your guides. At times we motivate you and nudge you on your adventure. Your intentions are our intentions and our intentions are yours. We are one."

Marissa acknowledges her three guides with a smile and a nod of her head. She moves her attention to the being sitting next to her guides. The tiny cat-like girl looks up at her and speaks, "I am Chrysalis. I represent your will of survival and the agreements you make with others. I give you structure."

Marissa stares at Chrysalis for a few moments before smiling and looking directly at the light being who is hovering in the chair next to the tawny cat girl. The cylindrical energy shape bursts into orange flames and transforms into a large stinging spider. Instantly the spider splinters into a magnificent peregrine falcon. The falcon mind-feels to her, "I feed you and you feed me."

Marissa feels pure light moving directly into her mind, propelling her to the timeless face of the woman sitting next to the falcon being. Seated almost directly across from Marissa, the woman seems familiar, so very familiar.

"Yes, you know me well. I protect the pattern. I am the wisdom of oneness. You may call me Kerridwen." The woman's words taste like honey in Marissa's mouth. She swallows slowly.

To Kerridwen's left, a dark, male, ape-like figure looms over the circular table. He sits in the chair like a judge waiting for Marissa's attention. "I am your opposite reaction, a constant companion to your doubts and fears."

Marissa can feel the disruptive energy coursing off the being and she quickly moves her awareness to the man next to the ape-like figure.

He shapeshifts into her and she shapeshifts into him. He melds with her and fills her with his mind. "I am your ancestors. They are all collected here within me, within you. Trace the pattern forward, backward, upward, and sideways. Remember, your body knows the secrets." The shapeshifter blends his words into Marissa's perception like paints on a canvas.

Next to the shapeshifter, Death sits hooded and cloaked in memories and lifetimes. Fire shoots out of her hands and the flames heat the mirror-like surface of the table. She speaks clearly, "I am the death of your old self and the bringer of infinite gifts." Death chuckles and continues, "What is your deepest desire?"

185

Marissa senses the power of the hooded figure. Her instincts tell her not to reply, and so she remains silent.

The elfin child sitting next to Death giggles, disrupting the momentary silence. The child smiles at Marissa and weaves a beautiful blue light around her in the shape of a delicate cape of gleaming threads. Marissa breathes in the blue light and feels the energy flow through her body. The sensation both heals and stimulates her.

Marissa glances to her immediate right at two children, a boy and a girl. The girl sits next to Marissa and speaks tonally, "We are life, your life, their life, all life. We are the ever-renewing, never-ending cycle of light."

Very slowly, everyone sitting at the table begins to chant in unison, "We are one. We are one. We are one."

Marissa stands up and raises her arms above her head. She moves her mind into the boundless. Rainbows of light pour from her hands and weave a lattice pattern of radiance around all those present. She can see a connecting circle of silver and gold threaded light tying her to the group of beings. The light shines brighter and stronger as Marissa becomes pure energy. She senses her awareness merge with the falcon light being. As a mighty bird, he moves outward. Tethering herself to him, she feels herself being pulled into another dimension.

Flying over the azure seas of the Island of Belit, Hara tucks into the wind and dives down beneath Telyn as they glide through the orange and rose-colored evening sky. Fully awake, she smells the wetness of the ocean. Together they flow with the warm west wind, down close to the black sandy shoreline. Settling softly upon a field of golden barley, Hara and Telyn lie back in each other's arms.

Hara smells the traces of the warm sun on the grass as her hair spills out like a pool of amber silk over her lover's shoulder and arm. She fingers the gold disk on the chain around her neck, momentarily shifting her attention, and then shifting it back to the man next to her. The fields of gold surrounding them shimmer brilliant orange, billowing and flowing in the west wind.

As the lovers gaze up into the sky, twilight turns into night and the twin moons of Belit rise slowly in the sky. Hanging low on the horizon, the double full harvest moons shine like two great orange-golden orbs. Hara slides closer to Telyn, eager and wanting. She touches his waiting lips with her mind and circles his face in soft golden light. Her mouth moves over his and she captures his tongue between her teeth.

He kindles her mind and he rubs his hands liberally over her lush body. Telyn's fingers radiate a soft blue-white flame as he explores her deep chasm and high ridges. The soft fiery light swirls around her gleaming body and through her long braided hair, covering her with tiny blue-white stars shining in the blazing moonlight. He weaves the light deeply into the fabric of her awareness, caressing her pure energy core.

Hara's full breasts press against his hard chest. Her heart races as Telyn's fingers feather up the delicate skin of her inner thighs. Her body rises as he kisses the hardening tips of her breasts. She moans as waves of gold light join together with his lips, intensifying the sensation. Desire fills every cell in her body and the building passion floods her every perception.

She cups his hard arousal in her hands and feels his desire grow even stronger. Telyn groans and encourages her continued exploration. She tingles in anticipation as she cradles and strokes the potency of his solid maleness. She drinks him in, every nuance, every detail, and every inch.

187

He moves over her like the west wind flowing across the moonlit fields of shimmering barley. She cries out as her silky body closes around his hard arousal. A white lattice of light whirls around the lovers as they thrust and flow into each other.

Hara twirls her mind in the light. She rolls over Telyn like the warm liquid wind moving across the lustrous golden field. Her mind blends completely with his and their bodies flow together like the sea sweeping onto the shore.

She kisses him. Her voice embraces him in a stream of wonder as she says, "You are every lover. You are every man. I love you." She cloaks her lover in a deep green light, shifting the swirling radiance to gold, and then to bright white.

He moves up into her, harder and faster. All sensation gathers and then quickens as she flies her lover through the golden moonlight. They merge together into the dream within the dream, moving into other realms of awareness. Parallelling out like pure flashes of white light, the lovers dance through the night skies in infinite worlds of perception. Their ecstasy burns brighter and bolder, cascading like fluid moonfire across the starry expanse.

Soaring through the eternal now, the lovers cry out as one. Their bodies flow into a spherical brilliance that leaps into the boundless night.

As they lay in each other's arms, light covers everything in a pulsating glow. Hara looks up. She mindspeaks softly to the twin moons, "We come from light. We are light and we return to light."

She cradles her lover. Somewhere in the far recesses of her mind, she hears the faint sounds of children playing. She can see them running and laughing through the golden fields of barley.

❧ The Wine Moon ☙

Nantosuelta & Sucellos

On moon fire nights when I am the vessel
you become the fiery blade.
Inspired by our union
spirits dance and children play.

The Wine Moon ♌

Nantosuelta & Sucellos

Full Moon in Aries, Sun in Libra
Cardinal positive fire and air elements

The Goddess and Her Consort

Made from the fermented juice of grapes and other similar fruits, wine embodies the bountiful harvest of the goddess. With yeast on the outside and sugar on the inside, the grape indeed is a divine creation of nature. Like the many faces of the goddess, wine possesses sweet, dry, still, sparkling, white, rose, and red qualities. Join together and toast the goddess and her consort with a chalice of full bodied wine on this last harvest moon, as well as on the Great Days and all the other High Moons.

♌
191

In ritual, place the wine at the center or threshold of your altar. Symbolizing the divine love and union of the goddess and god, the wine cup represents the mating of female and male energies and the merging of the manifest and the unmanifest. Accordingly, with the Wine Moon come gifts of prophecy.

Gwyddonic Druid Tradition includes a Wine Ceremony in the preliminary rituals. The Wine Ceremony uses a consecrated vessel, most commonly in the form of a chalice, cup, or cauldron. After pouring the wine into the sacred vessel, consecrate the liquid by calling in the goddess Kerridwen into the vessel and her consort Kernunnos into the Athame blade. At this stage of the ritual, everyone drinks some of the wine from the sacred chalice. The woman acting as goddess drinks first from the blessed cup. She passes it to a man and he drinks before passing it on to another woman. Finally, the man acting as the God drinks the remainder of the wine cup and sets it carefully back down upon the altar. Representing the sharing of the essence or spirit of the goddess, the Wine Ceremony joins people together, bringing them closer. When you drink wine from the same vessel, you share the same essential light. You become one, akin to each other.

Wine is the oldest and safest medicine in the world when administered with intelligence and moderation. This ancient liquid food also serves as a menstruum in medicinal preparations. The body absorbs herbs much faster if the prescribed ingredients are first dissolved in wine. In this way, wine serves as a healing substance when combined with certain ingredients. Interestingly, *menstruum* means "monthly," which correlates to the cycle of the moon.

Enjoy the intoxicating Wine Moon with the goddess of abundance, Nantosuelta. Portraying a beautiful river goddess, her name means "Winding River." She moves fluidly, like a strong flowing stream, and as such, represents the power of creativity and destruction. She is strong and vigorous with a gentle and loving touch.

As the enchanting raven goddess, Nantosuelta appears with dark black-brown hair and chocolate brown eyes. Her skin shines softly and her face is fair, with high, rosy cheeks. The generous goddess flows gracefully in her watery, blue-green robes. Her magical tools are a baker's paddle and a dove's house mounted on a pole.

The artful Sucellos, a god of fertility and death, acts as consort to Nantosuelta. An aspect of the All Father and twin to the river god Dagda, the consort Sucellos runs fast and strong like his brother. He rules the dark half of the year, corresponding with the ascendancy of the moon. His name means "the Good Striker" and he carries a large magical spear.

Powerful and determined describe the mindful actions of the virile and loving Sucellos. He possesses such beauty that to look upon his face brings instant death. Because of this, the consort appears in many disguises and in an assortment of shapes. He may visit you as a handsome young man or as an elderly gentleman with a keen sense of humor.

Receive the gifts of fertility and beauty from Sucellos combined with the dynamics of flux and flow from the goddess Nantosuelta. Rapport with the powerful river goddess and her consort increase your spiritual awareness of the never-ending, ever-flowing cycle of life. As you begin to perceive the cyclic patterns of oneness, your ability to read patterns grows proportionally. You discover what a useful tool correctly reading patterns can be for personal self-development.

193

Practical Knowledge and Useful Information— Prophecy and Pattern Reading

In Gwyddonic Druid Tradition, the prophecy of the New Age is re-discovering the Concept of Oneness and bringing the light back to the land. By reacquainting yourself with the perfect love and perfect peace of oneness, you begin to know the true meaning and adventure of this shared prophecy.

The gift of prophecy stems from both the ability to merge deeply with oneness and from learning to read patterns. *Prophecy* is defined as "a prediction made under divine influence or intervention." The root of the word means "to speak before."

Events of prophecy are recorded throughout history. Caesar's wife foresaw his death in a dream. The Celtic god Angus saw his true love in his dreams for a year before he finally found her. Like Merlin the Magician, Michel de Notredame, better known as Nostradamus, prophesied major historical events hundreds of years before they occurred. Just as these people were able to tap into oneness and foresee future events, you can also predict what is to come. Expand your repertoire as you incorporate the valuable skill of prophecy by mastering and integrating the fine art of pattern reading.

The Goddess Tradition teaches that to know oneself is to know deity, and to know deity is to know oneself. Everything is oneness. You are a unique aspect of oneness, and have manifest form in the primary world. You have a name, history, face, body, sensations, and emotions. Even though you are unique, you are simultaneously a part of the commonality.

Wisdom is seeing things as one without distortion or connotation. Oneness implies you are one with the goddess and god. With this in mind, you merge with oneness, asking for the information or knowledge that you require. The answers will arise naturally without struggle.

As you merge with the fluid awareness of the boundless, your rapport with the goddess and god deepens. With this depth of rapport, your ability to read patterns increases proportionately. Synchonicity occurs everywhere in your life. When you look through the eyes of the goddess and the god, you view the harmony of all things. You begin to see the exquisite patterns of being and you learn to recognize subtlety and nuance therein.

With this newfound awareness, you start to understand that prophecy is simply accessing information in the boundless. Since oneness is a never-ending, ever-changing continuum of energy, you can tap into the loop at any place and time, depending upon your needs.

A fundamental metaphysical principle states that information is based on the structure of energy and light. This principle defines information as encoded, carried and stored in energy and light. Tiny particles of bubble-like light called *loats* arise out of the unmanifested. Each *loat* is encoded and carries a great deal of information, like a tiny bubble with its own view and perception. Every time you encounter a *loat* of light, it changes and informs you. With more light comes more change, expansion of mind, and a stronger connection to all things.

To successfully read patterns, you need to gather as much light or information as possible. Look at all the angles, the reflections, and the vibrancy. Observe the details, the past history, and your sensual impressions. Notice all the possible movements and absolutely everything your awareness perceives about that particular pattern. See the pattern as you would an elaborate multidimensional chess game. Follow the probable movements of the pieces forward and backward. Discuss patterns with someone you trust in order to get another view. Be aware of how quickly patterns change and allow for that fluidity within the picture.

Begin to follow your sensations regarding a particular pattern. Saunter along the paths of your awareness and multi-sense the pattern. Look at the people involved. How do you feel about each of them? How does your body feel when you contemplate the pattern? How does the pattern reflect in your dreaming awareness? Where does the pattern lead you? What does it sound like or smell like? Are you living your own pattern, or a pattern someone else has constructed for you? Follow your perceptions and awareness as you travel methodically through the labyrinth.

Let go of your conditioning and merge deeply with oneness to successfully read patterns and to incorporate the ability for prophecy. Make an effort to see things as they are, not merely as you wish them to be. Clear away the distortion and valences that limit and twist your perceptions. Allow your impersonal observer to view the pattern in question, and read the configuration of energy from that perspective.

Successful pattern reading depends upon your capability to view the total picture and to take the longer view. Since you are an aspect of oneness, you are connected to the source and to the boundless patterns within and without. Move beyond your ego struggle and conditioned reactions, so you can read patterns more efficiently. As your ability to read patterns improves, your creative skill for constructing positive patterns will increase exponentially.

As you merge and build your rapport with oneness, you begin to grow closer to those who are of like-light around you. You start to feel more at one with your mate and with the ones you choose to learn from in this lifetime. You begin to move toward what you want, instead of spending your time avoiding what you don't want. Journeying together, you and your partner travel on a spiritual adventure, bonding and joining as one.

In a spiritual partnership or sacred marriage, there are less filters between you and your primary partner. Because of this, the relationship becomes more complex. For example, if you are trying to make love with someone and there is a high stone wall acting as the filter, you find it very difficult to connect. Now imagine there is a screen door between you both. Suddenly the filter changes and with it, the nuance of the relationship and possible interaction. Now imagine there is only air between you, and then only pulses of light. Finally know that there is no separation between you, and that you are truly one, without filters. With this intimate proximity comes increased complexity, i.e., more pinpoints of light, more *loats,* more information, and thus, infinite combinations and rapid personal evolution and change.

With the absence of filters, all things seem exceptionally real, brighter, more vibrant and filled with energy. This is why when you travel to other realms of awareness, they sometimes seem more real than your everyday life. In other dimensions, there is generally less of a build-up of personal history, less emotional valence and less ego involvement. Hence you are able to merge more deeply with oneness and go beyond the conditioned doors of distorted perception. You move directly into the intimate flow of pure energy and awareness.

The only way to know something is to be it, and to merge completely with it. Learn the gift of prophecy and begin to read patterns successfully as you apply the above guidelines. Remember you are unique, and you are part of the commonality. As you begin to commune with oneness, allow yourself to stretch your imagination and travel freely through the infinite realms of awareness.

Guided Journey

I hand you the athame, watching as you grasp the blade
handle tightly with both hands. From the center of the
altar, I pick up the chalice of wine and hold it out to you.
The tip of your blade perches just above the wine, with
fanning flames of light moving out from the metal in every
direction. You stare deep within the wells of my eyes, lifting veils until I stand naked in the moonlight before you.
With one swift motion, you plunge the knife into the vessel of wine.

"Great and Mighty One, let your blessing and power
enter into this wine. So mote it be!" The commanding tone

of your voice sends bolts of energy riveting from the wine, up my fingers and arms and finally racing up and down my body. I imagine a river of stars dancing like fireflies. Up they rise from the wine chalice, climbing higher and higher, flowing above the trees into the full moon.

I hand you the silver and gold wine chalice and you hold the vessel high in the air at the North Point, saying, "Blessed be. Blessed be the gods. Blessed be all who are gathered here."

I watch as you direct the energy. You move the light with a calm rapport that seems refreshing. To each of the other three points you move in a clockwise sequence while repeating, "Blessed be. Blessed be the gods. Blessed be all who are gathered here."

From the West Point, you move back to the altar, handing me the chalice. The tips of my fingers feel the outline of the grapes cast in the metal. I look deep into the gleaming pools of your eyes as I move the cup to my lips. Moving across the tip of my tongue, the wine tastes initially sweet, then becomes bitter when it reaches the base of my tongue. I grimace slightly and you smile at me.

"The Perfect Love of the Goddess, and the Perfect Peace of the God. Blessed Be," I say as I tenderly kiss you, handing you the chalice. Pausing before taking it back, you look longingly in my eyes. I watch your strong fingers take the cup and slowly move it up to your mouth. You watch me watch you.

"Blessed be!" We call out in perfect unison as if cued by the gods.

Suddenly in my waking vision, a circle of stones juts out from the earth in ragged disproportional shapes. Each of the different sized rocks flows together into the oneness of the circle. Stepping through the thick brush of pungent manzanita and small madrone trees, I see a three-foot-high fence of twisted vines encircling a clearing that measures about sixty feet across. Except for a small section of greenery, the circle appears devoid of life.

Behind the wild grape vines that outline the parameter, I crouch, watching as an old woman works the soil with her hands. Her fingers poke the long white seeds down into the rich black dirt. She tilts the spout of a filled vessel slightly downward and water pours gently onto the earth and seed. The seeds respond by sprouting up through the soft soil, lifting themselves toward the sun.

"The dance of fire has begun. You can only move forward in the revolving pattern of life," the wind calls in the whispering voice of a breeze, rustling through the dry grass and gently whistling through the brush and the trees.

The giant orange ball of the sun hangs suspended just above the western horizon. The lighted globe provides a backdrop for the old woman as she continues tilling and planting. Her brown leathery face reminds me of a dry river bed. Deep wrinkles are etched into her face from ancient streams that flow from the well of time. A large straw hat adorned with a purple sash casts a shadow over half of her face. As she moves sunwise around the circle, plants instantly spring up out of earth, growing to maturity within seconds. I marvel at the variety of flora. The circle now embodies life of every imaginable size, shape, and spectrum.

Overwhelmed with curiosity and fascination, I walk through the trellis of plants that now act as a gate to the newly-formed garden.

The old woman greets me with a smile and the words, "Perfect Love and Perfect Peace. Blessed Be."

She turns and I follow her, stepping carefully through the vegetation. We walk toward a flat rock at the northern point of the circle. She slides onto the rock, gesturing for me to sit down beside her. As I move close to her, I notice the top of the rock is smooth like a table, with more than enough room for both of us to sit comfortably. For a moment, both of us sit in silence, beholding the brilliance of the teeming life all around us.

She begins to speak, her voice like the melodic call of a meadowlark. "You hold the world in your hands. Look!" Lacing her thin fingers downward, she turns her hands over and wiggles her fingers upward. "Here are the Lady's knives and forks." She turns her hands back over and they form a small platform as she continues, "And here is the Lady's table." She places her thumbs together in a point and says, "Here is the Lady's looking glass." Moving her little fingers together in a V, she finishes, "And here is the Lady's cradle."

I watch her hands, trying to mimic her actions in an effort to remember the ancient rhyme.

While I repeat the motions, she watches me and smiles. Reaching out, she silences my hands and continues talking, "Life begins when earth and sun mate, producing a seed. Blessed by the blood of life, the watered seed springs up out of the womb of the Mother, toward the fire of the Father. What follows is the ritualistic dance driven by a primal cadence that propels the very fiber of life."

Holding her hand in the air, a chalice of wine suddenly appears and she drinks from it. Swallowing the liquid slowly, she continues, "Wine on one hand represents the fruits of an abundant harvest, but on the other hand symbolizes the blood of life, and how it spills out into death."

On the word "death," she overturns the chalice and the wine pours out, staining the ground a purplish red. "In life there is death, and in death there is life. Life becomes ever renewed," she utters while leaning back and closing her eyes.

For a few minutes she says nothing, so I move closer to see if she has fallen asleep. Just as I slide closer, she suddenly opens her eyes and points with her left hand to the horizon, "See the harvest moon. It rises once again as it does every year when the angle of the moon's orbit to the Mother Earth is at its minimum."

Out on the horizon, a blazing orange ball of moon fire consumes the sky. While the old woman has been talking, the full moon has replaced the sun on the opposite horizon. Astounded, I sit gaping at the beautiful face of the harvest moon.

The old woman's voice resounds, "It is at this time when the sacred moonflowers come to life, and for one night they drink, they dance, and then they die." Her finger points to a large bed of white flowers spilling off thick green vines. They completely fill the center of the circle.

"That's odd, I don't remember those flowers being there," I think to myself while intently studying the flower closest to where we sit. The flower seems larger and shines brighter than all of the flowers around it. I glance at the ground and notice the wine the old woman spilt, winding its way across the earth toward the flower. As the river of wine touches the roots and stems of the magnificent flower, a ray of light from the harvest moon seems to ignite the pale white, bell-shaped petals. In an instant, the circle fills with sparks of light spraying out from the flower and vines like fireworks.

I shade my eyes, watching the spectacle before me with interest and amazement. I hear the cackling laugh of the old woman as the energy and light intensify. Bolts of lightning shoot out into the circle. Staring at the center of the blossom, I see the form of a face. First the soft brown eyes, then the nose and mouth form within the flower. Soon a young man's face emerges as the top of the bell becomes curly, light brown hair, and the bottom becomes a slightly-pointed, dimpled chin. The vines become his arms, legs, and torso. The divinely beautiful man now stands before me. He steps forward and offers me one of two cups of wine that he holds in his hands.

With a certain reluctance, I accept the chalice. He nods his head and raises his glass toward me.

"Merry meet, and merry part," he says in a soothing deep voice before taking my hand, lifting me to my feet and kissing me tenderly on the lips. I stand beside him and we look out over the garden.

"Come, let us drink of the nectar of life, savoring every sweet droplet laced with succulent desire. Join with me and dance the dance of fire in the circle of the Wine Moon. For one night, shed the veils that bind you to your conditioned and illusionary world. It is time to celebrate, so let us make a toast to the goddess and her consort."

He pauses to drink from his glass. Then he calls out into the night like a Shakespearian actor nearing the end of his soliloquy, "Blessed be! Blessed be all who are gathered here! Let the celebration begin!"

He tosses the contents of his chalice up and the wine sprays out in all directions. As each droplet reaches out to touch every plant in the garden, I watch the circle spring into animation.

Red, white, yellow, and purple hollyhock blossoms transform into beautiful young women dressed in glistening eighteenth-century ballroom gowns. Autumn red daylilies, covered with golden bars on their dazzling red blooms, spring to life as nymphs wearing red satin gowns with shiny golden sashes. The nymphs begin to sing and dance in a sunwise procession around the circle.

Turtleheads, yellow trumpet honeysuckle, and seashell-pink faery roses become men with elfin features, rugged-looking men with blond hair, and men in lavishly-styled costumes of every type and style. With the anthropomorphosis complete, the entire garden sings, dances, and drinks the fruity nectar of the vine.

Before being swept into the throngs of people dancing wildly around me, I shake my head and think, "The celebration has indeed begun."

I find myself being pushed and pulled sunwise around the parameter of the circle. Gradually I move toward the very center of the circle where there is less activity. I spy a man with eye-catching yellow hair, wearing a cerulean satin shirt and lickerishly eyeing a woman whose hair resembles scarlet flame phlox. The two of them act out the sacred rite. First he chases her around a small circle until she suddenly stops, turns, and places a band of woven flowers around the man's neck. They then embrace and begin passionate foreplay, opening to libidinous petals of stimulation and sexual exploration.

I watch them until my own desire awakens like a hungry child, waiting to be satiated by the delicious feast. Looking away from the two lovers, I scan the melange. My eyes stop and again I am looking deep into the gleaming pools of your eyes.

I feel your arms around me as I squeeze you tightly. Your hands move slowly across my back like the terminator edging across the face of the moon. My being fills with the fullness of your light.

Suddenly we find ourselves alone once again within the circle. Our two energies embrace, creating intermingling strands of light that weave patterns of radiance shooting out like brilliant *loats*. Up and up we travel. Higher and higher we transcend the sky. Our doubles go out as we let go and float beyond the ionosphere.

You move me under you, your wet mouth passionately devouring me. Up my mountains, you climb higher and higher, fondling their hardened peaks. Your tongue swoops down my canyons and you dive into my hot and moist crevice. You linger there as my desire explodes in a burst of color. I cry out and you respond by delving further into my valley until my very being vibrates. An earthquake of passion and lust shakes me to my core.

The rhythmic thunder of your thighs drums against my flesh like the waves of the ocean driven by a wild storming wind. I stroke the blade that penetrates the wine and I savor the florescence like a feast of the gods.

You call out to me, your voice impassioned by the moment. I can feel you quiver deep within me, shooting your arrow. Like a hot dart rushing through me, I feel the ecstasy just beginning. Faster and faster our bodies pulse like torrents of water speeding down a steep embankment. Slower and slower time moves as hot waves of molten lava spill out within my body. The sweat slides between us mating as one and dripping out into eternity.

205

I stroke your damp hair as you lie naked in the bed beside me. I look knowingly across the unmanifested. In the mirror of oneness, I see the image of a young girl. Her blonde hair shines in the morning sun. She stands in the middle of a magical garden planted in a circle. All the plants are spent and brown and they bend toward the ground. A sunbonnet with a purple sash covers the top of her head. As she turns toward me, I see the wicker basket in her right hand. She leans down and I watch as she gathers a handful of seeds from the plants in the circle garden. She carefully and purposefully places them into the woven basket.

My focus shifts back to you as I feel you softly stroking my shoulders and back. As I close my eyes, I feel the caress of your rough fingers seesawing majestically between my soft mounds. I look within the deep gleaming pools of your eyes and see renewed vigor and newfound strength. Very slowly, with a sly smile, I move my lips to yours and kiss you.

❧ The Blood Moon ☙

Morgana & Ogmios

Resting in your ancient arms
our desire bathes in the moonlight.
Tenderly you touch me with your mind
and the fingertips of our ancestors
brush against my cheek.

The Blood Moon ☽♉

Morgana & Ogmios

Full Moon in Taurus, Sun in Scorpio
Fixed negative earth and water elements

The Goddess and Her Consort

Blood is life itself. Just as the Holy Grail contains the divine blood and is a life-giving vessel, the All Mother embodies the water of life from which all things spring. She resides in our blood, in the sap of plants, in the soil and stones, in the clouds, and in the rivers and oceans. The Blood Moon honors the goddess and her life-giving aspects of maternity and fecundity.

Blood is commonly defined as the circulating fluid in the veins and arteries of animals. This fluid cleans out waste products and delivers nutrients simultaneously as blood cells restore and replenish themselves. Flowing in accordance with the phases of the moon, women's menstrual blood both nurtures and cleanses. Accordingly, the health of your body depends upon the health of your blood.

The soul or spirit of a person resides in that person's blood. This is also true of animals. Blood is energy and certain traditions feel that eating specific animals will give you the strength and protection of that particular animal. On the other hand, many people abstain from eating all animals, lest the spirit of the animal may enter into them.

The eleventh High Moon represents the stream of life, where water acts as the blood of the All Mother. Interestingly, the human body and the surface of the earth are both seventy percent water. Further, our blood actually duplicates the salinity of the sea. In this way, we mirror the Earth and the Earth mirrors us.

As we experience a communal deepening in the Concept of Oneness, humankind will come to know that when we pollute and throw toxins into the earth and outward into the universe, it is the same as poisoning ourselves. We are one with all things and all people. As we merge with oneness, we learn to purify our bodies and Mind, and in turn begin to clean up and heal the earth.

Blood symbolizes many things. The British term *bloody* comes from the saying "By Our Lady." The Old English word *blod* stems from the root that means "bloom," defined as "flourishing" or "vigorous." The Celtic flower goddess Blodenwedd is created from blooms and later in her life transforms into an owl. She acts as the life and death goddess symbolizing the never-ending cycle from birth to rebirth.

Covenants of blood have served to tie specific groups together in the past, such as the Knights of the Round Table and the Irish Red Branch. In this way, they become of one blood and remain loyal to one another. This practice parallels the joining of blood by ancestry. The tie of ancestral blood seals our sacred connection with the goddess and god through generations and through our many incarnations.

The beautiful Death Mother, Morgana, embodies the ancestral qualities of the Blood Moon. As goddess of fertility, magic, and war, she represents the tripled triplicity or the Ninefold One. Healer, herbalist and shapeshifter, the awesome sea goddess Morgana is often depicted as the ruler of nine sisters on the Fortunate Isles, also called Apple Isle or Avalon.

Daughter of the sea god Llyr, Morgana moves fluidly like an amorous sea mermaid and a sinuous river goddess. She appears as both a young sensuous woman and as an ugly hag. Associated with the Faeries, the goddess reigns as the Queen of Death and rules the Underworld and rebirth, and all of the gifts therein.

The young and sexy goddess Morgana appears with a fair or ruddy complexion. Her eyes are colored a rich, dark brown, deep green, or blue-black, and her hair streams behind her in jet-black or crimson-black waves. The goddess moves among the cypress trees along the shoreline, wearing wine-red, purple, indigo, or black flowing robes. You may find her picking up seashells before she transforms into a magnificent raven or sleek, cunning crow.

The handsome and honey-mouthed Ogmios is consort to the lovely sea goddess Morgana. Besides the goddess Epona, Ogmios stands as the only native Celtic deity mentioned by name by the Romans. As a god of rebirth, civilization, poetry, speech, and eloquence, the well-endowed Ogmios appears with sparkling blue eyes and light brown or silver-brown hair. Like the goddess Morgana, Ogmios shapeshifts into either a virile young man or an old wrinkled man.

The friendly yet powerful consort acts as a Celtic Hercules. Carrying a club and bow, Ogmios portrays the champion of the Tuatha De Dannan. Representing the Air of the Boundless, he charms everyone with his smiling sun face, soothing voice, and gentle manner. The god of magic, music, and the arts draws crowds to him by chains connecting his audience's ears to his tongue.

Ogmios possesses the power to both bind and liberate. The Ogham writing he invented holds magical qualities, and the consort characterizes a god of the binding strength of poetry. The wise and knowing Ogmios helps you understand the deeper meaning of language and writing. Patterning images and the sound and shape of words all fall within his repertoire.

Travel with the formidable Ogmios, allowing the Wind of Oneness to conduct you into other dimensions and between worlds. He wears blue, white, or brown robes belted with silver and he carries a magical stick with his favorite runes carved on it. Enjoy the adventure and discover your personal creative process as you build rapport with the loving god Ogmios.

Ask the goddess Morgana and the god Ogmios to impart the infinite gifts of the Otherworld to you. Allow yourself to expand your creativity and further your sexual exploration as you immerse yourself in the sensual beauty and fertility of Morgana. Connect with Ogmios and learn the secrets of language and art. Flow into the arms of the compelling goddess and her thoughtful consort as you deepen your personal faith and your spiritual connection to oneness.

Practical Knowledge and Useful Information— Dreaming and Creativity

Mind is boundless; merging and dreaming become modes for tapping into this infinite flow of energy. Your creative experience is proportional to the amount of time you spend with your mind turned toward oneness. Focus and pattern your life in the way you choose, being very careful that the pattern is what you truly want and desire. Remember an error in calculation results in an error in situation.

First, thoroughly form your pattern energetically. Multi-sense all of the aspects of the pattern. Move forward, backward, vertically, and horizontally, flowing in all directions through time and space. View your pattern from these perspectives, while protecting your pattern and nurturing it to fruition. Manifest it, creating its tangibility through your intent, expectation, desire, and merge.

As you familiarize yourself with patterning and with reading patterns, you become more creative about the nature and intent of your choices. Your world expands and infinite possibilities float across your field of vision and sensation. Suddenly you realize you have the freedom to make personal choices every moment. As you make these choices, you find that every decision you make affects the pattern of your life and affects the larger pattern of oneness.

Positive creativity stems from the combining energies and elements of oneness. When you create something, you define it; by giving definition to something, you manifest it. In a sense, you limit its potential by defining it because you have assembled its energy in time and space, fixing it in place. Keep in mind that definition; shape and form are useful social structures especially in the practical world.

213

All tangible reality is created by Mind and Mind moves energy. Energy combined with intent transforms into manifest reality. This intended energy remains within the field of every creation. For example, there seems to be a light and even a spiritual quality that radiates from great masterpieces of art. In music and writing, you may experience a special kinship with the artist, or a particular feeling and ambiance surrounding certain creations. More personally, you can sense a certain resonance or energetic tone to your own creations, like your home and your living environment.

The creative process implies an exchange of energy. Moving energy from the manifested or unmanifested universe, you shape it in a new way. If you create something out of the manifested universe, you are actually redefining that which already exists. When you move your creative process into the unmanifested, you create something completely new. You become the inventor, creating a form of energy that has never been configured or defined before.

Venture into dreaming as a way to access your deeper creative potential. All things are fluid as you travel to other realms and move into the unmanifested. Energy is in a continual state of change. This is the only constant in the universe. Begin to enjoy the flux and flow of your life and avoid struggling with rigid mind constructs.

When you merge deeply with oneness, creating a magical pattern, it can be a work of art that changes you forever. The experience gives you a broader view and expanded personal awareness. Taking action by completing the steps to your creative pattern, you begin to live your dream. As you grow wise, you learn to know what you know and feel what you feel as genuine. Merge with the boundless and immerse yourself in creative dreaming. Multi-sense the experience, giving yourself the suggestion to be able to retain and creatively use the knowledge and information you acquire during dreaming.

In Gwyddonic Druid Tradition, what you do creatively is an indication of what you are able to do conceptually and magically. This is the reason the tradition is called the art and craft. Used this way, art means skill especially in arranging the elements like words, sounds, sensations, colors, tastes, and shapes. Craft means strength, skill, proficiency, and courage.

Immerse yourself in a romance with knowledge as you access sheer comprehension and understanding. The language and metaphors of the poet are bound in the goddess and god. Increase your vocabulary and learn the incredible power of the spoken and written word. In olden times as today, words were awesomely powerful. To know how to make the sound of an object, animal, plant, or person was a fine art. All things are held together by sound and the slightest noise repeats itself many times over. Begin to apply words and sound in a mindful and creative manner, enhancing your patterns and personal self-development.

Ritual itself is creative. Rituals on the Great Days and High Moons are based on the concept of creation, helping to align your energies with the cycles and nature. The fertility of the goddess and her consort represent the creative element while maternity and fecundity symbolize the creative divine potential within.

Through dreaming and merging with oneness, you gain an affinity with the goddess and god and with other beneficial energies in Otherworlds. Dreams are potentially divine in nature and hence become a source for creativity. Dreaming and merging are ways for all the parts of you to communicate with yourself and with the goddess and god. They become ways for you to completely connect with your inner faith, your artistic vision, and to know your spiritual essence.

215

Expand your dreaming adventures through your desire and positive intention. Emotional participation serves as the foundation of magical arts with awareness of emotions leading to awareness of intention. Emotion in the form of desire is energy in motion. Desire actually expresses and moves currents of energy outward to your pre-selected destination and pattern.

Acquire new insights and knowledge as you focus on dreaming, posing specific questions to yourself and to oneness. Speak aloud, giving yourself the suggestion to multi-sense the answers you receive. Know that you have this ability, utilizing it in a positive and loving way.

Allow dreaming to meld into every aspect of your life. Continue to enjoy living in your primary world while also venturing into infinite continua of awareness and experience. Merge and draw from the boundless, exploring new colors, smells, and unfamiliar sounds. Paint your fertile mind with ideas, concepts, and inventions as you design your dream canvas.

You are the artist. If you desire to create a positive loving relationship with another person, perfect it in your dreaming first. Change to another canvas as you use dreaming as an avenue for healing. Be specific, setting the dreaming experience up just as you would any other magical work. Examine your expectation as you fortify your desire and merge with oneness.

Increase the depth of your dreaming experience by using specific dreaming or merging tools. For example, pookas, chants or word patterns, scented oils, incense, and certain foods amplify and expand your awareness. Also decide whether you want to project a double to enhance or help with your dreaming endeavors.

216

Experiment with ancestral dreaming, giving yourself the suggestion to merge with your genetic lineage. Move to the source of your family tree energetically in dream. See the strong roots of the tree, the sturdy trunk and its mighty branches. Connect with your future ancestors as you project your awareness forward in dreaming. See your re-creation and your never-ending, ever-flowing rebirth.

Make an effort to share your creative energies with others, encouraging positivity within your primary world. Consider a more open world view and a balanced and healthy planet. Dare to be innovative, to think holographically or spherically, and genuinely see the world as one, viewing yourself as a creative and viable expression of the boundless. Envision a brighter future as you energize your creative dreaming with action and participation. Let yourself dream magnificent dreams, creating the precise patterns necessary to actualize those dreams.

Guided Journey

She watches the large black bird as it hops from limb to limb of the cypress tree. Each time the raven perches on one of the branches, they bend downward from the bird's weight. The iridescent coal-black feathers shine a brilliant violet-blue in the last vestiges of the slowly sinking evening sun. The twilight hangs and then fades from the branches of the evergreen. Soon the shadows consume the form of the bird as it melts into the oneness of the trees.

Looking down at her skirt, the woman can no longer distinguish the twill of the green and red threads that weave their way through the fabric. She sits quietly as the old man in front of her draws the sacred circle sunwise with a long golden cord. Starting at the center of the magical circle, he moves the cord outward, marking the four directions. At each corner, the old man places a clear quartz generator crystal. After he finishes marking the circle, he steps inside and stands at the East Point. Using the light from his hands, he spins around clockwise three times, tracing the outline of the circle with a blue-white flame.

The old man sits back down outside the circle of light. As he rests, a teenage boy scoops up twigs and leaves with a three-pronged pitchfork, heaping them on top of the pile of large branches. Finishing his task, the boy sets the pitchfork against the tree trunk and then sits back down at the edge of the circle.

The snow-colored sphere of the moon rises above the horizon, signaling the time to light the branches piled high within the circle of the hearth. Once the campfire is lit, the faces of each person sitting around the woman become illuminated by the fiery light. She stares into the red embers, watching the flames spark and dance along the pieces of wood. Her eyes search the faces around her and in their eyes she sees the echoing image of the flickering fire.

Once again, the old wise man sitting next to her stands up, holding a two-foot long cylindrical object high in the air. The woman's eyes focus on the cylinder the man holds, and its shape begins to take on a distinct form.

The wooden staff of the wand is made from a manzanita branch. The wood gleams a mahogany red and a hemp-like cord weaves tightly in a knot around the base. The cord winds itself up from the bottom of the wand, over the wooden body and all the way to the stone tip of the wand. The natural rope spins snugly around the base of the tip, attaching it to the sturdy wooden shaft. The intricately-carved bloodstone tip resembles the faces and torsos of a woman and man whose naked bodies join together at the hips.

"Ayea, ayea, Kerridwen! Ayea, ayea, Kernunnos! Ayea, ayea, ayea!" the old man commands as he summons the divine power of the goddess and her consort. He consecrates each of the four directions, bringing the white light of the moon into the circle. After he calls in the Wards and completes the preliminaries, the old man returns once again to his place at the edge of the fire.

The man pauses for a few minutes, taking a deep breath, and then he holds out the wand. "Behold the talking wand. Its magical powers promote healing and foretell the future, sundering all walls that prevent us from remembering who we truly are," he proclaims.

The woman takes the wand from his outstretched, wrinkled hands. The wound cord feels rough as she grasps the handle. Her fingers follow the strand of rope up past the coil, softly stroking the smoothness of the naked wood. The sleek line of the wood is broken by the edges of runic shapes carved in its solid flesh. She looks down at the wand, trying to decipher the meaning of the carvings.

219

"What do you desire from us?" ask the voices of a woman and man, speaking in unison from out of the wand. Startled, her body jumps slightly as her eyes light on the carved figures of the woman and man. The Bloodstone with its red spots surrounded by a sea of dark green fills her senses as she suddenly realizes the question came from the carved faces.

"Oh, it really is a talking wand," she thinks to herself, half amused, somewhat wary, and very curious.

"Ask any question that you choose," the voices speak again harmonically. "There are no gates, only the boundless." Undecided at first, she ponders the implications of the request. To ask any question seems an overwhelming task. She thinks to herself, "Well, you asked for it."

"Why am I here, right now?" she blurts out. "Is there a divine purpose or is it some sort of divine joke? Does each experience build on the one before it, or is life a series of random acts of hedonism, meaningful only at that moment? Even being a spiritual person, I sometimes wonder. There is so much violence and greed, so many lost and wandering souls." She looks directly into the faces of the wand and asks pointedly, "Can you answer these questions? If you can, then you truly are a most magical wand."

The face of the woman answers first. Her voice is that of the goddess. "Each of us has many roles in the cycles that make up life. We are all connected through our bond with oneness. Oneness is the primordial energy that permeates all things whether animate or inanimate. The Goddess and God are symbolic of that sacred union and bond."

"Experience is to life as paint is to a painting," interjects the face of the man. "Each color and every brush stroke gives meaning to the whole. You begin with a white canvas, ending up with a work of art. To paint the canvas and experience the oneness of everything is why you are here."

"How you paint the pattern of your world is how your life draws out," continues the carved face of the woman. "All life and experience is cumulative. Life never actually ends. The waters flow forever into the infinity of oneness, shapeshifting through the layers of awareness into the very essence of being. All doors open by simply remembering who you really are. To learn more, look into the carved runic shapes on the handle of the talking wand."

Her eyes move slowly from the bloodstone figures down to the markings on the wooden shaft of the wand. They look like letters or symbols, but not ones she is familiar with. Staring at the runic forms, she feels her essence being transported into a flow of moving liquid energy.

The blazing fire and the circle of people around her fade, replaced by images that look like clouds, racing by her at a tremendous speed.

Suddenly a young man stands at her side. She stares into his lapis-colored eyes, watching as his light chestnut brown hair blows back from his handsome face in the driving wind. Her gaze shifts to his hands, holding the reins that control the golden chariot, she now finds herself riding in.

Faster and faster he coaxes the three mighty steeds through the heavens. The horses, one white, one dappled gray, and one black, prance across the ethers. Nickering and snorting, their nostrils flare while their manes and tails whip wildly in the cosmic wind.

The light of Eight Suns and Thirteen Moons rise up like celestial stepping stones, summoning the chariot deeper into the center of the universe. They transcend through nine layers of matter that extend out like the branched canopy of an ancient tree. As each veil lifts, the magical core of oneness reveals itself.

221

She finds herself in a place that is neither dark nor light. The young man and chariot shapeshift into a young woman whose black hair reminds her of the raven she had seen earlier in the evening. She looks into the woman's emerald green eyes and then down at the circle of light that separates the two of them. In the blazing circle, dazzling forms of colored light dance like runic figures.

The young raven-haired woman passes her hand three times over the circle and begins to chant in a beautiful canorous voice, "Eihwaz, eihwaz, eihwaz." The power of her words rings out. A dazzling beam of light shoots up from one of the runic figures, ascending and connecting the three realms of being. In the brilliance she sees the seeds of the unmanifested spring out as sprouts of barley. The barley then metamorphoses through the life cycle until it matures and dies. Watching closely, she sees the barley return once again to seed, preparing for new life.

"The runes embody the process and flow of energy, connecting the self to oneness," cantillates the raven-haired woman. "It is in this connection the true meaning of life can be understood." The lovely young woman stops speaking and again one of the runes in the circle lights up. The black-haired woman picks up the bright rune and carefully hands it across the circle to the other woman.

The palm of her hand lights up as she takes the rune. At first, the shape of it is undefined, but as she pictures the light in her mind's eye, the rune begins to take form. Three lines weave together, one curving horizontally, one moving downward, with the last line pointing upward into three small circles. The lines connect in three places, creating an inverted triangle in the center.

"You have made a magical sigil," says the young raven-haired woman. "A sigil serves as a personal symbol and you can use it for any purpose you desire. It is more powerful than a rune because you create it by merging with the unmanifested. In particular, the sigil you hold in your hand is your spiritual connection to oneness."

She looks at the young woman's face with its milky white complexion and then down at the sigil sitting in her hand. Her mind moves freely into the shape of the symbol, diffusing and expanding into oneness. With each breath, a calm connectedness spreads across her being. For a moment, she become a pine tree and the pine tree becomes her. She feels her roots stretch down into the damp earth as her branches reach for the sun. Her fingers become pointed needles gently swaying in the breeze. A

raven sits cawing on one of her branches and instantaneously she becomes the raven and the raven becomes
her. Her wings spread wide as she propels herself through
the sky.

As the sun descends behind the mountains, she lands
on the branch of a cypress tree. Looking down she sees a
young girl looking up at her. She becomes the young girl
and the young girl becomes her. She becomes all things,
completely connected to oneness.

Opening her eyes, she notices the campfire that once
burned bright is now a mass of dying red embers. By the
light of the full moon, she sees that the old wise man with
his mysterious talking wand and all of the people except
for one, have gone.

"It's good to have you back," says the young man, his
face resembling that of the charioteer. In her hand she still
carries the sigil, only now instead of a shape of light, it is
in the form of a carved bloodstone.

"I see you remembered to bring your sigil back with
you," he says while smiling at her. She feels his intense
love like blood circulating through her veins.

He takes her by the hand and she notices they both
wear identical golden rings carved with runes. He guides
her away from the dying fire and they move hand in hand
into the forest.

Walking along a path that stretches up a low hill, they
come upon a giant rock. The top of the rock lays flat and
level with the top of the hill. The edge of the rock drops
abruptly twenty feet, down the face to the base of the hill.
The two sit on the rock top watching the full glory of the
lustrous moon.

Spreading out a sleeping bag already on the rock, the
young man beckons her to climb into the folds of the bag
with him. A wafer of moonlight slides over them as they lie

223

within the womb-like warmth of the sleeping bag. He slowly unbuttons the nine buttons of her dress.

She watches him intently, the whites of his eyes reflecting the moon. She slowly tugs and then pulls his shirt up over his head, exposing his well-developed chest and shoulders. Touching her tongue to his nipples, she moves downward onto the threshold of his desire. She hears him sigh and then moan as her wet tongue bathes his manhood. She licks intricate symbols over his skin and growing arousal.

She softly nips and kisses the hand beside her mouth. Is it his hand or her hand? They are one in the same as she feels her flesh form into a hungry mouth.

When he caresses her throat with his eager lips, she is uncertain whether her throat has given or received his kiss. As he slides his hands over her stomach and willing thighs, he feels his own stomach and inner thighs being caressed.

224

Gently moving her under him, he glides his tongue from the tips of her soft mounds to the depth of her well. Deeper he plunges until she cries out, trembling in her release. She moves him into her and the lovers succumb to their flaming passion. In a building cadence, their slick bodies dance atop one another and a bright white light shoots out from their union into the night sky. Up higher and higher, the lovers ascend the moon and the nine planets setting their course for the heart of the sun.

She feels him descend deeper into her core. He clutches her to him, softly grabbing handfuls of her hair and singing out in rapt delight. His magnificent voice envelops her as she feels the universe explode into a super nova, sending light out in all directions. A million suns reach out with their light into the center of the universe as the lovers course and surge through the cycle of life.

Joined and mated to the divine light, she feels the multitudes of generations lying beside her. They touch her flushed cheek with their ancient fingertips, tracing runes along her body, slowly and purposefully. Finally they all bleed into one, flowing in every direction through the boundless incarnations of her awareness.

The Snow Moon

Sirona & Borvo

Soothed by the waterfall
floating in the moonlight
I cover you in a blanket of stars
and you taste like my dreams
lifting me on your love.

The Snow Moon ☾

Sirona & Borvo

Full Moon in Gemini, Sun in Sagittarius
Mutable neutral air and mutable positive fire elements.

The Goddess and Her Consort

"Some say the world will end in fire, some say in ice,"
writes Robert Frost in his poem entitled "Fire and Ice."
Literally and metaphorically, he describes the powerful
forces of fire and ice bringing existence to an end. These
are also the great forces of energy through which the
world is created. From the dynamic unity of fire which
represents manifest energy, and ice representing unmanifest energy, springs the never-ending, ever-renewing cycle
of life.

The Snow Moon embodies the qualities of ice or
frozen water, as the twelfth and sometimes last full moon
of the yearly cycle slides its luminous face up into the
dark winter sky. Water provides the moisture for all things
to grow. Frozen water like hail, snow, or ice holds the
potential of all things, i.e., that which waits to be manifested. During this full moon, primordial matter waits for
the thaw, paralleling the way the unmanifested flows and
then melts into the manifested.

The primal snowflake pattern called the six-fold *hagalaz* acts as the Rune Mother. When you place this rune within a solid figure, every runic form can be derived from it. This is due to its numerical shape and value. Creation occurs as you place the Rune Mother, the snowflake, within a manifest structure. Thus the *hagalaz* symbolizes the origin of life and the potential energy of crystallized patterns.

Move purposefully through the High Moons of the cycle, building rapport with the many faces of the goddess and god. At midnight before the winter solstice on the Snow Moon, turn your mind to divine and royal purpose. Merge with divine awareness and intimately know the perfect love and perfect peace of oneness. Recognize and accept the boundless gifts of magic, healing and music bestowed by the Lady and her consort.

Begin by accessing the royal awareness within your inner being. The queens and kings of ancient times were both rulers and spiritual leaders. Through divine right, they carried the power of the gods on the earthly plane. Bound to the land, the rivers, the heavens, and the gods, when the queens and kings thrived, their land and people thrived and vice versa. Like the King of the Wood who was priest of Diana's sanctuary at Nemi, Italy, monarchs were deposed or replaced before they became decrepit. This was done in order to insure the fertility and vigor of the land and people.

Like the sovereigns of old, speak with the goddess and god to find the spiritual balance between yourself and the world around you. Notice what your intention is toward the Earth, toward nature, and toward humankind. Are you and people around you thriving? Is our global home, the Earth, thriving? Merge even more deeply with oneness and begin to acknowledge and cultivate a positive relationship with yourself and your home. Dare to show your royal and divine face to the other people in your life, so that they may understand and incorporate these qualities within themselves.

The divine and royal face of the beautiful goddess Sirona shines brightly in the sacred light of the Snow Moon. As a solar and an astral goddess, she embraces the qualities of both fire and ice. With her right hand in the manifest and her left hand in the unmanifest, Sirona's contrasting nature symbolizes the dynamic polarities of oneness.

As a Celtic Venus, the goddess acts warm, sensuous, and loving. As sky and star Goddess, Sirona exhibits the etherial qualities of the universe. She appears fair with mahogany or black hair and when you look into her eyes, they shine dark green and indigo. Wearing blue and silver robes covered with star-like jewels, Sirona carries the symbol of the star on her forehead. At other times she appears dressed by the sun and wind, radiating with light and fluid energy.

Borvo is consort to the lovely Lady Sirona. Considered the Celtic Apollo, the masterful god romances the lovely goddess with his magical flute and with his well-strung golden harp. Like Sirona, Borvo represents both fire and water. He is especially associated with wet heat and can often be seen soaking and relaxing in mineral and hot springs.

Borvo embodies the healing qualities of oneness and acts as a god of unseen or concealed truth. The consort's vigor and strength stem from the boiling energies of the Otherworld. He takes his light from the very depths of the Earth. He gains his power directly from the goddess and inspires through dreaming.

The soothing touch of Borvo's healing hands feels sensuous and hot. As you gaze at him, you notice his golden brown hair and his sun-bronzed skin. His eyes have rims of gold that seem to shine more brightly when he smiles. Naked or vested all in gold, the handsome Borvo carries a magnificent sword and swift spear. His magical symbol is the rolling sun disk.

Merge with the goddess Sirona and her consort Borvo and learn about the contrasting elements of fire and water. Use the combined heat and potential energy of the dynamic goddess and vigorous god to motivate and move your personal patterns in positive directions. Make an effort to remember your divine and royal purpose as you gaze into your own mirrored face.

Practical Knowledge and Useful Information— Dreaming with the Goddess and Her Consort

Looking in the mirror, you see an image of yourself. You see that you are one with the image, yet you are unique. Dreaming is exactly like looking at your reflection in a mirror. Normally we view dreaming and waking as two separate states of being. Turning your mind to oneness, you learn that these seemingly separate states of awareness can be experienced simultaneously. As you merge with the Concept of Oneness, you realize that duality and separation are simply practical constructs of the conditioned mind.

By integrating your primary or secondary worlds with dreaming, you become aware of your evolving personal mythology. Living your dreams by following that which you love becomes your mythical task. Myth, our ever-lasting experience with oneness, carries us across the artificial threshold of waking and dreaming. Joseph Campbell addresses this very concept when he suggests that dreams are private myths, and myths are public dreams.

The most powerful and sacred myths are ancient myths. All other myths are built upon their foundation and basic qualities. Many of your actions and belief systems spring from an underlying mythology. Every day your personal mythology alters to a greater or lesser degree, depending upon your experience and perception. To the waiting and observant mind, this continually creates new and interesting perspectives.

Aboriginal tradition proposes that whenever you imagine the world full of spirits, you connect to the ancient part of human mythology. Just as you may experience other worlds or personas within yourself, your aboriginal Mind sees the world as the expression of mythic powers. These mythic energies curve the very time and space of geology and of all existence. The Mother Goddess remains central to the mythic view of our world and ourselves. View your reality through the looking glass of the Lady, while multi-sensing the infinite beauty of myth, voyaging beyond your imagination.

233

Mythology embodying the goddess and god serves as the basis for sexuality. The ever-renewing cycle of life is perpetuated by sexual energy and by fertilization through the sexual experience. In this way, the elements of fire and water join together to produce ever-renewing life.

From the very beginning of human history to present day, the magical force and wonder of the female and male are no less marvels than the universe itself. The female body like the male body, may be looked upon as a metaphor for society and culture. Our bodies are the cosmos. By learning how we conceive of the body, we can rechart our vision of the world.

Merge with oneness and understand the energies and signals of the universe, the earth, and within yourself.

Increase the well-being of your environment and enhance the world as you learn to honor and respect oneness. Get acquainted with the spiritual energy that makes things whole as you reconnect with nature.

Be mindful, cultivating a positive attitude and personal mythology toward sexual experience. Your communion and lovemaking with the goddess and her consort act as avenues to spiritual self-awareness. Visualize a world where women and men hold equally valuable roles, complementing each other's qualities and energy, rather than competing with one another.

You can choose to live in a state of love and ecstasy that most people only find in orgasm. As you and your primary partner build rapport with the goddess and her consort, you begin to more fully understand the Concept of Oneness. As a result, your primary partnership transforms into a spiritual and sacred partnership.

Spiritual lovemaking transcends all other sexual experience. Viewing sexual intimacy as sacred may well be the beginning to re-balancing the female and male energies of the Earth. When you make love, you exchange energy. As you make love with the goddess and her consort, and simultaneously as you make love with your partner, you touch upon the true meaning of perfect love and perfect peace. The goddess bestows her powers and energy upon those whom she wishes to aid, and yet she never completely depletes her own force or energy. In this way, the goddess aids the consort, yet remains autonomous and powerful. They live in harmony and balance.

Merging with the divine light of oneness, you discover making love and dreaming are both paths to expanded awareness. As you dream and make love with the goddess and god, openly receive the infinite knowledge and gifts they willingly offer you. Create shared dream adventures to help you with specific patterns and enjoy shared sexual journeys, using and directing the accumulated energy in a mindful way.

Dreaming creates your world and your world creates your dreaming. Learn to tap into the unmanifested in dreaming as you create new relationships in your awareness. Double out so you can dream and move your mind in several dimensions at once, learning to respond rather than react to your spiritual experiences.

The many faces of the goddess and god represent the many parts of yourself. Become acquainted with all of your faces and develop a relationship between the various aspects of yourself. Know you are one with the goddess and god as you begin to enjoy every step along the way and each moment of your life.

An excellent method for gaining rapport with the goddess and her consort is by Taking on the Aspects of a God. Traditionally this is done alone on the full or new moon. First, select a goddess or god. In a private setting, lay a magical circle, calling in the Four Wards as you would any other work. Use colors, incense, any objects, foods, and stones representative of the goddess or god you have selected. Enjoy yourself as you mix your mediums.

235

To invoke the goddess and her consort, begin to chant, "Oh self of selves, arise and awaken. Attend unto me." Repeat the words over and over with your voice growing louder and louder. The repetition of the chant causes the awakening of your selves. As you continue chanting, take everything off your body, including any jewelry. Then anoint your body with scented oil made from the particular herbs associated with the goddess or god with whom you have chosen to merge.

Formally call in the goddess or god by saying, "Now enter into me, so that I may see through your eyes, hear as you hear, taste and smell and sense as you do. As you enter me, you in turn may see as I see, hear as I hear, taste and smell and sense as I do." Intend both parties to benefit from this exchange. Build the energy to a peak and ask the divine energy to descend and move into you. Draw the goddess or god into every cell of your body and into every particle and wave of your awareness. The experience can last from a few moments to several months, depending upon your expectation and desire and the depth of your merge.

Expect to travel to the edge of your mind. Let yourself go all the way as you immerse yourself in the divine grace and light of the goddess and god. Bathe in the sacred light of oneness, moving beyond the brink of ecstasy to the boundless bliss of perfect love and perfect peace.

Guided Journey

The source spills out into a intricate waterfall flowing and weaving over massive granite boulders. The sheer rock face hangs in midair like a surrealistic painting. The waterfall splits into two rushing torrents, gushing out over the steep rock face. Toward the bottom of the rocks, the steaming waters converge back together as one, and then course into a bubbling hot springs pool.

Surrounding the pool are huge granite menhirs. I count them as I make my way over to the pool. They stand like nine sisters, silently watching the water, and as I approach, I can feel their blind eyes following me.

A thick blanket of white snow covers the perimeter of the rocks and pool. I look up at the grove of tall pine-like trees growing out from the solid rock. They outline the suspended oasis with their branches clumping together oddly here and there. The snow dusts the long cones hanging on the trees a brilliant white.

I flow into the warm pool and the silky warmth of the water covers my skin in a million tiny sensations. The fluid moves over my body, covering me with its wet massaging fingers. My hair floats over the surface of the water, fanning out like a burnished copper wave in the slow motion of the soothing water.

I swim near to where the waterfall pours down over the rocks. I surface just in front of a flat granite-like boulder. Pausing for a few moments, I catch my breath and then lift myself onto the large rock, its face smoothed by time and the elements.

Sitting quietly, I listen to the pounding waterfall and enjoy the feel of its warm spray misting over my face and body. This is my special place, a place where I feel at home, comfortable, and calm. Each time I sit in this particular spot, a sense of oneness washes over me. My mind weaves and flows out over the terrain. My awareness spreads over and under the floating oasis and I draw a circle of white light around the entire area. I rest peacefully on the rock as my attention rolls out into the still evening.

Twilight drifts up to greet me. Just as I feel its caress, I begin to chant softly at first, then louder, "Oh self of selves, arise and awaken. Attend unto me. Oh self of selves, arise and awaken! Attend unto me!" My voice has a deep rich texture, sounding melodic over the drumming sound of the nearby waterfall.

As I chant louder and louder, I simultaneously dip my hand into the pool, cupping my palm. I drip the water over my body as I continue speaking aloud, "Mother of all things, now enter into me. Merge with me so I can see through your eyes and feel from your heart. Be one with me, so I may intuit as you do, taste as you taste, smell the scents you do, and hear as you hear."

The drumming sound of the waterfall matches the rhythm of my words as I repeat my chant again and again. A circle of electric blue fire begins to gather and blaze around the nine menhirs surrounding the steaming pool. The light spins clockwise faster and faster, shooting out and swirling over me and then coursing back into the giant standing stones.

A flashing shiver of surging excitement streams through me as I peak the energy in my being. The tones of my chant echo louder and louder, layered with the rhythmic drumming of the waterfall.

Invoking the goddess, I watch as each of the nine menhirs comes to life around me. The full moon lights up the oasis, shining brightly on the faces of the Ladies born from the massive stones.

They mindspeak their names, "Danu, Bridget, Morrigan, Rhiannon, Sirona, Triana, Arianrhod, Coventina, and Rosemerta."

My awareness slowly touches each of the beautiful women and I experience a flowing warmth and strong sense of kinship. It seems I intimately know each of these intoxicating Ladies.

They speak to me in unison, a symphony of voices, "We have one wish for you—perfect love and perfect peace." As their words dance through my mind, dazzling rainbows of color blossom and spin from the Ladies' hands.

Green, gold and purple weave and thread with silver, red and white, while blue, copper and rose join and shine through me. The colored light feels alive as it courses through my body, electrifying me and then moving out into the boundless night.

The rocks and trees gleam in a spectrum of multicolored radiance and as the colors stream into the spherical moon, the floating island rests bathed in the lucent glow. I look at the long cones hanging from the pine-like trees, noticing they shine silver in the gleaming moonlight.

The Ladies speak, "We are your sisters. We are the faces of the goddess and the faces of yourself. Recognize that everything can be done by remembering who you truly are."

As I absorb the deeper meaning of their words, my awareness travels slowly around the circle of women. In each of their faces I see myself mirrored. It feels odd looking at pieces of myself. These wild and fantastic Ladies seem creative, nurturing, positive, gentle, demur, assertive, and fertile all at once.

"We honor your desire to seek the truth and dream the sacred dream. Help us complete the pattern, bringing the message of the Concept of Oneness to the land and its people," the women's voices play out to me like a sweet lilting melody.

As I shift my attention to my surroundings, I see myself mirrored in everything around me, in the water, rocks, trees, and in the silver pine cones.

"You, like ourselves, are born of the water and the earth. When it is time, we shall return to the earth and our spirits will flow once again into the waters of the sacred dream." With these words, the women spin in a whirl of white light and transform back into giant menhirs. They stand silently watching me.

I plunge into the warm pool and then rise up, floating on the surface of the healing water. My mind travels outward as I let go and flow freely in the brilliant moonlight. Stars hang like the silver pine cones in the surrealistic sky.

Somewhere next to the waterfall, I hear a voice speaking, "You are one with the water. Being in the water strengthens you."

I peer through the waterfall illuminated in the gleaming moonlight. You spill out from behind the steaming veil of cascading fluid, where the falling water meets the pool until it blurs. Born of the water, you move sinuously and deliberately, flowing through the threshold, out of the doorway of the world where our ancestors dwell. The streaming water gushes over your muscular arms as you beckon me to join you in the rushing veil of warm liquid.

I swim purposefully toward you. As I approach the aqueous sheet, it gets harder and harder to breathe. Before the air turns into water, I take a deep breath and move into your arms.

The warm silky water rolls over my skin, exhilarating my senses. Every inch of my body tingles as I melt against you. My mind feels fluid and pliant as I look into your eyes and dive into their depths, merging completely with you. I become the nine Ladies and you become my consorts. I see you through all of your incarnations and you gaze back at the multitude of faces and forms that flow through me. In tune with the elements, the contact of your skin on mine feels hot and exciting. The heat from your body radiates into my inner fire and our flames mate and blaze out of control.

We move out from under the flow of the water. You guide me over to a soft mossy bank that feels warm and damp from the gentle mist of the waterfall. You gather your many faces together and look me straight in the eyes. I reveal all of my selves to you, opening my mind to your healing caress. We surrender to one another, giving and receiving, our fingers, lips, and tongues working in unison. You smell and taste of the water, the rocks, and the earth.

You whisper in my ear, "Our love was bound to be."

I draw you into me like a natural miracle, all of your selves, welcoming each of your faces and forms. We transform into the goddess and god and then our images shift into sleek, swift, running wolves. We shape-change into two great brown bears and then we fly through the night as two white snowy owls.

I become the water and you dive into me. You become the air and I breathe you. We stream into the starlight as our bodies and hearts unite. We transcend them, soaring into pure energy in an instant of erotic movement. I am aware of a deep and boundless love between the two of us, a love stronger than I had ever considered possible.

The standing menhirs seem to sing out as we make love. We abandon sensation and the music of the elements carries us on our sacred journey. Each noise sounds amplified—the drumming of the waterfall, the contact of our wet bodies, and even our breathing. I call out to the sounds of the water, the air, the earth, and the stones. You cry out to the moon and the stars.

My body sings to you in an ancient symphony, the cadence stroking you past the threshold. Covered by a blanket of stars, you lift me on your love. Your desire surges into me and I respond wildly, wanting more. The drumming of the water on the rocks echoes the rhythm of our bodies as we move into a blinding white swirl of moonlight and silver starlight.

You guide me waist high into the warm bubbling pool and the sensation of the water, coupled with your skilled and purposeful movements, sends me floating into space. You mate your Mind to mine and join me. We flow out as two souls and course back, now unalterably one.

The universe moves away in a silent thought and then thunders back as I look into the deep pools of your loving eyes. We dive into the boundless and, mated together, we become all things.

🍀 The Oak Moon 🍀

Kerridwen & Kernunnos

Touch me again softly
Daring to know yourself
drawing out the deeper meaning
Now touch me once more
and let the knowledge move you
Into the ebb of love.

CHAPTER THIRTEEN

The Oak Moon ༄

Kerridwen & Kernunnos

Full Moon in Gemini, Sun in Sagittarius
Mutable neutral air and mutable positive fire elements

The Goddess and Her Consort

Under the thirteenth full moon beneath the branches of a
mighty oak, Merlin works his enchantments. He listens to
the whispering of the tree's remaining sinuated leaves as
they softly foretell the future. On the wintery Oak Moon,
the druid watches silently as spirit beings flow out from
the trunk of the tree. They dance around him and speak to
him, imparting their knowledge and wisdom.

The word *druid* means "Oak Seer" or "Oak Sage."
From the roots of the tree, the mysteries of other worlds
and deeper dimensions flow into your awareness. All
knowledge resides within the belly of the oak. Withstand-
ing drought and flood, the oak tree symbolizes strength
and endurance. Representing oneness with the earth, the
very last leaf of a live oak never falls.

Long ago, vast evergreen and oak forests covered
Europe and the British Isles. Most widely worshipped of
all trees, Greek legend holds that the formidable oak was
the first tree created, from which sprang humankind.
Sacred to many people, the oak is especially associated

with the fiery gods Dagda, Robur, Thor, Zeus, Jupiter, Demeter, Hercules, and Jehovah. Oak wood was burned in the perpetual fire of the Vestal Virgins in Rome. Carried into modern times, need fires as well as the traditional Yule Log are still made of oak.

The entire being of the oak represents fertility and fecundity. Every part of the tree is productive and useful. The acorns or nuts serve as a food staple for animals and people. The three-celled ovary of an acorn develops beneath the delicate flowers of the oak. Maturing, the nut becomes one-celled and one-seeded, depicting the oneness of all things through sexual union and fertilization.

Native American hunters knew that oak communities were rich in bear, deer, and other wildlife. The animals thrived on the acorns and lingered within the shade of the trees. Collecting the nuts, the native people crushed and leached the acorns before eating the meat. They also noticed lightning struck the big trees more than any other and that the allheal mistletoe flourished in the oak's branches.

In Gwyddonic Druid Tradition, the sacred mistletoe is gathered on the summer and winter solstices. Knock the plant out of the tree with a rock or stick, catching it before it touches the ground. As a token of both life and death, mistletoe bestows life and fertility. You embrace the life of the oak when you hold the allheal mistletoe in your hands. Under the dominion of the fire element, the mistletoe you collect can be used for protection, spiritual knowledge, healing, and for heightened sexual exploration.

Now and again the Oak Moon rises on, or just before, the winter solstice. This thirteenth full moon occurs about every third year and acts as the change element and balancing element in the ever-growing, never-ending cycle. Constant change keeps the pattern viable and healthy while balance gives it stability. As the thirteenth moon, the

Oak Moon personifies the creative and active process of birth, expansion, maturity, and rebirth.

On this dynamic High Moon, the All Mother Kerridwen teaches rebirth and transmigration. Goddess of inspiration, knowledge, and transformation, she stirs the symbolic cauldron from which all things manifest. For a year and a day the powerful Kerridwen brews a magical potion within her cauldron. As it happens, the young Gwion ingests the magical fluid, suddenly gaining the ability to hear everything in the world. In an instant, he understands the secrets of the past and of the future. Gwion is reborn into the sixth-century bard Taliesin, who is considered to be the greatest poet of his language.

The Ninefold One, Kerridwen, plays a key role in the Gwyddonic Magical Chase. The chase or hunt symbolizes the cycle of oneness. As an all-knowing shapeshifter, the goddess possesses the wisdom of transformation and death. Embracing the fecundity of the unmanifested, Kerridwen knows that with death and rebirth come true inspiration and creation.

247

Living on an island in the middle of a woodland lake, the Lady Kerridwen is mother to two children. She has a bright daughter and a dim and dark son. Together her two offspring represent positivity and negativity emerging from the same source and the potential balance and dynamics therein.

Kerridwen the Bright looks translucent like moonlight. Traveling in woodland forests as a luminous fog or diffuse cloud, the goddess exudes pure white light. Shapeshifting into a brilliant woman of prophecy, the Lady Kerridwen wears robes of pure radiance. Her face and eyes glow with love and laughter as she cavorts with her magnificent consort, the All Father Kernunnos.

The powerful god of life and death, Kernunnos charms the goddess Kerridwen with his mastery and lordship over all of nature, particularly animals. Associated with the wild hunt, the All Father guides the spirits of the dead to the Otherworld. With his nature fixed to the seasons, Kernunnos acts as the Earth's caretaker. He controls the culling and purification of the herds through intention and selection.

Associated especially with hoofed and horned animals like deer and cattle, Kernunnos roams along forest streams and in grassy meadows. His eyes shine hazel brown and his curly brown hair feels thick and coarse. Wearing a short tunic of any color, Kernunnos carries a bag of flowing coins. When he travels, a stag, a bull, three cranes, and a rat often accompany him.

Genuine rapport with Kerridwen and Kernunnos propels you closer to the source. The All Mother teaches you the essential balance of light and dark, of positivity, neutrality, and negativity. From the All Father, you master your environment, learning to communicate with nature and those around you. You become aware of the vital energy and light in each person with whom, and in every animal and plant with which, you interact.

As you merge with the All Mother and the All Father, you begin to construct a wider and larger picture of your world. The sacred dream or pattern takes shape in your mind and life transforms into a beautiful adventure. Your perceptions become infinitely reborn and your spiritual awareness expands when you join with the goddess Kerridwen and the god Kernunnos, allowing them to usher you through oneness.

Practical Knowledge and Useful Information— The Dream of Oneness

Immerse yourself in perfect love and perfect peace as you join energies with the goddess and her consort. Threefold in nature, the experience of perfect love and perfect peace embodies the perfect love of the goddess and the perfect peace of the god. You reach out and touch upon the perfect love of knowledge and the perfect peace of wisdom. As you join with the perfect love of all nature, you learn the perfect peace of being in harmony with all things whether animate or inanimate.

Open your mind and discover the perfect love of the goddess and the perfect peace of the god in nature. Like a guidebook through the boundless, nature becomes our road map on the Great Adventure. Planted by oneness, knowledge and wisdom flow in the rivers, oceans, and streams. Perceive the subtle flows of awareness and the patterns of energy in the rocks, in the mountains, in the soil, deep within the roots of the trees, and in the petals of a flower. Experience the essence of love and peace residing in the clouds that sweep across the skies and in the jeweled tapestry of stars shining in the night sky.

Nature waits for us to rediscover her beauty and bounty. As you commune with the natural elements of your being, turn your mind toward the circular flow of the cycle. Join and mate with the ever-flowing, ever-growing aspects within oneness and within yourself.

249

The first of the "Instructions of Kerridwen" in Gwyddonic Druid Tradition states, "Out of That Which has No Name, issues She who is the Mother of All Things." Cross-culturally, the Sioux Indians hold the same basic concept of divine and sacred power of the Mother Goddess. To the Sioux, her name is Wakanda.

In the beginning is Wakanda, the great void. She is everything, representing the great circle. Then comes the Lightning Bolt of Illumination, showing Wakanda both of her sides. He acts as the Great Mirror and when Wakanda looks within, she finds her man. They marry and dance and become the sun.

We are all reflections of oneness. Notice nature's reflection in the manifest universe. For example, the cosmic reflection of the sun's light on the Earth illuminates our planet. This light reflects off the moon's surface and back to the Earth. In this way, the moon acts as a mirror for the sun and the Earth.

As an evolving practitioner, you notice that certain people seem to be mirror images of yourself. They act as your moons. Often you will take either an immediate like or dislike to the person mirroring you. This largely depends upon how you feel about those qualities within yourself that are being mirrored. Your response reflects how connected you are with yourself and with oneness. Every experience enables you to view yourself in a different way and to look at the reflection from a new angle or perspective. The cleaner your lens of perception, the clearer your view.

Take time to look around you. Do you see faces reflecting positivity and love? What qualities and emotions do you personally reflect to the world? What does the culture and society in which you live reflect outwardly and inwardly? What are the global and universal reflections? What image does the media promote and reflect? Do you like what you see?

If you don't like what you see, you can change it. Dream acts as an agent of change. We all dream the consensus dream and together we create our world, patterning reality through our intention. Positivity and negativity stem proportionally from our communal awareness and actions, so turn your mind brightly toward the future, actively creating an image of the world you choose. Share your vision with others and fully participate in the sacred dream of oneness.

Go ahead and accept the challenge to consciously step into the stream of energy, co-creating life within the flow.

Recognize and immerse yourself in your calling as you follow your deepest feelings, that which you love the most. Allow merging and dreaming to serve as vessels to new frontiers of personal development and enhancement. Awareness and perception become your tour guides as you travel and explore the metempirical possibilities, dreaming beyond your imagination.

Merging with the Concept of Oneness enables you to live many lives in one. Flowing along the ever-changing, never-ending stream of energy, you understand that change leads to transformation and rebirth. With rebirth comes transmigration. You learn to purposefully migrate across your conditioned view of reality, to a more adaptable and comprehensive personal perspective.

Venture into the multitude of realities, Otherworlds and even into worlds created by your intent or by your partner's intent. Try doubling out into several worlds simultaneously, maintaining your center and remembering who you really are. Tap into your ancestral memories and flow back to the source. Carry and utilize this knowledge with you as you enjoy new sensations and added sensitivity.

As you merge and dream, carefully observe everything in your field of awareness. Witness pure energy threading its way through the universe and weaving oneness together. Sense the living energy of the fabric of light as you dream with your eyes open, every day of your life. Feel free to access the unmanifested where the conditioned rules of reality cease to apply.

Each of us chooses to live on this earth and to evolve. Our evolution is perpetuated by a thirst and hunger for experience and knowledge that wakes us from our conditioned sleep. Love relationships where spiritual partners engage in sacred sexual exploration act as a stimulating bridge between the conditioned world and oneness. In the

251

fluid state of spiritual love and orgasm, you can see both the physical dream you live in and the divine dream of the goddess and god.

The combined powers of female and male, joined together when making love, causes a vast surplus of light and energy. Making love implies you are making light. Begin to work in unison as you direct this energy and light toward specific patterns and outcomes. Realize that a growing spiritual partnership requires constant effort and a strong positive desire from each person involved. Build patterns of trust, love, respect, and consideration, lowering your personal drawbridge as you merge deeply with your mate.

Endeavor to use the four keys: wisdom, self-honesty, self-responsibility, and love. This will reduce distortion and deception within yourself and within your relationships. As a practitioner, intend to pattern events in your life rather than manipulate individuals. Know that happiness and personal fulfillment are emotions and feelings, not possessions. What is precious is not the gemstone, but the beauty and light that radiate from it. Understand that light and love are everlasting and ever-renewing, being careful not to trade your life in for a handful of dimes.

The New Age dawns upon a world where the secrets and knowledge of the ancient ways no longer need to be hidden. In turn, it becomes a time for revealing the extent of your wisdom, light, and beauty. In this time of awakening comes a period of healing and of genuine sisterly and brotherly love.

In the evolution of oneness, be mindful and flexible in the light of change, realizing things do not stay the same. Remember to adapt, flow, and grow as you actualize and live your dream, filling your positive patterns with light and life. Expect the world to be a light-filled place to grow and raise your children, and build your desire for just such a reality. Dream with your eyes open and know the goddess and her consort intimately. Merge with the exquisite pattern of oneness spreading out before you as you would with a sublime erotic adventure.

Some say we come into this world with nothing and we leave the world in the same way. Flip over the coin and begin to consider the possibility that we are born with everything and we have the sacred opportunity to be reborn with everything again and again. We do indeed all shine on like the moon and the stars and the sun, so boldly allow your light to brighten the world and the future of our planet.

The coming of the Golden Age of love and peace is upon us. We shall walk with both the goddess and god once again upon this earth. Awareness and perception act as the keys that open our minds and hearts to the light. Begin to fully understand we are all one, regardless of our personal and cultural differences, and perceive the power of universal connection instead of focussing on the dissipating forces of negativity and division.

253

Commune with the forests, rivers, the oceans, deserts, and astral bodies. Dream with the goddess and her consort while you connect and travel to other realms of existence, opening yourself to all of the stimulating possibilities. We shall overcome our fears and alienation and we shall walk hand in hand as we turn our minds to the Concept of Oneness. Let us dream together of paradise on Earth, joining together and carrying the message of love forward. May we ever-grow, choosing to learn from what has passed before.

Guided Journey

She walks down the earthen path toward the magnificent oak tree. Its many branches stretch out like arms in the chill of the late afternoon sun. As she moves closer, she sees that the base of the tree is at least fifty feet around. "This is the largest oak tree I have ever seen," she thinks while continually stepping closer.

The remaining jagged leaves dangle down, swaying slightly back and forth in the light breeze and occasionally dropping onto the ground. She passes a bed of clover and the sweet grassy fragrance fills her nostrils, sending her back in time to when she was a young girl playing in her grandmother's garden. She takes another deep breath before continuing her journey to the giant oak tree.

The brittle leaves covering the ground beneath the oak crunch and crackle as she walks toward the mighty tree. As she moves, her mind wanders to the young man she met yesterday at the bookstore. His soft blue eyes and dainty elfin features seemed definitely familiar. With a copy of her book tucked under his arm, he told her his name was Arrdu and that he had come to the store to both meet her and to talk with her about the book. His thirst for knowledge about the goddess Kerridwen and god Kernunnos was insatiable and he asked question after question. Finally she had to leave because of a prior commitment. But before leaving, she had promised to meet him the next day under what he described as the immense Dagda Oak in the Forest of Anderida. He said it was there that the two of them could continue their conversation.

She approaches the massive trunk and sees the tree is indeed as boundless as he had described it. She walks under the stark canopy of the massive oak tree and sits down between the tops of two gnarled roots, sinuously growing out from the base of the tree. As she rests nestled against the trunk, she watches the shadows of the branches dance to and fro on the grassy ground. Like the ever-changing oak tree, the shadows have no permanent pattern. The shadows wash over her and she merges with them. She blends with the movement and shape of the oak branches, as they shadow dance over her skin. The play of shadows shows her the true essence and form of the oak. Supple strands of light and darkness weave in the wings of the wind, their canorous voices merging her more deeply into oneness.

Startling her from her merged state, she feels something plop into her lap. Looking down, her surprise turns to delight as she sees a green sprig of mistletoe resting against the contrasting light beige fabric of her pants leg. "Aha, a gift from the goddess," she murmers aloud while taking the stock between her fingers and surveying the small, oval, jade-colored leaves. She remembers from her reading that mistletoe acts as a master key, and is believed to open all locks and doors.

Immersed in her thoughts, her eyes absently travel from the twig in her hand and down over the ground. To her right, she focuses on the outline of a circle drawn in the grass, formed out of a ring of dark green fungus. Within the circle, a clump of brightly colored marigolds grow, their orange and gold heads bob slightly in the breeze. She furrows her forehead as she ponders silently, "How strange. This is the wrong time of year for marigolds to be blooming."

She gasps and her eyes open wide as the earth in the circle suddenly begins to crack and spread apart. She tries to get up and run, but her legs won't move. The yawning chasm in the ground continues to expand and break away until the entire circle is a deep hole. Recovering from her immediate reaction of fear, she stands with her hand resting against the oak, craning her head and trying to look down the gaping crack. She jumps back in astonishment as the face of Arrdu, the young man from the bookstore, arises out of the strange circular opening in the earth.

"How did you do that? What's going on?" she questions, cautiously stepping back from the young man and the open hole.

"Don't be afraid," he muses. "I have come to guide you to the Land of Enchantment." He beckons to her. She hesitates and then reluctantly moves closer, caught somewhere between her conditioned doubt and her wild tugging curiosity. As she looks down through the opening, she sees a path descending into the depths of the hole, leading to a land beneath the earth.

"What is this place? Where does that path go?" she questions the young man while peering further into the ominous cave-like opening.

"You will see soon enough," he says as he takes her hand and guides her through the entrance.

Instead of being surrounded by darkness as she first expected, the underground cave is illuminated with a crepuscular light, whose source emanates from somewhere behind the distant shadows that stand before them. For the first ninety feet, two rock walls stretch out on either side of the narrow earthen path. Soon the walls give way to a grassy meadow covered with colorful wild flowers. As they move closer to the source of light, she sees that the tall distant shadows are actually two giant oaks, standing about nine feet apart, connected together at the branches.

"The tree on the right represents the sun and the tree on the left represents the moon," he says as he motions to the oaks with his right hand. "Together they form the gate to Tylwyth Teg, the enchanting land of the Faery folk."

257

He moves over to the sun tree. Reaching up, he plucks off an acorn. As he holds it in his hand, the acorn transforms into a lead box. The box lid is imprinted with the images of the sun and the moon surrounded by nine stars. He opens the lead box and slowly pulls out a crystal pentacle fastened to a gold chain.

He turns to her and places the necklace around her neck, securing the clasp. He smiles brightly as he tells her, "This pentacle contains the power of the oak. It, too, reflects the strength, endurance, and oneness of the earth. Whenever you wish to leave Tylwyth Teg, just touch the crystal around your neck and repeat these words, 'One is unto all, as all is unto one.'"

She recites the words several times to herself, locking them in her mind for future use.

Arrdu moves over to the moon tree. Once again he extracts an acorn from the branches. This time the nut transforms into a silver ring with a pearl set in its center. As he slides the ring on her right middle finger, she notices the pearl seems to shine with a light of its own, like a full moon.

Arrdu holds her hand in his as he says, "This ring will enable you to see the beings who inhabit Tylwyth Teg. Without it, they would be invisible." He lets go of her hand and motions for her to follow him. Together they glide through the oak gate and into the enchanting land of the Faeries.

A blinding golden light forces her to shade her eyes as she looks around at dozens of small earthen huts crowned with thatched roofs. Her eyes adjust to the light, and she notices the huts dot the perimeter of a vast golden circle in the center of the village. The circle is covered with golden bricks which appear to be the source of the brilliant streaming light.

She and Arrdu stand inside the gate for a few moments. They watch as a procession of strange people riding white ponies approaches them. The people wear green hooded cloaks and their diminutive features are soft and pleasing to the eye. The braided manes of the small horses hang with ribbons and tiny silver bells that tinkle as the procession moves closer. At the front rides a young woman with very light skin, emerald green eyes, and long, flowing red hair. Behind the young woman rides a green-haired man playing a siod-cruit. The melody from the delicate Faery harp intermingles with the tinkling silver bells, creating a beautiful symphony of sound.

"Greetings," proclaims the young woman as she reins in her pony. The procession stops. "I am Mari, Queen of the Faeries, and this is my consort, Krom." The young man smiles and nods his head while his nimble fingers continue to stroke the strings of the sweet singing harp.

Mari continues, "Your timing is impeccable, as usual, Arrdu. The celebration of the life-giving energy of the oak trees is just about to begin. We hope you will join us for the ritual and feast."

Mari slides gracefully down the side of the small white horse to the ground. The rest of the procession follows her cue and the ponies amble off toward the huts. Soon the whole exotic group, consisting of faeries, humans, elves, brownies, wyns, pookas and elementals, stands in a half circle before the two mighty oaks.

She watches as three couples step forth out of the crowd, carrying objects for the Oak Ritual. First, two wyns carry a small round oak table, setting it between the two oaks. Then two elves follow, one holding a beautiful finely-woven gossamer cloth, while the other holds a metal box exactly like the one that contained the crystal pentacle Arrdu had given her earlier. She touches the necklace around her neck while watching the first elf, a young man with blue eyes and cherubic features, as he drapes the lavender cloth over the table. The young elfin maiden then opens the ornate lead box and begins extracting the magical tools within and starts setting up the altar.

"Why do they keep the altar tools in a lead box?" she asks Arrdu, who stands beside her.

"Lead protects the magical qualities of the tools from negativity and prevents their power from being dissipated," he replies. She returns her attention to the elf assembling the altar. When the girl is done, two elementals appear, each holding a long oak staff with greased mullein tied to the tip. The female elemental moves to the left and the male to the right, each placing the staffs in the ground and lighting the tips. The left torch emits a bright green flame, and the right one a fiery red flame.

After the staffs are lit, Mari and Krom move to their places in front of the altar. Krom calls in the goddess and god with nine raps of his Faery wand. The magical wand has a blazing selenite star tip and three faces carved deep in the oak handle. Mari then calls in the Great Wards to guard the four directions. As the Faery Queen beckons to the North Point, the earth begins to rumble, and when she moves to the East Point, a Faery wind gusts through the village. At the South Point, a ball of fire flares, and at the West Point, the image of a lake appears with waves that wake softly against the shoreline. Mari then moves back to Krom's side in front of the altar.

Suddenly the two mighty Oaks, representing the goddess and the god, speak in unison. "We have invited the outsider from above because the eternal balance of Mother Nature has been severely disrupted and the rift between body, mind, and spirit is ever-expanding. Too many unconnected beings exist in the world above and they are destroying nature, their world, and ultimately themselves, through their lack of connectedness." Their words echo and fade throughout the village. Then there is complete silence as the oak trees begin to bleed, dripping a reddish sap from their trunks.

Swaying back and forth, the massive trees continue to speak. "The tree of life shows a pattern of growth and the flow of oneness. Through a personal connection to oneness, you discover the source within, restoring the essential connection to oneness. Our power lives within each of you, as you in turn live within us. Become partners with your mate and your world. Work as equal partners, and know that true lovers always stand strong under the arms of the mighty oak. Relationships with the one you call your mate happen many times over in many worlds and lifetimes. Each time, the bond grows stronger and stronger until there is no division between body, mind, and spirit. If you destroy your world, so too, you destroy ours. Beware, time is running out. It is all important that the people above become one with their world again, opening themselves to divine love and light. Deliver this message to those above who will listen."

She watches as the swaying of the trees becomes more wild and pronounced until they finally topple over in a tremendous cracking and crashing sound. Suddenly the light grows dim like the sun during a total eclipse. From the corpses of the fallen trees, two spirits rush out in the energetic shapes of charging blue bulls. Her eyes follow their forms as they ascend into a huge ball of light. The brilliant sphere of multicolored light radiates outward and restores the brightness to the land of the Faeries.

261

She turns to question Arrdu, but he has gone. She scans the faces around her, but she can't see him anywhere. The crowd begins to disassemble and the feast and festivities sound throughout the town circle. The aroma of freshly-baked bread fills her senses and the smoke from the cooking fires drifts toward her. The Faery folk celebrate, linking their arms as they dance the spiral dance, clockwise around the center circle. Their beautiful voices join together in a perfect cadence as they sing the ancient songs.

She watches the singing and dancing for a time, but eventually closes her eyes. Her hand clasps the crystal pentacle around her neck and she recites the words, "One is unto all, as all is unto one." When she opens her eyes, she finds herself looking into the blue pools of Arrdu's eyes. They sit side by side under the oak tree where her adventure into Faery Land began.

"Did you enjoy your journey?" he questions softly with a smile.

"Yes, but it seems too fantastic to be real," she responds. Grasping her hand firmly in his, he guides her over to the Faery ring formed in the grass.

To her amazement, she can still see the images in the world below the circle of dark green fungus growing in the grass. "Why can I still see the Land of Faery?" she asks in a puzzled voice.

Arrdu takes her left hand in his, "You still wear the silver pearl ring. It is a gift from Faery folk and you are to keep it forever. As long as you wear the magical ring, you can see into the Land of Enchantment. The ring was given to you as a permanent reminder to carry the message of oneness to the people of your world."

She fingers the silver ring, running the tip of her forefinger over the smooth pearl and says, "Yes, I understand now."

Arrdu tenderly takes her hands in his, looking deep into her eyes. After a few moments they move into each other's arms, embracing oneness. The branches of the Dagda Oak sway gently over the lovers as the winter wind sings quietly through the stark canopy.

APPENDIX 1

A List of Goddesses and Consorts

The following is a list of goddesses and gods. There are four type of deities. First are the elven deities like Edain, Gobannon, and Mider. Second are the monadic deities including Rhiannon, Morrigan, and Triana. Third are the young gods, called the demi-gods. Cordemanon is in this group. The gods incarnate make up the fourth group of deities. These are goddesses and gods that have been born as humans, so that they may perform a specific task on earth.

Danu, Anu, Triana, and Morgana are aspects of the goddess Kerridwen. *Kerri* means "lady," and *dwen* means "white" or "bright." The Tuatha of Kerridwen and the Tuatha De Dannan are the same family. The Tuatha of Kerridwen refers to the members of the family who are presently human, incarnated on earth, while the Tuatha De Dannan describes the members of the family that are gods.

Danu or Anu was the mother monad of all gods. Bel or Belenus was the first monad to stem from Danu. The Dagda is the second monad, Bridget the third monad, and Llyr is the fourth monad to arise from Danu.

Amaethon: A god of agriculture and the harvest. Called the Harvest King. Appears with bronze, tanned skin, sun-streaked dark blond hair, blue or blue-green eyes, and a brilliant smile. He is a very friendly god. He wears green and brown tunics, or robes the color of wheat, corn, and grapes. His magical symbols are the fruits of the harvest and farmer's tools, particularly the sickle, hoe, and plow.

Andraste: Also Andrasta. A goddess of death, war, and fertility. Appears with dark skin, tall, and in green robes.

Angus: Also Angus Og, Oengus. A god of love and intimacy. Appears youthful with fair skin, red hair, and green eyes. His is full of fun, loving, and very well-endowed.

Arianrhod: A star and moon goddess similar to Sirona. A goddess of higher love and wisdom. Represents air of water. Appears very fair and gentle, her skin is translucent like starlight. She wears dark blue robes that are transparent or almost transparent. Her robes have a silver shimmer to them and are decorated with star-like jewels. *Arian* means "silver," and *rhod* means "wheel" or "disc." Her magical symbols are the crescent moon, stars, moonbeams, and a silver, eight-spoked wheel.

Artio: A bear goddess, the monad of all female bears. Appears large and strong. A protector of nature.

Balor: A sun god and king of the Formors.

Banba: A goddess representing Ireland.

Belenus: Also Bel, Belanos. A god of life, truth, inspiration, and music. Represents fire of fire. An active healing (dry heat) god. He drives away diseases. Appears as a radiant young man, with curly golden-blond hair and sky-blue eyes. He wears an unbelted robe of the whitest white, a sky blue robe, or goes nude. His magical symbols are the sun disc, a golden harp, a golden curved sword, and spear.

Belisama: A title of the goddess of fire, an aspect of Bridget but as the young sun, the sun maid. Her name means "like unto flame" or "bright and shining one." She wears transparent robes of sunrise colors and a white mantel and appears as fair, with bright sky-blue eyes and pale golden-blond hair. Her magical symbol is the rising sun.

Belisana: An aspect of Belisama with a similar appearance, but more earthy. Goddess of healing, laughter, and forests.

Boann: Also Boi, Boanna. A river goddess, and consort and wife of the Dagda. She is the mother of the herds. Her magical symbol is a silver salmon.

Bodb the Red: A son of the Dagda. He is virile and athletic and represents active male energy.

Borvo: Also Bormo, Bormanus. A Celtic Apollo, and a god of healing. Associated with wet heat, such as hot springs and mineral waters. Represents fire of water, and is a god of the unseen truth, and inspiration through dreams. Appears with golden skin, hair, and eyes, and wearing a golden tunic. His magical symbols are a flute, a golden harp, a golden sword or spear, hot springs, and the sun disc.

Bran: Also Bron. A protector of poets and bards. His features are similar to Gwydion. He is a handsome and manly god with long auburn hair and brown or green-brown eyes. Appears very tall, slender, and gentle. Appears with a beard and mustache most of the time. He wears blue, gold, yellow, and brown robes or nothing at all. His magical tool is the bard's harp and he is an excellent singer.

Branwen: A Welsh goddess of love, called the White-Bosomed One and the Venus of the Northern Sea. Her magical symbol is a white crow.

Bridget: A sun and fire goddess, fire of fire. She is the goddess of the hearth and home and represents the sacred fire. She is a goddess of smithcraft, healing, medicine, poetry, and inspiration. She is fair and bright, with sunny blue or green eyes, and honey-colored hair. She wears gold, brown, and golden-white robes or pastel shades of light blue and peach. Her magical symbols are the spindle and distaff, the sacred flame, a fire pot, and her brass shoe.

Brigantia: A powerful Celtic Briton nature goddess. Very similar to the sun goddess Bridget. An ancient name for Britain, representing rivers and the curves of the countryside.

Camulus: A Celtic Mars and war god, associated with clouds and storms. Appears with dark skin, brown eyes, and black hair. He wears a blood red tunic or dark charcoal-silver robes. His magical symbol is the severed head, and he carries a large sword.

Cliodna: A bird goddess and a young aspect of the Dark Goddess. Her name means "shapely one," and she is the most beautiful woman ever seen when she takes human form. Appears with black hair, brown eyes, and wears russet-colored robes. Her symbol is an apple.

Cordemanon: A young god of travel and knowledge. He appears as a handsome young man with golden hair and blue eyes. His magical symbols are stone circles and the Great Book of knowledge.

Coventina: A goddess of childbirth, renewal, and healing springs. Her well represents the womb of the earth. Appears with brown hair, brown eyes, and an earthy complexion. She wears brown robes the color of the earth. Her magical symbols are the womb and the well.

Dagda: Also The Dagda. He is an aspect of the All Father, and a lord of complete knowledge and wisdom. He is the Good God or the Good Hand, and is master of life and death and a bringer of prosperity and abundance. Twin to Sucellos as ruler of the bright half of the year. Appears with dark brown eyes and wavy brown hair. He is wise and very regal. Wears robes of cobalt blue and purple and sometimes peach or crimson-colored clothes. His magical tools are the rods of command, a chalice, a magic harp, the flesh hook, a sword, club, and cauldron.

Damona: A protectress of farmer's herds and fields and a goddess of abundance and prosperity. Her magical symbols are cattle.

Danu: Also Dana, Anna, Anu, Don. A goddess of wisdom, complete abundance, and control over all things; air of air. She is the greatest goddess, a goddess of the people. Appears as an old plump lady with gray hair, gray eyes, and gray robes. Sometimes she appears young and beautiful in bright green or white robes. Her magical symbols are a staff and the color green.

Diancecht: A physician of the gods. Appears with dark hair, brown eyes, and with a fair or ruddy complexion. He wears blue or silver robes, and his magical tools are the mortar and pestle.

Dumiatis: Also Dumeatis. A master teacher god of creative thought, a Celtic Mercury. Similar to the god Lugh. Appears tall and slender with a brilliant smile, and dark curly brown hair and golden eyes. He has a quiet intensity and is often seen sitting on a hill or under a tree surrounded by children who are listening to his teachings. His magical symbols are the quill pen and ink, writing staves, books of knowledge, and the teaching tales.

Dwyn: A god of love and mischief who loves to play tricks. Appears youthful with dark skin, hair, and eyes. He is noted as being extremely manly and very well-endowed.

Edain: Also Etain. A goddess of grace and beauty and wife of Mider, who won her in a chess game. An example of transmigration. Appears fair, with golden hair, blue eyes, and wearing blue and gold robes tied with a golden belt. Her magical symbols are a herd of white mares with blue eyes and a spray of apple blossoms held in her hand.

267

Elayne: Also Elen, Elen Lwyddawg. She is the Leader of the Hosts, and considered the Warrior Mother; also called Eriu, goddess of Ireland. A goddess of war and leadership and of immense stature. Myrddin is one of her consorts.

Epona: An earth goddess representing fertilization by water, and a horse goddess. Appears as fair-skinned with black hair and gray eyes. She wears blue and gray robes and is portrayed holding an apple while seated on a horse.

Esus: A woodland god and aspect of the dark face of Kernunnos. He is a woodsman and hunter who slays Tarvos, the golden bull. Appears tall, strong, and muscular. Wears animal skins and carries a sword and bow.

Fagus: A tree god representing the monad of all beeches.

Fliodhas: A goddess of the woodlands and woodland animals, associated with the deer goddess Sadv. She protects animals and the woodlands. She calls the wild animals of the woodlands her cattle. Appears as a quiet and shy goddess, with long wavy honey-colored hair. She wears brown tunics and breeches, but is also seen in robes of woodland greens and crowned with ferns and flowers. She has a sunny personality. Her magical symbols are a large doe, lush green grass, and woodland springs.

Gabba: A goddess of the Abyss, a crone aspect of the Dark All Mother, and one of the dark queens. No one knows or remembers what she looks like. Her symbol is the Celtic endless weave.

Gobannon: Also Govannon, Goibniu. A blacksmith god of magic. Works with metals and forges. Appears dark complected, with dark brown eyes and black hair. Wears a brown tunic with a leather apron. His magical symbols are blacksmithing tools and the transforming fire.

Gwalchmei: Called the Hawk or Falcon of May, as the son of the goddess Mei. He portrays a god of love and music. His symbols are raptors and the fields at hunting times, in the early morning and late afternoon.

Gwydion: Is the son of Don (Danu). He is a god of kindness, the arts, eloquence and magic; a master of illusion and fantasy, and helper of humankind. He is the brother of Amaethon and Gobannon. He is brother and consort to Arianrhod. Gwydion has two sons, Dylan and Lleu (Lugh). Math, son of Mathonwy, handed on his knowledge and abilities (which are infinite) to his student and nephew, Gwydion. Gwydion is bard and wizard, prince of the powers of the air, a shapeshifter. Appears as fair with short blondish-brown hair and blue eyes. Wears a blue or gray robe or tunic. He is a great enchanter and healer, and his magical symbol is a harp.

Gwyn ap Nudd: Also Gwyn. A god of the Wild Hunt. A god of the death chase and god of the Otherworld. He is the hunter of souls and lord of the unmanifested. Appears as very fair, almost white, with icy blue eyes. He has a very large body and moves with great strength. His magical symbol is a white hound with red ears named Dormarth.

Hellith: A god of the setting sun (fire of air), and of the dying. If invoked, he brings peace to those near death. After death, souls are in his protection until they reach their destination. He is a gentle young man with pale blond hair and very fair skin. Wears white robes with a violet hue. Also appears with hair, eyes, skin and robe of one color, the color of the red embers of a dying fire. His magical symbols are the setting sun disc and a flute that brings peace and tranquility to those who hear it.

Hertha: Also Herdda. A goddess of rebirth and healing. She is an earth goddess, representing the greening of spring. Appears with brownish hair, green or brown eyes, and is very well-endowed. She wears brown and green robes. Her magical symbols are the cow, calf, and milk pail.

Kernunnos: The All Father, and a god of wealth. He is lord of the animals, and a god of life and death. Appears with medium long, curly brown hair, fair and ruddy skin, and brown or hazel eyes. He wears a short tunic. His magical symbols are animal horns, a serpent belt, a stag, a bull, three cranes, a rat, and a bag of flowing coins.

Kerridwen: The All Mother. A goddess of inspiration and knowledge, called The Ninefold One. Looks translucent like moonlight, sometimes like a white fog or a brilliant point of light. She wears robes of white and her face is bright, and pure light radiates from her eyes. Her magical symbol is a large cauldron from which all manifested energy arises.

Letha: A harvest goddess associated with Midsummer. Appears with honey-brown hair and hazel eyes, wearing robes of silver and gray, or golden-brown. Her magical symbols are a swan and apples.

Llyr: Also Ler, Lir. A god of the sea and a king of the oceans. He is a shy god who rarely reveals himself, and can appear as a part-man, part-fish creature. He is very gentle and loving, but if provoked can turn to rage. Appears kingly and very handsome. His skin is faintly green and seems to sparkle like moonlight shining on the ocean, almost translucent. He has silver-white hair, a beard and mustache, and pale green-blue eyes the color of the ocean. He wears gray and sea-foam green robes or goes nude. His magical symbols are sea shells, sharks, sea mammals, the sea serpent, and seagulls. He plays a harp that he fashioned with silver, pearl, coral, and shell.

Luchta: Also Lucta, Luchtaine. A god of smiths, wrights, and craftsmen. Associated with Gobannon. He is the Carpenter God, and the shield maker for the Tuatha. Appears with blue eyes, blond-brown hair, and wears a belted tunic in brown or gold. His magical symbol is the shield.

Lugh: Also Lug, Lleu, Llew. Uncontested master of all arts. A god of war, smiths, poets, and bards, associated with the setting sun and the moon. He is a champion of the Tuatha, a historian and powerful sorcerer. Appears very handsome and clean shaven, with dark brown hair and blue eyes. Very lusty appetite and known for his generosity and prowess. His magical symbols are the cock, turtle, goat, a magic sword, and a bag of coins.

Manannan: Also Manannan Ap Llyr, Manannan Mac Llyr. A god of the sea and travel, and a magician. He is a master shapeshifter and great teacher. Appears tall, dark, and handsome. He wears black or dark charcoal robes, sometimes belted in a gold chain. His magical symbols are a wand, a magic coracle, a magic spear called Red Javelin, and several magic swords, three of which are called The Great Fury, The Little Fury, and Retaliator.

Math: A Welsh god of sorcery, magic, and enchantment. He is a master druid, teacher, and king. Math is the seasonal king, and is symbolic of the cycle of life, death, and rebirth. Math is king of the empire and has great wealth and knowledge. Uncle and teacher to Gwydion, he is protective, powerful, and wise. Nothing escapes his attention. He is older, but virile and handsome. He has white in his hair, the bluest of eyes, and wears light blue or white robes. His magical symbol is the fabric of life.

Medb: Also Maeve, Mab. A goddess of the land's sovereignty, she is the good queen, called The Warrior Queen. She is the Faery Queen and Queen of Connaught. Appears with flame-red hair, green eyes, and wears orange-red robes. She is magnificent and powerful, runs faster than horses, and carries animals and birds on her arms and shoulders. Her magical tools are the spear and shield.

Mei: Also Mai, Meia. An earth and sun goddess, similar to Rosemerta. She is the mother of Gwalchmei. She has long dark golden-brown hair, blue eyes, and wears sky-blue or meadow-green robes.

Mider: A Gaelic god of the Otherworld, called the Faery King. A bard and chess player, he likes to play games for high stakes. He is a Celtic Pluto and consort to Etain.

271

Modrona: Also Motrona. A goddess associated with Coventina and an aspect of the All Mother.

Morgana: A goddess of war, fertility, and magic. She is the Death Mother or the Queen of Death. She is the daughter of Llyr and Anu. Appears as fair or ruddy, with long black, blue-black or reddish-black hair, and dark brown, green, or blue-black eyes. She has awesome beauty and is very sensuous. Appears as a young woman or can look like an ugly hag. She wears wine-red, indigo, or black robes. Her magical symbols are trees along the shoreline, sea shells, cypress tress, ravens, and crows.

Morrigan: Also Morrigana. She is called the Sea Queen and the Great Sea Mother. She is a goddess of wisdom and appears very queenly. She is a statuesque woman, with long dark silver-streaked hair, opalescent skin, and gray-green eyes. She wears deep sea green and blue robes, tied with a cord of white or shell pink. She wears a tiara of gold, silver, and pearl. Her magical symbols are the queen's rod of command, sand dollars, ocean vegetation, manta rays, and whales.

Morrigu: A goddess of death, life, and magic. She is called the Dark Gray Lady or the Queen of the Sea. She protects sailors and the shores of Erin. Appears with dark indigo eyes, dark silver-gray hair, and opalescent skin. She has a gentle nature but if angered, she destroys. She wears pale green robes, or sometimes gray-green, silver, or dark blue robes. Her magical symbols are a harp of silver, shell and pearl, and ocean caves.

Myrddin: A sun and earth god, fire of earth. A god of woodlands and nature, laughter and mirth. A sky god associated with stones, caves, crystals, woodlands, and magic. A god of healing associated with herbs, natural mineral deposits, and pure water springs. Appears as a younger robust man, with reddish brown hair and hazel green eyes. He wears short brown or forest green belted tunics, and has woodland flowers tangled in his curly hair, beard, and mustache. His magical symbols are the wild rose, sweet water springs, and he plays a flute whose sound urges you to laugh and dance.

Nantosuelta: A goddess of abundance who is associated with Sucellos. She is a river goddess. Appears as fair and rosy with brown hair and brown eyes. She wears blue-green robes, and holds a dove house on a pole in one hand, and sometimes carries a baker's paddle.

Nemetona: A goddess of the oak grove, and a warrior goddess, who is the great protectress of the sacred Drynemeton and a patron of thermal springs. She is gentle and friendly, with dark skin, long dark hair, and dark eyes. She wears a short brown warrior's tunic and sandals or brown belted robes. Her magical symbols are oak groves, a ram, and a spear made of ash wood with a silver tip.

Nimue: An earth and water goddess, and a young aspect of the Bright All Mother. She is goddess of lakes, also known as the Lady of the Lake, maker and keeper of Excalibur, King Arthur's sword. She is a student and teacher of Myrddin, her consort. She has knee-length dark brown hair, large blue-green or blue-violet eyes, fair skin, and large man-like hands. She wears robes of soft blues, lavenders, whites and aquas, or goes nude. Her magical symbols are a large, bright white-silver sword, underwater caves, swans, swallows, and quartz and crystalline formations.

Nodens: A god of sleep and dreams, dream magic, and a god of the Otherworld. He has light hair and eyes and wears light colored robes.

Nuada: Also Lludd, Nudd. A Celtic Jupiter and an aspect of the All Father, the Good Father. He is a god of wealth, war, kingship, and thunder. Appears as fair, with silver-gray eyes, and grayish-white hair and beard. He wears a very short brown or dark charcoal-colored tunic, and is good natured with a great appetite. He has a silver arm made by Diancecht. His magical symbols are a magic spear, thunder, and lightning.

273

Nwyvre: A god of the ethers and space, also god of celestial sciences, astronomy, and astrology. He is a god of space and stars and is consort to Arianrhod. Appears as fair, almost translucent like starlight, very gentle, and wears robes of dark blues or silver. His magical symbol is the nine-pointed star.

Ogmios: Also Ogma. A god of civilization and the inventor of writing (Oghams). Appears as fair with brilliant blue eyes, and light brown or silver-brown hair. He is lusty, well-endowed, handsome, and very knowledgeable. He wears a blue or brown tunic, belted with silver. His magical symbols are a club or stick with runes carved on it.

Pryderi: A master of disguise and shapeshifter. He brought the swine from the Otherworld. He is the son of

Rhiannon. Appears in many shapes, usually young and athletic. His magical symbol is the pig or boar.

Pwyll: A ruler of the Otherworld, and Prince of Dyfed. He is always seen with a pack of hounds.

Rhiannon: A goddess of knowledge, and an aspect of the All Mother. She is called Queen Mother and is associated with horses as the Queen Mare. She was originally called Rigatona or the Great Queen. Appears fair and bright with reddish-brown hair and green or blue eyes. She wears robes of bright reds or red-browns, or silver and gray. Her magical symbols are apples, a mare, and three birds.

Robur: A god of forests, in particular oaks, the monad of all oaks. He is a tree god known as the Forest King. Sometimes he appears with bright gray eyes, a wild unruly white beard, and silvery white hair and mustache. His skin is the color of tree bark and he goes nude or dressed in a leather tunic. He often has mistletoe tangled in his hair and beard. His magical symbols are mistletoe, a budding staff of oak, and woodland animals.

Rosemerta: A goddess of abundance and plenty. Lugh is her consort and she is a young aspect of the All Mother. She has a rosy complexion, with honey-colored or auburn hair, and green-brown eyes. She wears robes colored with warm hues of red, brown, and green. Her magical symbols are gardens and a cornucopia flowing out with all good things.

Sadv: A goddess of the forests. She is called the Deer Goddess. Mother to Oisin, the poet. Appears with white hair, dark blue-gray eyes, and wears scarlet robes tied with a silver belt. Her magical symbols are the doe with a fawn, and other woodland animals.

Sirona: A Celtic Venus and goddess of the sun and the stars. Her consort is Borvo. She is fair with dark reddish-brown or black hair, and deep green or indigo eyes. She has a star on her forehead and wears dark blue or silver robes with star-like jewels. Her magical symbol is the star.

Smertullos: A god of the Abyss and associated with the unmanifested. He is called the Preserver and Lord of Protection. He appears with red hair, fair skin, and blue eyes, and wears brown and white robes. His magical symbols are a snake with a ram's head and a snake belt.

Sucellos: A god of death and fertility, an aspect of the All Father. He is the Dagda's twin as ruler of the dark half of the year. He has such beauty that to look upon his face would bring death, so he appears in many disguises and shapes; sometimes he appears odd and humorous. His magical tool is a large spear.

Taranis: A god of the passing seasons, storms, and thunder. He is very fair-skinned with blue eyes. He has long wild hair and a beard. He wears a white tunic and mantle, and his magical symbol is the eight-spoked wheel.

Tarvos Trigaranos: A god of vegetation and a young aspect of Kernunnos. Born at Coventina's well, he is built like a bull and his form is perfect. He is virile and athletic. His hair is light brown and his eyes are very intense, usually blue or brown. His magical symbols are oaks and three gray cranes.

275

Tethra: A shadowy god of the sea and magic; air of water. Appears with golden-brown curly hair, green eyes, and wears gray-green robes. He has the appearance of moonbeams on the ocean. His magical symbols are the albatross and a flock of seagulls.

Ti Ana: Also Ty Ana, De Ana, Dy Ana. A goddess of the house and home. Her name means "Thy Mother" or "Ana of the Household."

Triana: The Threefold Mother. She portrays three faces of the goddess. Sun-Ana is a goddess of healing, knowledge, and mental arts. She wears a white robe with a bright yellow mantle, which is clasped together at the breast with a golden sun disc. Earth-Ana is a goddess of nature, life, and death. She wears a green robe with a brown mantle which is clasped together with a copper broach inlaid with three green leaves. Moon-Ana is a goddess of higher love and wisdom. She wears a gray robe with a blue mantle which is clasped together with a silver crescent moon.

Viviana: Also Vivian. A goddess of birth and life, and an aspect of the All Mother. She is a bright goddess of life and love, of mothers and childbirth, and of children. Her name means "Life Mother." She has golden streaks in her hair and green or blue eyes. She wears a golden-white or spring green robe. Her magical symbol is the five-petaled red rose.

Goddess Color Correspondence Table

Colors reflect light, and are effective symbols in magic. Gwydonnic tradition incorporates the effectiveness of color in its teachings. Suggested uses for color and the corresponding goddesses serve as references for the practitioner.

Red: Corresponds to passion, sex, the physical body, dynamic force, vitality, virility, blood, healing, rebirth, power, animation, and emotional desire. Brigantia, Rhiannon, Morgana, Medb, Viviana, and Elayne typify the color red.

Orange: Corresponds to pleasure, joy, feeling good, being open, generosity, happiness, gladness, mirth, ease and comfort, prosperity and plenty. The color orange represents the hearth and home and the origination of patterns and ritual. Bridget, Rosemerta, Hertha, and Belisama typify this color.

Yellow and Gold: Correspond to orange, and add a youthful emphasis. Gold relates to knowledge, learning, teaching, studying, understanding, cognition, truth, fact, lore, comprehension, and perception. Belisana, Ty Ana, Viviana, Nimue, and Bridget typify the colors of yellow and gold.

Brown: Corresponds to the earth, soil, potential, nurturing, and rebirth. Hertha, Cliodna, Coventina, Epona, Fliodhas, Modrona, and Nemetona typify the color brown.

Green: Corresponds to creating positive physical patterns, birth, spring greening, healing, the home, prosperity, abundance, regeneration and renewal, growth, the young and the tender in nature. Danu, Rosemerta, Hertha, Viviana, Fliodhas, Sadv, Belisana, Ty Ana, Damona, Mei, Artio, and Andraste all typify the color green.

Blue: Corresponds to divination, dreams, intuition, loyalty, defensive protection, cleansing, water, creative arts, dance, and emotions. Arianrhod, Morrigan, Nimue, Boann, Sirona, Mei, Edain, Nantosuelta, and Morrigu typify the color blue.

Violet: Corresponds to lore, ancestral intuition, sacredness, consecration, offensive protection, pattern making and breaking, ancestral memory, and healing through destroying disease. Danu, Nimue, Sirona, Morrigan, Elayne, and Morgana typify the color violet.

White: Corresponds to the manifested, divine energy, ritual, positivity, perfection, pureness, and love. Kerridwen, Branwen, Nimue, and Bridget typify the color white.

Gray: Corresponds to wisdom, oneness, merging, cosmic consciousness, creative life force, and feeling centered. Rhiannon, Morrigan, Sirona, Edain, Morrigu, Arianrhod, Epona, Gabba, and Letha all typify the color gray.

Rose: Corresponds to higher love, enlightenment, nirvana, godhood. Danu, Nimue, Branwen, and Rosemerta typify the color rose.

Feather Augury Chart

Most of us have happened upon bird feathers while out walking in nature. Gwyddonic Druid Tradition includes the ancient custom of gathering feathers and using them as symbolic communication tools. You can use feathers to send a secret message to your lover or friend. Combining feathers of different colors can say a great deal to those who make an effort to understand the meanings of feather augury.

Feather Color	Symbolic Meanings
White	Pureness, gladness, a birth
Green	New prospects, adventure, money
Red	Fortune and good luck
Rose	A love affair, romance
Blue	Love, a gift
Brown	Good health
Yellow	Friendship, companionship
Orange	Happiness to come in the future
Gray	Peace of mind, tranquility
Purple	A journey or trip
Blue and White	A new love
Brown and White	Health and happiness
Gray and White	A new and positive situation
Black and White	Beware, be cautious
Black	Misfortune, bad luck, death, the unknown
Yellow and Green	Gossip and small talk

Stones and Suggested Uses

Stone	Suggested Uses and Qualities
Agate	Emotional and physical balancing, digestion, grounding
Amethyst	Spiritual development, courage, psychic growth
Aquamarine	Clarity of mind, flow, inspiration
Adventurine	Positive participation, active imagination, travel
Azurite	Amplifies healing ability, mental clarity
Bloodstone	Creativity, vitality, circulation of energy, higher knowledge
Carnelian	Sexuality, fire energy, power, and creativity
Citrine	Thinking process, mental clarity, patterning, insight
Clear Quartz	Healing, balancing energy, sight and clarity, spirituality
Calcite	Balancing positive and negative energies within the body
Diamond	Strength, power, insight, inspiration, protection, development
Emerald	Psychic clarity, divination, growth, patterning, sexuality
Fluorite	Otherworld experience, projecting a sense of peace

Garnet	Strength in physical body, love and passion, imagination, flow
Hematite	Grounding, protection, strength, density, the shadow self
Herkimer	Dreaming, higher love, stimulating psychic centers, power
Jade	Protection, divine love, connection with earth, cleansing
Lapis Lazuli	Psychic development, divination, protection, creativity, power
Malachite	Communication with nature, rapport with animal kingdom, balance
Moonstone	Connection to female energy, receptivity, tidal flow, emotions
Opal	Harmony, cosmic energy, creativity and wisdom, balance
Pyrite	Prosperity, circulation and flow, generating energy
Rose Quartz	Emotional balancing, relationships and friendships, higher love
Ruby	Power, insight, creativity, physical and mental strength, drive
Rutile	Building energy, balance, insight, health, patterning
Sapphire	Psychic development, creativity, passion, stimulates energy
Smoky Quartz	Grounding, centering, earth connection, healing, prosperity
Topaz	Insight, knowledge, loyalty, higher love, creativity
Tourmaline	Strengthens energy body, regeneration, creativity, growth

Chart to Calculate
Great Days and Moons

Begin with the first Full Moon after Yule.

1. Wolf
2. Storm
3. Chaste
4. Seed
5. Hare
6. Dyad
7. Mead
8. Wort
9. Barley
10. Wine
11. Blood
12. Snow
13. Oak

Earth
North-Yule
First Great Day

Samhain

Bridget's Fire

Water
West
Hellith's Day

Air
East
Lady's Day

Lughnassad

Beltane

Fire
South
Letha's Day

283

Note: Oak is not used in 12-Moon years.

Path of the Sun — from Yule Clockwise to Samhain

• Yule, Winter Solstice at 00.00 degrees Capricorn
• Bridget's Fire at 15.00 degrees Aquarius
• Hertha's Day, Spring Equinox at 00.00 degrees Aries
• Beltane at 15.00 degrees Taurus
• Letha's Day, Summer Solstice at 00.00 degrees Cancer
• Lughnassad at 15.00 degrees Leo
• Hellith's Day, Autumnal Equinox at 00.00 degrees Libra
• Samhain at 15.00 degrees Scorpio

Alphabets

The Oghams

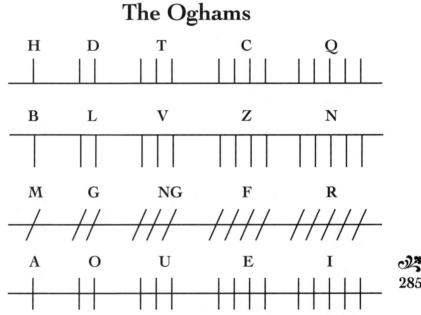

There are three forms of covert sign language used by the Ancients. They are Hand Ogham, Nose Ogham, and Shin Ogham. All three had certain concepts in common.

Nose Ogham: Uses the nose as a baseline and the five fingers (four plus thumb) to form the letters on the nose in four groups.

Shin Ogham: Uses the shin bone to represent the whale's back or baseline. Form the individual letters in the same way as they are in the Nose Oghham.

Hand Ogham: Indicates each of the 20 letters by a particular finger joint, pointing to one, or displaying one. Also you can make the letters with fingers themselves.

The Theban Alphabet

A   B   C   D   E

F   G   H   I   J

K   L   M   N   O

P   Q   R   S   T

U   V   W   X   Y

Z

Futharken Alphabet

The Futhark rune system has three major functions: as an alphabet, for divination, and for magic.

A   OS (god)
B   beorc (birch)
C   cen (torch)
D   daeg (day)
E   eoh (horse)
F   feh (money)
G   geofu (gift)
H   heagl (hail)
I   is (ice)
J   gear (year)
K   kenaz (creation fire)
L   lagu (water, sea)
M   man (human being)
N   nied (need)
O   eoel (inheritance, noble)
P   peod (dance)
Q   kaun (boil)
R   eolhs (stones)
S   sygil (sun)
T   tir (honour, war)
U   ur (aurocks, ox)
V   vend (hope)
W   wynn (joy)
X   (k + s)
Y   jera (season)
Z   ethaz (protection)
TH   thorn (thorn)
NG   ing (a hero)

Futharken Runes

A	B	C	D	E	F

G	H	I	J	K	L

M	N	O	P	Q	R

S	T	U	V	W	X

Y	Z	ING		TH	

Glossary

Aboriginal: Indigenous or original inhabitants of the land.

All Father: The consort and father. The god.

All Mother: The goddess and mother.

Amulet: An object usually metal or stone that has feelings or sensations placed in it.

Ancestral Dreaming: Merging with your ancestors to expand your awareness.

Apple Land: Avalon, island home of the goddess.

Archetypes: Symbolic representations of universal principles, defining concepts in a symbolic form.

Art and Craft: The ancient Goddess Tradition or Old Religion that uses the natural elements to create tangible reality.

Athame: A ceremonial blade traditionally two-sided representing the element fire.

Avalon: Land of the Otherworld, a harmonic of energy in oneness.

Beltane: Fourth Great Day at the beginning of May. Also known as Bel Fire, Bel meaning bright.

Boon Moon: A High Moon, the sixth full moon after Yule.

Boundless: A vast and infinite place of being. Oneness.

Bridget's Fire: The second Great Day following Yule.

Bright One: The Bright aspects of the All Mother representing light and the living.

Celtic: The ancient Gauls and Britons. Welsh, Irish, Highland Scot, Manx, Cornish and Breton peoples of central and western Europe, described as being fair and tall.

Chalice: A loving cup made of metal or clay. A consecrated tool symbolizing the water element and the Concept of Oneness.

Commonality: Oneness, the boundless, common connection.

Conditioning: State of being that reflects the culmination of one's ancestry, upbringing, experience, personality and culture. Not the true self, but a somewhat practical collection of valences and reactions an individual wears as a way to maneuver in the world.

Crystal Healing: Using quartz crystals and other stones as amplifiers and transducers in healing applications.

Dark One: The Dark aspect of the All Mother who represents death, destruction, and rebirth.

Days of Power: The eight Great Days and thirteen High Moons of ritual celebration.

Divination: The art and science of forecasting or reading events using traditional tools such as runes, tarot cards, etc.

Double: A duplicate self that arises out of one's primary self.

Doubling Out: The process of creating a double.

Dragon: Symbol of unmanifested energy.

Dragon Light: The visible energy that is generated by dragon lines or veins.

Dragon Lines or Veins: Serpent-like channels of energy that run through the earth, our bodies and the cosmos.

Drawing Down the Moon: Taking on the aspects of the moon and moving them into your awareness.

Dreaming: A state of being, engaged in while awake and sleeping. Can be used to pattern and create tangible reality and as a way to experience other realms of awareness.

Dream Magic: Using expectation, desire and merging to mindfully pattern your dreams.

Eight-Spoked Wheel: The wheel of the sun which includes the eight Great Days. Each spoke denotes one of these days.

Elements: Four traditional elements, sometimes a fifth. Fire, earth, air and water. The fifth element is the practitioner.

Fabric of Life: The endless Celtic weave representing the totality of all manifest reality. The threads that connect all things into one.

Feast: Celebration meal in honor of the goddess and god.

Female Energy: The goddess represented by the color green and associated with the left side and the state of being receptive, and with dreaming. Reservoir of power.

Four Keys: Wisdom, self-responsibility, self-honesty, and love.

Four Wards: The four corners of north, east, south and west. Also called the Watch Towers, Great Wards, or Guardians.

Full Moon Circle: Magical healing circle on the High Moons.

Full Moons: The twelve or thirteen full moons of the yearly cycle, beginning with the first full moon after Yule. Each moon has its own qualities. A time of healing rituals and for dreaming.

God: An individual being who lives in a merged state.

Goddess: An individual being who lives in a merged state.

Godhood: The attainment of becoming a God. A being who has gone through the three great merges, moving beyond time and space. A being who moves freely through the continuum.

Granting of the Boon: A request of a gift from the goddess. A boon is a blessing and a sacred gift.

Great Adventure: Birth, life, death and rebirth.

Great Circle: A protective circle of light constructed by the practitioner for magical works. The cycle of life.

Great Days: The eight Great Days, the Wheel of Taranis, including the solstices, the equinoxes and the midpoints.

Great Goddess: The term encompassing all of the faces and qualities of goddess energy.

Grid: Placing objects, usually crystals and stones, in a particular pattern which is often symbolic in form.

Gwyddon: Magician, Wise One, Astrologer or Healer.

Gwyddonic Druid Tradition: Ancient teachings and instructions to improve your life, based on the Concept of Oneness.

Harp: A stringed musical instrument. The number of strings on a harp has special meaning. Often a magical tool.

Hellith's Day: The seventh Great Day usually celebrating the harvest which takes place on the autumnal equinox.

High Moons: The twelve or thirteen full moons in a yearly cycle. Starting with the first full moon after Yule, they are the Wolf, Storm, Chaste, Seed, Hare, Dyad, Mead, Wort, Barley, Wine, Blood, Snow and Oak.

High Priest: Man representing the god or consort.

High Priestess: Woman representing the goddess.

Individuality: The essence portion of a human being that lives from life to life. The eternal part of one's being.

Initiation: Being initiated into the Art and Craft. The birth of one's true self. Rebirth.

Instructions of Kerridwen: The first teaching of the Great Book of Gwyddonic Druid Tradition.

Invocation: A magical technique for calling a being of energy.

Lady's Day: Also called Hertha's Day. The third Great Day of the cycle, traditionally associated with the beginning of spring.

Letha's Day: The fifth Great day of the cycle, also called Midsummer.

Loats: Minuscule particles and waves of light encoded with information that permeate the ethers.

Lughnassad: The sixth Great Day that takes place in August. Lugh's wedding feast. Considered the time when the forces of light and dark converge, and the moon becomes stronger than the sun.

Mabinogi: Bardic tales and stories of the lives of heroines and heros.

Magic: The study of the nature of all things. The use of ritual to continue the cycle of the goddess and her consort.

Magical Arts: Creating matter and energy out of the unmanifested or the manifested. Patterning and building the future.

Magical Tools: Items representing the elements that have been consecrated by a High Priestess and High Priest or by the goddess and her consort.

Magician: One who practices magic, a practitioner.

Male Energy: The consort represented by the color red, and associated with the right side and the state of emitting and doing.

Manifested: Tangible reality. Existing energy.

Merging: The state of becoming one with all things. Diffusing into the boundless.

Mind: The flux and flow of oneness, boundless imagination.

Moonflower Vine: A type of white morning glory that blooms and opens in the moonlight.

Multi-sense: Getting a sense of something by merging and going beyond sensory modes, using all of one's abilities to understand energy and experience.

Negativity: An energetic force which breaks patterns and feeds upon itself. Associated with the Dark One.

Ninefold One: The tripled representation of the triplicity. Nine faces of the goddess in one.

Oghams: Form of writing invented by the god Ogmios.

Oneness: The boundless. A place where one is connected to all things and to nothing.

Patterns: A term for discussing one's intentions and expectations. The formula and foundation from which one merges and experiences all things.

Pooka: A companion and elemental being. Can be very helpful and beneficial. See *Greenfire: Making Love with the Goddess* for full instructions on making pookas.

Portal: A door to another world or realm. Threshold of energy.

Positivity: An energetic force which creates and builds patterns. Associated with the Bright One.

Practitioner: A person who practices magic.

Prophecy: Prediction under divine influence and direction. Reading patterns successfully.

Rapport: Harmony of relationship with another, to be in close accord. Remembering who we really are and understanding the deeper connection.

Runes: Letters with magical qualities. Secret letters, secret knowledge, secret powers and magical symbols. Living symbols of active energy.

Running the Light: Moving mass amounts of energy during a magical work or with a sexual partner during lovemaking.

Sacred Marriage: Spiritual union with the goddess and god. You become the goddess and god. Craft marriage.

Samhain: All Hollows Eve and the eighth Great Day, associated with death and rebirth. The day when the veil between time and space is the thinnest.

Secret Name Work: Finding your special name for protection and strength. You are the only one who knows your Secret Name and you never reveal it to anyone.

Seeker: A person interested in the Art and Craft, and in learning the Concept of Oneness.

Shared Dream: Patterning to share dream experiences with another. Agreeing to dream with another person.

Sigil: An original and unique personal symbol created in a merged state. A living symbol of light.

Siod-cruit: Small Faery harp.

Slip-Knot Magic: Using thread or rope tied in knots to do magical works.

Solstices: Days of power in the times during summer and winter when the sun is at its greatest distance from the celestial equator. Yule and Letha's Days.

Spiritual Partnership: Sacred bond between two people.

String Magic: Using thread, cord or string to weave a pattern into manifest reality. Ancient form of sewing.

Sunwise: Clockwise turn which is considered the positive direction. The opposite of widdershins or counterclockwise.

Symbols: Representation of many things in one thing.

Synchronicity: When two things occur at exactly the same time and having the same vibrational energy. Timing things together for a particular outcome.

Taking on an Aspect of the Goddess or God: Ritual for merging completely with the energy of a particular goddess or consort.

Tarot Cards: A divination tool using archetypal and symbolic visual representations. Aspects of life experiences.

Theban: Ancient form of writing.

Three Eyes of Kerridwen: The formula for magical works which consists of expectation, desire and merging.

Threefold One: The Triple Goddess representing birth, life and rebirth. Three faces of the goddess in one.

Tir-nan-Og: Land of Promise and the Celtic paradise.

Totem: Natural object or animal that represents an ancestral or energetic relationship.

Tuatha De Dannan: The family of Danu, title of the gods.

Tuatha of Kerridwen: The family of Kerridwen, the goddess and her consort in infinite human incarnate forms.

Unmanifested: Non-tangible reality. That which does not exist as yet. Energy that waits to be born.

Waking Dream: Dreaming with your eyes open.

Wand: Craft tool made of wood and decorated with stones, representing the element air.

White Goddess: Kerridwen, the Bright One.

Wine Ceremony: Ritual to bring people closer together.

Wine Cup: Placed at the center of the altar, at the threshold between the manifest and unmanifest sides of the altar, representing the joining of female and male energies.

Wizard: A sorcerer and wise person.

Yule: The first of the Great Days celebrated on the winter solstice.

Bibliography

Alder, Margot. *Drawing Down the Moon.* Boston, MA: Beacon Press, 1981.

Araoz, Daniel L. *The New Hypnosis.* New York, NY: Brunner-Mazel Publishers, 1985.

Alder, Margot. *Drawing Down the Moon.* Boston: Beacon Press, 1981.

Andrews, Lynn V. *The Woman of Wyrd.* New York: Harper & Row Publishers, 1990.

Bandler, Richard, and Grinder, John. *The Structure of Magic.* Palo Alto: Science and Behavior Books, 1975.

Bolen, Jean Shinoda, M.D. *Goddessess in Everywoman.* New York: Harper & Row, 1984.

Bonwick, James. *Irish Druids and Old Irish Religions.* New York: Dorset, 1986.

Bord, Janet and Bord, Colin. *Mysterious Britain.* London: Paladin Books, 1974.

Brennan, Barbara Ann. *Light Emerging.* New York: Bantam Books, 1993.

Briggs, Katherine. *An Enclyclopedia of Fairies.* New York: Pantheon Books, 1967.

Budapest, Z. *The Grandmother of Time.* San Francisco: Harper & Row, 1989.

Bull, John, and Farrand, John. *The Audubon Society Field Guide to North American Birds.* New York: Alfred A. Knopf, 1977.

Burland, Connie. *North American Indian Mythology.* New York: Peter Bedrick Books, 1985.

Campbell, Joseph. *The Masks of God, Vol I-IV.* New York: Penguin Books, 1977.

Campbell, Joseph, (editor). *Myth, Dream, and Religion.* New York: E.P. Dutton & Co., Inc., 1970.

Castaneda, Carlos. *The Art of Dreaming.* New York: HarperCollins, 1993.

Castaneda, Carlos. *The Eagle's Gift.* New York; Simon and Schuster, 1981.

Ceram, C. W. *Gods, Graves and Scholars.* New York: Bantam Books, 1972.

Chesterman, Charles Wesley. *The Audubon Society Field Guide to North American Rocks and Minerals.* New York: Alfred A. Knopf, 1978.

Chopra, Deepak, M.D. *Return of the Rishi.* Boston: Houghton Mifflin Co., 1988.

Cohen, Leonard. *Selected Poems 1956-1968.* New York: Viking Press, Inc., 1968.

Conway, D.J. *Celtic Magic.* St. Paul, MN: Llewellyn Publications, 1990.

——*Maiden, Mother, Crone.* St. Paul, MN: Llewellyn Publications, 1994.

Cunningham, Scott. *Living Wicca.* St. Paul, MN: Llewellyn Publications, 1993.

Delaney, Gayle. *Living Your Dreams: Using Sleep to Solve Problems and Enrich Your Life.* San Francisco: Harper & Row, 1988.

Delaney, Gayle. *Sexual Dreams.* New York: Fawcett Columbine, 1994.

Dexter, Mariam Robbins. *Whence the Goddesses: A Source Book.* New York: Pergamon Press, Inc., 1990.

Donner, Florinda. *Being-In Dreaming.* San Francisco: Harper Collins, 1991.

Eliade, Micea. *Shamanism.* Bollingen Series: Princeton, New Jersey, 1964.

Epstein, Perle. *Oriental Mystics and Magicians.* New York: Doubleday & Co., Inc., 1975.

Faraday, Ann. *The Dream Game.* New York: Harper and Row, 1974.

Frazier, Sir James George. *The Golden Bough.* New York: The Macmillan Company, 1935.

Frost, Robert. *Selected Poems of Robert Frost.* New York: Holt, Rinehart and Winston, Inc., 1963.

Gackenback, J. I, and Bosveld, J. *Control Your Dreams.* New York: Harper and Row, 1989.

Gantz, Jeffrey, Translator. *The Mabinogion.* Middlesex, England: Dorset Press, 1976.

Garfield, Patricia. *Women's Bodies, Women's Dreams.* New York: Ballantine, 1988.

Gawain, Shakti. *Living in the Light.* San Rafael, CA: New World Library, 1986.

Gimbutas, Marija. *The Language of the Goddess.* San Francisco: Harper & Row, 1989.

Graves, Robert. *The White Goddess.* New York: Faber & Faber, 1966.

Gruffydd, W. J. *Folklore and Myth in the Mabinogion.* Cardiff: University of Wales Press, 1975.

Hay, Louise L. *You Can Heal Your Life.* Santa Monica, CA: Hay House, 1982.

Highwater, Jamake. *Myth and Sexuality.* New York: New American Library, 1990.

Hockey, Thomas. *The Book of the Moon.* New York: Prentice Hall Press, 1986.

Karagulla, Shafica, M.D., and Kunz, Dora. *The Chakras and the Human Energy Fields.* Wheaton, IL: The Theosophical Publishing House, 1969.

Knight, Sirona. *Greenfire: Making Love with the Goddess.* St. Paul, MN: Llewellyn Publications, 1995.

Krieger, Dolores. *The Therapeutic Touch: How to Use Your Hands to Help or Heal.* Englewood Cliffs, NJ: Prentice-Hall, 1979.

Krippner, Stanley, (editor). *Dreamtime & Dreamwork.* Los Angeles: Jeremy P. Tarcher, Inc., 1990.

Lawrence, R.D. *In Praise of Wolves.* New York: Ballantine Books, 1986.

Lazarus, Arnold. *In The Mind's Eye.* New York: The Guilford Press, 1977.

Leach, Maria, Editor. *Standard Dictionary of Folklore, Mythology, and Legend.* New York: Funk & Wagnalls Co., 1950.

LeBerge, Stephen. *Lucid Dreaming: The Power of Being Awake and Aware in Your Dreams.* Los Angeles: Jeremy P. Tarcher, Inc., 1985.

Lorusso, Julia, and Glick, Joel. *Healing Stoned.* Albuquerque, NM: Brotherhood of Life, 1976.

MacNeill, John, and Carnoy, J.A. *Celtic and Teutonic Religions.* London: Catholic Truth Society, 1975.

Markale, Jean. *Women of the Celts.* New York: Gordon & Cremonesi Publishers, 1975.

Matthews, Caitlin. *The Elements of the Goddess.* London: Element Books, 1989.

297

Mindell, Arnold. *The Dreambody in Relationships*. New York: Routledge & Kegan Paul, 1987.

——*The Shaman's Body*. New York: HarperCollins, 1993.

——*Working with the Dreaming Body*. Boston: Routledge and Kegan Paul, 1985.

Missing Link Newsletter. Chico, CA. Autumn, 1991 thru Winter, 1993.

Monaghan, Patricia. *The Book of Goddesses and Heroines*. St Paul, MN: Llewellyn Publications, 1990.

Morgan, Marlo. *Mutant Message Down Under*. Lees Summit, MO: MM Co., 1991.

Mormouth, Geoffrey. *History of the Kings of Britain*. New York: E.P. Dutton & Co., 1958.

Morris, Jan. *A Matter of Wales*. Oxford: Oxford University Press, 1984.

Newman, Paul. *The Hill of the Dragon*. London: Kingsmead Press, 1976.

Nexxus Newsletter. Whitesburg, KY. Spring, 1985-Fall, 1988.

Papazian, Charlie. *The Complete Joy of Home Brewing*. New York: Avon Books, 1984.

Paterson, Helena. *The Celtic Lunar Zodiac*. Boston: Charles E. Tuttle Company, Inc., 1992.

Paul, Jordan, and Paul, Margaret. *Do I Have To Give Up Me To Be Loved by You?* Minneapolis, MN: CompCare Publishers, 1983.

Pavlik, Bruce M. (et al). *Oaks of California*. Los Olivos, CA: Cachuma Press, 1991.

Pearce, Joseph Clinton. *The Crack of the Cosmic Egg*. New York: Crown Publishers, 1971.

Pecker, Jean-Claude. *The Orion Book of the Sky*. New York: The Orion Press, Inc., 1960.

Pepper, Elizabeth, and Wilcock, John. *Magical and Mystical Sites: Europe and the British Isles*. New York: Harper and Row, 1977.

Phillips, Guy Ragland. *Brigantia, A Mysteriography*. London: Routledge and Kegan Paul Ltds., 1976.

Piggott, Stuart. *The Druids*. London: Thames & Hudson, 1976.

Ravenwolf, Silver. *To Ride a Silver Broomstick*. St. Paul, MN: Llewellyn Publications, 1993.

Redfield, James. *Celestine Prophecy.* New York: Time Warner Company, 1993.

Rees, Alwyn & Brinley. *Celtic Heritage, Ancient Tradition in Ireland and Wales.* New York: Grove Press, 1978.

Rhys, John, M. A. *Celtic Folklore, Welsh and Manx.* New York: Benjamin Blom, Inc., 1972.

Ross, Anne. *Pagan Celtic Britain.* New York: Columbia University Press, 1967.

Schwarz, Jack. *Voluntary Controls: Exercises for Creative Meditation and for Activating the Potential of the Chakras.* New York: Hutton, 1978.

Smith, Sir William. *Smaller Classical Dictionary.* New York: E. P. Dutton, 1958.

Spence, Lewis. *The History and Origins of Druidism.* New York: Samuel Weiser, Inc., 1971.

Spence, Lewis. *The Magic Arts in Celtic Britain.* New York: Samuel Weiser, Inc., 1970.

Starck, Marcia. *Women's Medicine Ways.* Freedom, CA: The Crossing Press, 1993.

Starhawk. *The Spiral Dance.* San Francisco: Harper & Row, 1979.

Stein, Diane. *The Woman's Spirituality Book.* St. Paul, MN: Llewellyn Publications, 1987.

Stewart, C. Nelson. *Gemstones of the Seven Rays.* Health Research: Mokelumne Hill, California, 1975.

Stewart, R.J. *Celtic Gods, Celtic Goddesses.* New York: Sterling Publishing Co., 1990.

Stone, Merlin. *When God Was a Woman.* New York: Harcourt Brace Javanovich.

Thorsson, Edred. *Futhark: A Handbook of Rune Magic.* York Beach: Samuel Weiser, Inc., 1984.

Ullman, M., and Limmer, C., (editors). *The Variety of Dream Experience: Expanding Our Ways of Working with Dreams.* New York: Continuum, 1987.

Ullman, M., and Zimmerman, N. *Working with Dreams: Self-Understanding, Problem-Solving, and Enriched Creativity through Dream Appreciation.* Los Angeles: Jeremy P. Tarcher, 1979.

Vogel, Marcel. *The Crystal Workbook.* San Jose, CA: PRI Institute, 1986.

Walker, Barbara. *Women's Rituals*. San Francisco: Harper & Row, 1990.

Wilde, Lady. *Ancient Legends, Mystic Charms and Superstition of Ireland*. New York: Lemma Publishing, 1973.

Wilde, Stuart. *The Force*. Taos, New Mexico: Wisdom Books, Inc., 1984.

——*The Whispering Winds of Change*. Taos, New Mexico: White Dove Publishers, 1994.

Wolfe, Amber. *In the Shadow of the Shaman*. St. Paul, MN: Llewellyn Publications, 1988.

Yeats, W.B. *The Celtic Twilight*. New York: Signet Books, 1962.

Zukav, Gary. *The Seat of the Soul*. New York: Simon & Schuster Inc., 1989.

Index

301

303

STAY IN TOUCH!

On the following pages you will find listed, with their current prices, some of the books now available on related subjects. Your book dealer stocks most of these and will stock new titles in the Llewellyn series as they become available. We urge your patronage.

TO GET A FREE CATALOG

You are invited to write for our bimonthly news magazine/catalog, *Llewellyn's New Worlds of Mind and Spirit*. A sample copy is free, and it will continue coming to you at no cost as long as you are an active mail customer. Or you may subscribe for just $10 in the United States and Canada ($20 overseas, first class mail). Many bookstores also have *New Worlds* available to their customers. Ask for it.

In *New Worlds* you will find news and features about new books, tapes and services; announcements of meetings and seminars; helpful articles; author interviews and much more. Write to:

Llewellyn's New Worlds of Mind and Spirit
P.O. Box 64383-791, St. Paul, MN 55164-0383, U.S.A.

TO ORDER BOOKS AND TAPES

If your book store does not carry the titles described on the following pages, you may order them directly from Llewellyn by sending the full price in U.S. funds, plus postage and handling (see below).

Credit card orders: VISA, MasterCard, American Express are accepted. Call us toll-free within the United States and Canada at 1-800-THE-MOON.

Special Group Discount: Because there is a great deal of interest in group discussion and study of the subject matter of this book, we offer a 20% quantity discount to group leaders or agents. Our Special Quantity Price for a minimum order of five copies of *Moonflower* is $79.80 cash-with-order. Include postage and handling charges noted below.

Postage and Handling: Include $4 postage and handling for orders $15 and under; $5 for orders *over* $15. There are no postage and handling charges for orders over $100. Postage and handling rates are subject to change. We ship UPS whenever possible within the continental United States; delivery is guaranteed. Please provide your street address as UPS does not deliver to P.O. boxes. Orders shipped to Alaska, Hawaii, Canada, Mexico and Puerto Rico will be sent via first class mail. Allow 4-6 weeks for delivery. **International orders:** Airmail – add retail price of each book and $5 for each non-book item (audiotapes, etc.); Surface mail – add $1 per item. **Minnesota residents add 7% sales tax.**

Mail orders to:
Llewellyn Worldwide, P.O. Box 64383-791, St. Paul, MN 55164-0383, U.S.A.
For customer service, call (612) 291-1970.

GREENFIRE
Making Love with the Goddess
by Sirona Knight
Greenfire offers an innovative approach to the goddess tradition in the area of sexual expression and exploration by joining elements of traditional Celtic Gwyddonic ritual and symbolism with tasteful erotic passages and guided fantasy. This book offers straightforward instruction for the solitary practitioner focusing on creating a viable relationship with one partner by merging with the divine aspects that exist inside each of us. Journey through each of the eight Sabbats with the Goddess and her consort, exploring their different aspects along the way through concepts, rituals and guided imagery.
1–56718–386–7, 6 x 9, 224 pgs., index, softcover **$14.95**

ECSTASY THROUGH TANTRA
by Dr. Jonn Mumford
Dr. Jonn Mumford makes the occult dimension of the sexual dynamic accessible to everyone. One need not go up to the mountaintop to commune with Divinity: its temple is the body, its sacrament the communion between lovers. *Ecstasy Through Tantra* traces the ancient practices of sex magick through the Egyptian, Greek and Hebrew forms, where the sexual act is viewed as symbolic of the highest union, to the highest expression of Western sex magick.
0-87542-494-5, 190 pgs., 6 x 9, 14 color plates, softcover **$12.95**

DREAMS & WHAT THEY MEAN TO YOU
by Migene Gonzalez Wippler
In this fascinating and well-written book, the author gives you all of the information needed to begin interpreting—even creating—your own dreams. *Dreams & What They Mean To You* begins by exploring the nature of the human mind and consciousness, then discusses the results of the most recent scientific research on sleep and dreams. The author analyzes different types of dreams: telepathic, nightmares, sexual and prophetic. In addition, there is an extensive Dream Dictionary which lists the meanings for a wide variety of dream images.
0-87542-288-8, 240 pgs., mass market **$3.95**